Whose Holy Land?

Michael Wolffsohn

Whose Holy Land?

The Roots of the Conflict Between Jews and Arabs

 Springer

Michael Wolffsohn
Bundeswehr University Munich
Neubiberg, Germany

Translation from the German language edition: Wem gehört das Heilige Land? - Die Wurzeln des Streits zwischen Juden und Arabern by Michael Wolffsohn, © PIPER Verlag GmbH 2017. Published by PIPER. All Rights Reserved.

ISBN 978-3-030-74285-0   ISBN 978-3-030-74286-7   (eBook)
https://doi.org/10.1007/978-3-030-74286-7

This Springer imprint is published by the registered company Springer Nature Switzerland AG.
The registered company address is: Gewerbestrasse 11, 6330 Cham, Switzerland

This book is dedicated to all the people who have wanted to live *in the Holy Land—without killing others*

Foreword

To whom does the Holy Land—Israel, Palestine—belong? This question is millennia old, but reverberates (again) globally with renewed intensity during the last 200 years due to the dual impact of external, often imperial, ambitions and conflicting desires for national self-determination and statehood. From a religious angle, the land is dear, even holy, to several major religions, Judaism, Christianity, and Islam, but also the Bahai, Druze, and Samaritan faith. Michael Wolffsohn invites us in this fascinating book to embark on a journey: to explore and critically question the religious, and political, roots of all-too-often exclusive claims to this territory from the dawn of human civilization to the present era. The book is a fantastic orientation for everybody interested in a humanistic and at the same time historically informed analysis of this land located at the Eastern shores of the Mediterranean—the cradle of so much of humanity's religious, cultural, and social heritage.

The book is written in accessible and entertaining prose—while the depth of arguments presented in it speaks to the author's intellectual ambition and perspective. What one should not expect, though, is an argument in favor of a given religion, state, people, or political movement of more or less "owning" this land. As Wolffsohn makes clear: this is a book for all people who ever lived, live, or in fact will live in this land—or longed to do so. Following this credo, tolerance is required, and accepting the attachments and sincerity of senses of belonging of many diverse groups. Many of them are well known like Jews, Christians, and Muslims—or Israelis and Palestinians. Others less so, like the Samaritans, the Bahai, the Druze, and others. This land belongs to none of these groups exclusively, but what is exclusive are diverse forms of attachment each of these groups holds in relation to the land. The question then is, as Michael Wolffsohn accurately states, how the people and political movements in this land can—if ever—leave the history of relative tolerance behind, which characterized relations between people there over the last millennia (let alone periods of complete intolerance): how do people who feel like owning the land manage to arrive at a much more fundamental sense of togetherness, of exclusive but shared senses of belonging? Senses of belonging that respect each group's historically formed, and emotionally deep, senses of attachment. This is a deeper question to which this book speaks so convincingly.

Religion is—as politics—often associated with an impossibility to arrive at such senses of shared but diverse belonging. But is that true? One of the remarkable insights from this book is Michael Wolffsohn's analysis of different religious traditions, of course foremost in Judaism, Christianity, and Islam. He elaborates how all these three religions (often to the despair of religious people and fundamental leaders, reflecting the tendency of religious movements in the course of human history to descend on a path of intolerance) inhibit a deep sense of shared identity with the respective others. There is no clash of civilizations in what in fact are three religions connected, should one say, by their shared roots in what Karl Jaspers has much later coined axial time. The question then is, of course, how to engender political, cultural, and social structures across these three religions that would allow us to un-dig these roots, making them visible to large segments of believers, for them not to be seduced by those preaching eternal opposition. While religion in theory could play such a positive role, the reality in history has often been to the detriment of such a reconciliation. It need not to be so, and educational efforts such as this book could be a building block of such a much-needed undertaking.

The same could be said about politics. Political movements, first of all exclusive nationalism, have also again and again delegitimized other groups' political attachment to the land. In the closing pages of the book, Michael Wolffsohn discusses the possibility of federalism as a way forward—distinct from a classical two-state but also a one-state solution. How to institutionalize such a federal perspective in concrete political structures? This is a core impulse stemming from this book, in particular because any working supra-national federalism—think of European integration after World War II—not only established technocratic structures of political cooperation but, more importantly, a sense of shared European political identity from the Netherlands to the Balkan Peninsula and from Scandinavia to Portugal and real ownership of all these countries and people in European integration accepting each other as equals, leveling power asymmetries. National and sub-national identities do not fade away, but are enriched by this sense of togetherness in diversity. This might, at first sight, be a model hard to conceive of for the Holy Land, let alone the wider Middle East—but for this very reason it is a political objective not less worth fighting for. As European federalists did already one hundred years before, eventually, in the 1950s European integration became a political reality. Questions like these are posed to us on this journey, to which Michael Wolffsohn invites us. This allows also situating the Israeli–Palestinian conflict (and occasional coexistence) in broader historical perspective. That is why this book only partly deals with this modern history of the land in largely the twentieth century. While the reality of this conflict and the religious and national claims for ownership by Israelis and Palestinians are real and relevant today, they play out against a historical background for which the term *longue durée* even seems like a gross understatement. Traveling across the timeline from the dawn of human civilization until today not only helps in nurturing a deeper understanding of distinct forms of attachments. It also nurtures hopes that shared roots, either born but forgotten in history or growing as part of future agreements, might be the real promise the often-heard notion of a "holy" land entails.

University of the Bundeswehr Munich   Stephan Stetter
Neubiberg, Germany Munich, Germany/Florence, Italy
June 2021

About This Book

Whose Holy Land? Today, this question remains a political and historical "evergreen." Power struggles, conflicting interests, and prejudices continue to inflame minds and situations in the Middle East. In order to address such a charged issue, we need to first uncover the roots of the conflicts between Israel and its neighbors and to dispel a number of handed-down myths. With this best-selling book, Michael Wolffsohn has produced a comprehensive and standard work that is essential for any informed discussion about the political situation in the Middle East. Painstakingly researched and easy to read, it examines the historical background of the conflict between Jews and Arabs. It is "highly recommended as a knowledgeable introduction to the controversy over Palestine/Israel" (Schalom Ben-Chorin). 15 editions of this book were released by Piper publishers in Germany between 2002 and 2021; between 1992 and 2001, four editions were published by Bertelsmann and Goldmann.

Michael Wolffsohn

Contents

Holy Land? Israel? Palestine?   1

Part I   Religiosity and Politics   5

The Pious, the Zealous and a "Dead" God   7

Fundamentalism: A Shield for the Culture?   11

Is Zionism Blasphemy?   15

Zionism in the Quran?   23

Part II   The Holy Land, Religions and Politics   27

What Is the Holy Land?—Biblical Borders?   29

Why Is the Land Holy?   37

To Whom Is the Land Holy?   47

Where Is the Land Holy?   53
The Jewish Holy Places   56
The Christian Holy Places   69
The Muslim Holy Places   81

How Is the Land Holy?   95

By What Means Is the Land Acquired?   101

Part III   The History of Changing Ownership   105

Whose Possession? Whose Property?   107

Names and Power   109

The Patriarch Fathers   115

Jewish Settlement as "Conquest"   119

Kingdom and Kingdoms Come and Go   123

Exile, Return and Autonomy   127

The Europeanization of the Holy Land   133

Christians as Heirs and Owners   149

Re-orientalisation: Arabisation, Turkification   151

Re-europeanization   157

The Return of Islam   161

The Return to Zion   175

The British in the Holy Land   181

The Founding of Israel: Palestine Becomes Jordan   195

"Greater Israel": Jewish or Democratic? Of Federations and
Confederations   201

Injustice for Injustice—Conclusion—Solution?   207

Chronology   215

Recommended Reading   219

About the Author

Michael Wolffsohn was born in Tel Aviv to German Jewish parents in 1947, and has lived in Germany since 1954. He received his doctorate in 1975 and completed his postdoctoral degree (*Habilitation*) in 1980. He served as Professor of Modern History at the Bundeswehr University in Munich from 1981 to 2012. His books have been translated into numerous languages.

Holy Land? Israel? Palestine?

What is in a name? Is there more than sound and fury? There certainly is when it comes to the names of people, cities and countries. Depending on whether we use the name "Jerusalem" or "Al Quds" we choose either a Jewish-Israeli or an Arab-Islamic connection. In doing so, we are no longer playing with words but with highly explosive political issues.

Names are intimately tied to history. Two more recent examples: Following the Bolshevik revolution the czarist capital of St. Petersburg became Leningrad—and Leningrad reverted back to St. Petersburg in 1991. The old German city of Chemnitz re-emerged from the ruins of the Second World War as part of the German Democratic Republic and bearing a new name: Karl-Marx-City. The fall of the Wall and of the G.D.R. led to the resurrection of Chemnitz. Names mirror political programs and indicate to victors and vanquished. This also applies to the Holy Land. Is Israel the land of Israel, i.e. the Jewish people? Is Palestine the land of the Palestinians?

"The land" is the simple term employed by the Jews at the end of the period of the Second Temple (also the beginning of the Christian epoch). Of course, we find earlier references to "the land", for example in Leviticus 19:23: "When you come into the land …" and in Joshua 11:23: "So Joshua took the whole land …". The usage here is more that of an abbreviation than of a name. But it also expresses that, though there are many lands on this earth, for the Jews there is only one, "the land of Israel", in Hebrew: *Eretz Yisrael*. In earlier times, the different parts of the land also bore different names. Only in the later period was the term "the land" used, thus establishing a unity among land, people and religion: Israel, Jews and Judaism.

M. Wolffsohn, *Whose Holy Land?*, https://doi.org/10.1007/978-3-030-74286-7_1

At the very beginning, the Egyptians of the fourteenth and thirteenth centuries B.C.E. referred to the region as *Retenu*, which included what is today Syria and Lebanon. Later they used the name *Hurru*, which referred to the Hurrians (the Horites of the Bible), a people who had inhabited the region, especially Syria, since the seventeenth century. This designation is to be found as late as Ptolemaic texts of the third century B.C.E.

From the end of the fourteenth until the twelfth century the Egyptians spoke of *P-Knaana*, the land of Canaan. We finally find ourselves on more familiar ground, as this name is known to us from the Bible, where it refers to the lands west of the Jordan in particular and more generally to the western region of Syria. One Canaanite tribe was that of the Amorites and part of the area was also referred to as the "Land of the Amorites."

In searching for references to Jews or Hebrews we thus first encounter of other peoples and other names for various parts of the land.

Peoples come and go. The *Hebrews* came and they included, among others, the Israelites. "For I was stolen out of the land of the Hebrews," reports Joseph in Genesis 40:15.

The so often invoked—and fiercely contested—unity of land, people and religion is a product of the later conquest by the Israelites. The "land of the children of Israel" is mentioned for the first time in Joshua 11:22. It is into this "hill country" that Joshua led the children of Israel, where he eventually, as commanded, drove out or "utterly destroyed" (Joshua 11:20) the people who had lived there before, thus beginning the process of the Jewish conquest of the land.

Eretz Yisrael, the land of Israel, appears for the first time in the first book of Samuel (13:19), but refers only to the area settled by the children of Israel and not to the land as a whole.

As we know from the Bible, Saul, David and Solomon ruled over the *Kingdom of Israel*, but there is a consensus among scholars that the designation "land of Israel" was introduced retroactively for the period of King David (1 Chronicles 22:2 or 2 Chronicles 2:17).

In King David's time the names *Israel* and *Judea* were both applied to the land where the Jews lived. Both names already appear in Joshua (11:21), but Judea refers only to the "hill country". Most scholars regard this as an anticipation, as the land was not divided into *Israel* and *Judea* until after the death of King Solomon.

The confusion of language is thus Jewish-Israelite, not Babylonian. Names are like mirrors. They reflect a certain image of reality. But they are not reality. A multitude of names reflect the historical complications and struggles, the myriad of only incompletely known or ambiguous historical and political relationships of the region. In view of the hopelessly entangled ambivalancies, only the propagandist will claim clear vision.

In the year 538 B.C.E. the Persian King Cyrus permitted the Jews of Babylonia to return to their land, to *Judea*. For the first time, the words *Jew* and *Hebrew* carry the same meaning. Judea is the land of the Jews, specifically of those Jews who returned to Zion. Since then, Judaism refers to the movement back to the homeland which began in 538 as the "return to Zion".

Zion is the name of the ancient city of the Jebusites now known as Jerusalem. When the Jewish prophets spoke of Zion they always meant Jerusalem as a spiritual and religious symbol. "For out of Zion shall go forth the law, and the word of the Lord from Jerusalem." (Isaiah 2:3). Finally, in the Jewish Diaspora, that is outside the land of Israel, Zion became the symbol for the Jewish Holy Land.

Zionism, founded in the nineteenth century, was the national movement of the Jewish people. Its goal was the return of the Jewish people to their land, or, more cautiously stated, to the land which the Jewish people regarded as its own. But this jumps over millenniums of history.

From 538 B.C.E. on, Judea was more or less officially the autonomous region inhabited by Jews within the homeland from which they had been taken in captivity first by the Assyrians (in 722) and then by the Babylonians (in 586). In the second century B.C.E. the Jews of Judea, under the Hasmonean dynasty, succeeded in once again establishing an independent state, the Kingdom of Judea. The name survived even under King Herod. This Kingdom of Judea was considerably larger in area than its historical forerunner of the same name which had been extinguished in the Babylonian conquest of 586.

By King Herod's time, the real rulers of Judea were the Romans, against whom the Jews rose up in rebellion. The uprising was in vain. The Jewish rebels were defeated in the year 70 and again, this time disastrously, in 135, after which the Romans abolished even the name of Judea. Emperor Hadrian decreed a new name, *Syria-Palestine*, which soon became shortened to *Palestine*, the land of the Philistines. Everyone who remembers the story of David and Goliath will recall that the giant was a Philistine.

The symbolism chosen by the Romans was unambiguous. In Rome's view, the Jews had forfeited their right to the land. In the course of subsequent centuries, the Byzantine, Arab or Ottoman rulers added or subtracted various areas, but *Palestine* remained substantially intact—until the establishment of the Jewish State. The latter was proclaimed on May 14, 1948, and, as everyone knows, was given the name *Israel*.

Not all of Palestine became Israel. East of the Jordan river, due in part to the instigation of Winston Churchill, the *Emirate of Transjordan* had been created by a stroke of the pen in 1921. After 1946 it was known as the *Kingdom of Transjordan*. This kingdom took possession of the West Bank region and East Jerusalem in December 1948 and this amalgamation of cis- and trans-Jordanian lands has been subsequently known as the *Kingdom of Jordan*. Except for Great Britain and Pakistan, however, no other nations recognized the Jordanian annexation of the West Bank and Jerusalem. Since the 1967 Six Day War, Israel has occupied both the West Bank and East Jerusalem. The Gaza Strip came under Egyptian administration in 1949, but never formed part of the Egyptian state. In 1967 it came under Israeli occupation until attaining autonomy under the Palestinian Authority in 1994.

Today, the name *Israel* stands for the territory of the Jewish State established in 1948. In 1967, East Jerusalem was formally incorporated into the Jewish State. The Israelis speak of "reunification", the Arabs (and most other states) of "annexation". In 1981 Israel also annexed the area of the Golan Heights occupied since the 1967 war. This act has also not achieved international recognition.

Where does the name *Holy Land* come from? For both Jews and Christians the term expresses reverence and love toward the land. But it has never served as an official designation. For Jews, it is connected with the symbol of Zion as the spiritual and religious center, and augments the concept of the "land". In his Letter to the Hebrews (11:9), the apostle Paul wrote of the "land of promise" which the Lord had pledged to Abraham "as an inheritance".

Muslims revere holy places in this land as well, but as a whole it was never the "Holy Land" of Islam, which, as we shall explore further, has always been oriented to Arabia and the Arabic language. In its origins Islam is "Arabocentric". The emphasis on Palestine is a result of politics and, from a Muslim viewpoint, is both understandable and justifiable. But, as always, what is "justifiable" is not always automatically right. Usually, the justification is partisan and often serves more to provoke than to inform. This is part of the ritual of conflicts and thus ought to be left to the parties to the conflict. We shall attempt to exclude it from the following presentation.

Part I

Religiosity and Politics

The Pious, the Zealous and a "Dead" God

Whose Holy Land? "Ours, naturally," say Israelis and Jews. "No, ours, of course," reply Arabs and Muslims. "The land is not ours, but it is also holy to us, and we want to have a say regarding access to the holy places," explain Christians.

Are these the answers of the pious or the zealous? Undoubtedly they reflect the convictions of the piously motivated. Religious claims, longings and hopes with regard to the Holy Land are nurtured by Muslims and Christians, and especially by Jews. The bonds between people, religion and *this* land as *"our"* land, the Holy Land, the Promised Land, are clearly most pronounced among the Jews.

Neither Muslims nor Christians claim that it is *their* land, but it is equally evident that this land is indissolubly linked to their own religious history and therefore is also holy to them.

One would assume that those who use religious arguments ought to be religious, but this is all too often not the case. Frequently not piety but zealotry is the wellspring of religious argumentation with regard to the Holy Land. The zealots all too often fail to recognize that one of the purposes of all religion is to protect, not to destroy human life. The biblical fifth commandment is recognized by Jews, Christians and Muslims.

In October of 1991 the Islamic extremist Muslim Brotherhood, which forms the largest single faction in the Jordanian Parliament, and the Islamic fundamentalist Palestinian Hamas movement reiterated their opposition to the peace process and declared "Holy War" against the Jewish State in order to "liberate" Palestine. The view of the Iranian government, even since the passing of the Ayatollah Chomeini, is virtually identical. The pro-Iranian fanatics of the Lebanon-based Hisbollah proclaim their intention to drive out the Zionists and to create an Islamic state modeled on the laws of the Quran. When four Hisbollah followers were dispatched into northern Israel in November 1991 their orders were "Shoot as many Jews as possible." Such dire and un-holy tones echo the Third Reich, where people were murdered simply because they were Jews.

We read in the Bible that mankind was created in God's image. Is murder thus to be considered an act of religious liberation? In the final analysis, can God really be alive for those who preach death? The language used is, in any case, anything but secular: "Those who die fighting for the liberation of Palestine will go directly to Paradise." The echo here is that of the European crusaders of the middle ages.

"Holy warriors" have always been something of a plague upon human society, be they Christian Crusaders, Muslim Holy Warriors or Jewish-Israeli settlement fanatics. The latter do not refer to themselves as "holy warriors", but they are similarly convinced of the sacred nature of their mission and are quite prepared to accept that their use of bullets lead to Palestinian casualties.

Of course, we all know that religion can be used to justify rigid positions as well as compromises, but religion is not a viable political instrument or argument. Religion is there to give life moral depth and clarity, not to provoke man into murder and slaughter. Nevertheless, un-holy calamity and destruction have continued to descend upon the Holy Land in the form of countless wars. Sometimes the Holy Land appears to be a microcosm of an un-holy and malevolent world.

It is strange that increasing numbers of people in the Jewish, Islamic and Christian worlds protest that they want little or nothing to do with religion, but yet resort to religion in order to buttress their claim to the Holy Land. "Arab sovereignty must be re-established in the Old City of Jerusalem. Once peace has been re-established, Jerusalem will be the embodiment and the symbol of peace between the followers of the three great monotheistic religions." Thus proclaimed the Foreign Minister of the Kingdom of Jordan, Kamil Abu Jabir, at the Madrid Peace Conference on October 31, 1991. This secular politician (please note: not a cleric) also announced that the fact "that his historic city is so important to all [three religions] is God's will." The source of the Foreign Minister's knowledge was not revealed.

Similar phenomena may be observed on the Jewish side. For decades, around 70% of the Jewish citizens of Israel have responded in the polls that they consider themselves "not religious". Some are even militantly anti-religious and even state that they feel that their rights are being (literally) "violated" by the power of the extreme Orthodox. The non-religious majority are depriving Judaism of its religious substance. For them, the Jewish religion is nothing more than a superficial shell for the Jewish people. Their ties to "their" land are purely historical. The Jewish claim to the Holy Land is thus being historicized.

While the Arab-Islamic world displays its religious feelings with ever increasing intensity, in Jewish-Israeli society and in great parts of the Christian world—apart from the growing militancy of Orthodox groups—the process of secularization (the increasing distance and alienation from religion) continues.

The secularized Jewish-Israelis are thus undermining the foundation of their own legitimacy. To the extent that the people of the Book cast off their ties to their religious writings and laws, they therewith lose their claim to the Land of the Bible, their Holy Land, their Promised Land. They stand naked before the Arabs. The Jewish claim becomes "historicized" and, like all things historical, is no longer absolute, unchallenged and unchallengeable, but is relativized and opened to challenge. The modern, predominantly non-religious majority of Jewish Israelis are thus forced to steer a precarious course between fundamentalist orthodoxy and complete secularization.

Distance and alienation from religious roots provoke counter-reactions. *God's Revenge* is the title of a book by Gilles Kepel which appeared in 1991. Its subtitle: "Radical Muslims, Christians and Jews on the March". Certainly, fundamentalists are attracting more and more followers among Jews, Muslims and Christians. But have they really succeeded in reversing—or even slow-ing—the process of secularization which they so greatly fear? We may be per-mitted to doubt. Secularization continues inexorably, at least in the realms of technology and organization, less so in the intellectual-cultural sphere.

Perhaps religious fundamentalism is merely an offensive tactic in a defen-sive strategy. In the last two centuries the Jewish, Islamic and Christian worlds have witnessed many comparable actions and reactions. We may continue to view the theory of the offensive defense as valid until such time as it is conclu-sively disproved.

Fundamentalism: A Shield for the Culture?

The reason for the apparently irresistible advance of the religious fundamentalists is to be found in their attempt to re-establish religious and therewith cultural autonomy. The goal is autonomy in an increasingly standardized and homogenized world. This is a motive familiar to both the Jewish and Islamic worlds.

From the very beginning, Judaism, like Islam, was intent upon setting itself apart. The Prophet Mohammed nurtured close contacts with Jews and Christians, but as the founder of a religion he also had to create a distance between his and the other religions—even if the intention was not at all hostile. There were also political reasons. In Mohammed's time, Christianity was the religion of the Byzantine Empire and Judaism, with its center in Mesopotamia, was closely connected with Persian interests. Islam recommended itself, so to speak, as the bloc-free alternative.

Today's world is increasingly patterned after "Western", i.e. European-American civilization, or so it appears to many Islamic, Jewish and Christian fundamentalists, who are confused and feel threatened by what they perceive as a predominantly materialistic and technological civilization. They feel that their very spirits and souls are at peril. In their eyes, "Western" civilization is an assault on their culture, of which their religion is an inseparable part. To them, modern civilization represents a torrent of homogenized cultural swill which must be contained. Fundamentalism is one of their flood walls.

Culture concerns essentials, defines being itself. Civilization organizes and regulates the form of existence. Fundamentalists live in a polarity between

© The Author(s), under exclusive license to Springer Nature Switzerland AG 2021
M. Wolffsohn, *Whose Holy Land?*, https://doi.org/10.1007/978-3-030-74286-7_3

essence and existence. Their fear is that their own group or people is becoming more and more like all the others and will eventually be submerged in the mass. The notion of becoming a people "like all the others" causes an Orthodox Jew to shudder. But they are not alone in resisting the homogenization of civilization.

The failure of fundamentalist philosophy appears, however, to be pre-programmed, as the positive achievements of civilization are all too obvious. Moreover, this civilization can permit peoples to preserve and to further develop their individual cultures. Civilization must be recognized for what it is: an instrument to regulate the form of existence. This form does not necessarily determine being, as least not fully. Differing cultures and a uniform civilization are not necessarily mutually exclusive, provided the two are differentiated, for example, by dissolving the bonds between politics and religion.

Many have discovered that it is possible to utilize the advantages of civilization without relinquishing one's own cultural heritage. The Jewish Neo-Orthodoxy (which arose in Germany in the nineteenth century) recognized this, as do neo-orthodox Christians and Muslims.

"The Bible [Torah] in the things of this world [*derech eretz*]" may be regarded as the motto of Jewish neo-orthodoxy. It is not necessary to deny the one to have the other. The strict Orthodox Jew, for example, always wears his black coat and his black hat, even in the middle of summer. He follows his religious law down to the last detail, fully incorporating the Jewish culture and religion in his daily life. At the same time he may operate a high-technology business selling the newest in hard- and software. What is decisive for *this* neo-orthodoxy is the separation of religion from the political sphere.

As examples from the Muslim world we mention two Islamic modernists of the last century, both of whom, however, were militants in the sense that they did not separate religion and politics. Their goal was the modernization of religion in order to bring about a political and military revival. Gamaladdin Afghani (1839–1897) and his pupil Muhammad Abduh (1849–1905) transformed Islam into an anti-colonialist ideology intended to give rise to "political action against Europe" (Bassam Tibi). Neither was closed-minded about Europe "but they were only prepared to accept elements of bourgeoisie civilization and culture to the extent that these would strengthen Islam against Europe" (Bassam Tibi).

Among the less militant representatives of neo-orthodoxy we may count Mehdi Bazargan, the first prime minister of Iran under the Ayatollah

Chomeini. Bazargan was a devout Muslim but at the same time a pragmatic technocrat, not an ideologue. For this reason his term in office was very brief. Abdelkader Hachani of Algeria also personifies the mixture of technocrat and theocrat. Hachani, an oil engineer, heads Algeria's Salvation Front.

We note that the Islamic world has its representatives of neo-orthodoxy, although secularization or the separation of religion and politics are not part of the program. Religion was and remains a means of achieving political goals.

Fundamentalism is a sign of the crisis of civilization, for the threat of its collapse. Originally Christian, then increasingly non-religious, technological and European-American in nature, Western civilization is now challenged by Jewish and Islamic fundamentalism. The danger of collapse is greatest in the Muslim world, as the religious walls have long crumbled among Christians and Jews. The great majority of the latter are either secularized or have harmonized civilization and culture in neo-orthodox fashion. Only the fundamentalists continue the battle.

Is Zionism Blasphemy?

The Jewish religion provides nothing even remotely resembling a manual for the assertion of claims to Jewish statehood in the Holy Land. Some fundamentalists are even convinced that the land's very holiness enjoins against the establishment of Jewish statehood prior to the arrival of the Messiah.

Jewish fundamentalists can be roughly divided into two groups: the activists, who strive to help things along, and the passivists, who await the manifestation of God's will. While the activists have involved themselves in building the Jewish State, which they wish to ultimately transform into a Jewish theocracy, the passivists await the fulfillment of their wishes with the advent of the Messiah, who alone can establish a new covenant. In their eyes, the activists, who have already taken the first steps in the establishment of the Jewish state, have thus demonstrated their lack of trust in God and are thus guilt of blasphemy.

The passive Jewish fundamentalists are deeply religious and in some areas thoroughly modern. Involvement in politics, however, is, if at all, justified only as religious policy within the context of community policy. For them, Jewish statehood has nothing to do with the holiness of the Holy Land. To the contrary, they argue that "Zionism is blasphemy". Anyone who has visited Mea Shearim, the orthodox Jewish quarter in Jerusalem, has probably read this slogan on the walls and wondered why Orthodox Jews are opposed to the Jewish State and the Jewish national movement.

Extreme as well as religiously and politically militant Orthodox Jews tend to be doves when it comes to the Arab-Israeli conflict. On the eve of the Madrid Conference in October 1991, Rabbi Schach announced: "We are not bothered by Arabs living in Jerusalem." He was probably thinking of the

M. Wolffsohn, *Whose Holy Land?*, https://doi.org/10.1007/978-3-030-74286-7_4

Talmud passage Ketubbot 110b: "Our masters taught: A man should always live in the Land of Israel, even in a city where the greater number are strangers" [i.e. non-Jews] He should not live abroad. Not even in a city where the greater number are Jews." Why? Sota 14 gives at least a partial answer: [The people of] "Israel were given many laws which can only be fulfilled in the Land of Israel." And, concerning religious law, the Talmudic sage Rabbi Simlai added: "I want to enter the Land of Israel so that I may fulfill them all." Jewish religious life is thus decisive, not Jewish statehood. In other words, what counts is Jewish quality, not the quantity of Jews.

Rabbi Schach headed one of the most influential of the radical religious parties in Israel. For a time he was able to play the role of kingmaker in Israeli politics, tipping the delicate balance of power and thus strongly influencing who became prime minister.

At the Madrid conference in 1991, Israelis, Palestinians, Jordanians, Egyptians, Syrians and Lebanese for the first time came together to sit at a conference table and not to shoot at each other. Much impressed—but poorly informed—a German newspaper published a photograph depicting Rabbi Hirsch and Faisal Husseini together. The accompanying caption read: "At the beginning of a difficult conference a meeting in Jerusalem signals a spark of hope: Rabbi Hirsch, leader of the ultra-orthodox Neturei Karta meets with Palestinian leader Faisal Husseini." Apparently, the newspaper's reporters and editors were not aware of the fact that Neturei Karta is militantly anti-Zionist and denounces the State of Israel as blasphemous. Well-intentioned is not necessarily the same as well-informed.

The radicals of Neturei Karta are to be found in Mea Shearim and for years have maintained contacts with the Palestinian national movement. Neturei Karta also dispatched three advisors to the Israeli-Arab conference—as part of the Palestinian delegation. Neturei Karta's activities neither increase nor decrease the hope for a peaceful resolution of the Arab-Israeli conflict.

Numbers and proportions are important. About seventy percent of Jewish Israelis are non-religious. The religious Jews in Israel are thus a minority. Within this minority, the orthodox are again a minority. And Neturei Karta is but a tiny minority of this minority within a minority. Their exotic appearance and extreme militancy draws the attention of the media and the outside world. While dramatizing their peaceful disposition towards Muslim and Christian Palestinians, they are quite prepared to toss bombs at non-religious Jews who, for example, dare to open a swimming pool where men and women are not separated.

"Modern" and "enlightened" people, including this author, find it all but impossible to comprehend any form of religious orthodoxy. But anyone who wants to know whether the struggle over the Holy Land is a war of the religious and of religions or even possibly a battle *for* the religions must know something of the intricacies of the conflict. And these are confusing indeed, because the lines of conflict are highly confused. Knowledge of the multiplicity of the ambiguities involved is the prerequisite for an understanding of the conflict and, of course, for overcoming it.

Many will wonder if strict Jewish religious orthodoxy and anti-Zionism do not represent a fundamental contradiction. Making things even more confusing, a passive fundamentalist like Rabbi Schach acts as kingmaker in Israel's politics and another passive fundamentalist, Rabbi Hirsch, takes pains to distance himself from Israel and all things Israeli but yet cozies up to radical Palestinians who shoot at activist Jewish fundamentalists.

Let us attempt to at least partially unravel the facts.

For strict religious believers, the course of history is the manifestation of a plan of salvation. This applies to Jews, Muslims, Christians and others. The events of history are therefore not products of the work of man but of the will of God. Man's duty is to follow God's commandments, not to engage in politics.

Thus, if God desires to grant a people a piece of land, *He* will do so without requiring human assistance. To be truly convinced of this orthodox theory, one must be a true believer. Secularized people who have distanced themselves from religion—and they are now the great majority—will only be able to understand the concept intellectually, but at least this much is necessary if one wishes to concern oneself with the religious dimensions of the conflict over the Holy Land.

The decisive point is this: The emphasis of the religious dimension does not inevitably lead to the demand for the creation of a state for one's own religious group, be it Jewish, Muslim or Christian.

The holiness of the Holy Land is thus not dependent upon the factor statehood. This applies both to the religious and the historic dimensions of the conflict, as even during the centuries of their presence in the Holy Land, the Jewish people was organized as an independent state for only a very small portion of that time. In the more than 500-year-long period of the Second Temple (520 B.C.E. to the year 70) the Jewish people of the Holy Land continued to develop their religion and society in the Holy Land, but in political terms they were at best *autonomous,* that is they were able to exercise self-determination in internal matters, but they were not *sovereign*, i.e. they lacked self-determination in their external relations.

To put it more provocative terms, it is the *non*-religious who are more likely than the truly religious to speak in terms of a "battle for the Holy Land".

All theories, especially heretical ones such as this, must be substantiated. To this end, we shall briefly show for which Jewish believers holiness and political-secular statehood are mutually exclusive and for which believers this does not apply. In order to do so we must sketch the history of the tensions between the Jewish religion and Zionism.

The Zionist movement was proclaimed in 1897 by Theodor Herzl. The founding fathers of Zionism were anything but religious. Their longings for Zion were political, their goal a Jewish "homeland" and they quite deliberately avoided the term "state".

The early Zionists wanted to rescue threatened and persecuted Jews, not Judaism itself. The Holy Land was therefore not a fixation. In fact, some Zionist pioneers considered Argentina and even Uganda as possibilities for a Jewish homeland. Such plans, however, never gained wide acceptance. From both the religious and historical perspectives, Uganda and Argentina were pipe-dreams. The Holy Land, the Promised Land, was the only real alternative, even for the non-religious majority.

Nevertheless, the Zionists remained cautious; at first they even refrained from calling for the creation of a Jewish state. With good reason, as such a demand at that time would have been not only illusory but also self-destructive. How could this tiny band, which called itself the World Zionist Organization, hope to wrest the land for a Jewish state in Palestine from the then still powerful Ottoman Empire?

The decision for restraint was also wise from the intra-Jewish perspective. Strict religious Jews would have been incensed at what they could only regard as an attempt to usurp a role reserved to God alone: the return of the Jewish People to Zion.

But religious Jews were anything but united over the issue of mixing secular politics and religious history. Many religious leaders were interested in binding Zionism more closely to Judaism. Those who hoped to impart a greater Jewish religiosity to an originally non-religious, even anti-religious movement by working *from within* gave themselves the label "national-religious". To achieve the *Judaization of Zionism* they, of course, had to be integrated in the movement itself and thus set out on their own "march through the institutions". The most strictly religious groups, however, regarded even this approach as blasphemous and maintained their distance from the Zionist movement.

Those Zionists who called themselves national-religious also refrained from defining as their goal the establishment of a Jewish state in Zion, preferring instead to speak of creating a *spiritual center*. The Hebrew term is *Misrachi*; hence the name of their organization. Zion was to once again become the spiritual and religious center of the Jewish people. The issue of statehood was thus avoided.

To the national-religious, religion did not represent merely a means to a political goal. To the contrary, religious Jews joined Zionist organizations in order to prevent what they say as a weakening of the Jewish national movement.

For the majority of Zionists, Zion (Jerusalem) was the locality and the goal upon which their political efforts were focused. But their intention was to save Jewish lives, not souls, and religious Jews increasingly regarded these activities as provocations. In 1902 the Zionists decided that education, a traditional bastion of the religious, ought to be more secular and national—in other words: oriented to and controlled by the Zionist movement. The national-religious took this as a direct challenge and consolidated their hitherto loose constellation of groupings into an inner-Zionist "party". In its first program-matic platform, formulated in Pressburg (Bratislava) in 1904, the Misrachi party proclaimed that the survival of the Jewish People depended not only on its "return to the land of our fathers" but also on adhering to religious law.

Undeterred, the non-religious Zionist majority further escalated its demands, adding the control of cultural affairs to its list in 1911. For ortho-dox Jews this was tantamount to a declaration of war. One response was the formation of the Agudat Israel organization. From the Agudist viewpoint, the national-religious effort to make Zionism more Jewish was at best a waste of time, as the basic principles of Zionism were contrary to the Jewish religion.

In 1940, as the Nazi mass murder machinery was already going into high gear, the Agudist Rabbi Isaak Breuer polemicized: "It is nationalism which divides us from Zionism. … The concept of the nation in the Torah is con-trary to that of Zionism. … The Zionist idea of the nation is closer to that of the English than that of the people of God."

The orthodox groups also regarded a Jewish presence in the Holy Land as desirable, but statehood, in their view, violated the land's holiness—as long as the Messiah had not yet arrived. The orthodox were thus prepared to submit to virtually any secular authority other than Zionist rule, as this, they argued, could only serve to transform other-worldly, messianic expectations into pro-fane politics and was thus equivalent to blasphemy.

The emergence of the national-religious movement also brought forth another perspective: Liberating the Jewish people from the yoke of history and its diaspora existence was regarded as an integral part of the historical plan of salvation and thus as God's handiwork. But man could actively par-ticipate in "the beginning of salvation". In the national-religious perspective, Zionism and Israel took on the character of transitional stages between the sufferings of the diaspora and final salvation.

The experiences of the Holocaust served to modify the Augudists' view of the world and of salvation. Thus, Agudat Israel set out more or less enthusiastically on its own "march through Zionist organizations"—an effort which met with considerable success. The reasons Agudat Israel gave for its decision to participate in the Zionist movement were similar to those of the national-religious Misrachi. As the Agudist Rabbi Benjamin Minz put it succinctly in 1947: "Although we know that the Jewish State is not the complete solution we believe in, we know that this state will provide a means of rescue and relief for hundreds of thousands of Jews. It is thus perhaps possible to regard the Jewish State as the beginning of salvation." Saving lives thus appears as part of the process of saving souls. At least on this point an approach to the Zionist world view was accomplished.

The militantly orthodox members of Neturei Karta, however, continue to barricade themselves behind the ideological wall they have erected. For them, the Land of Israel is not a place of salvation in this world, but only in a metaphysical, other-worldly context. Displaying little interest in Israel's current affairs, in the past they went so far as to reject Zionism and Israel even as a means of rescue from the Holocaust. Refusing to resist the National-Socialist murderers, the ultra-orthodox accepted the "glory of martyrdom" as being "sent by God". An orthodox rabbi brought to Auschwitz described his fate as a "just punishment" for not having resisted Zionism more decisively.

This tradition continues: The fundamentalist Rabbi Schach placed himself at the forefront of an orthodox march through the Zionist institutions, but, as a believer in history as the manifestation of the plan of salvation, maintained a soft stance towards the Palestinians. During Israel's continuing political crisis in 1990 and 1991, Rabbi Schach produced a series of new variations on the meditations of the Hungarian orthodox rabbi in Auschwitz. Although more than 90 years old, Rabbi Schach proclaimed with youthful combativeness and zeal that the Holocaust was God's punishment for Jewish apostasy. To the non-religious majority in Israel, such pronouncements had an incredible ring to them, and they must appear even more astounding to non-Jews.

On the other hand, Schach and his followers never requested permission from Jordan's King Hussein, Yasir Arafat or his representative in Jerusalem, Faisal Husseini, when they planned to pray at the Western Wall (the "Wailing Wall") of the former Temple. Neturei Karta, of course, always requests permission, as it recognizes the Arabs as the legitimate political authority in Jerusalem.

There is no such thing as the *single* truth, not even among the religious, be they Jews or not. Only one thing is clear: The multiplicity of interconnections between religion and politics with regard to the Jewish return to the Holy

Land. It is only natural that the responses to this diversity vary widely among the Zionist majority on the one hand and fundamentalist-religious Jews on the other.

Jewish statehood and holiness are mutually exclusive—so claim the fundamentalists—as long as the "blasphemous" Zionists hold sway. The Zionists' dilemma lies in the fact that the legitimacy of their presence in Zion is inseparable from the Jewish religion. To give up the religion means to lose the automatic claim to Jewish statehood. This statehood *can* be based on and justified by the Jewish religion, but at the same time the Jewish religion can be used to negate the legitimacy of statehood.

Those striving to clothe their actions and missions in the Holy Land in holiness would do well to keep this ambiguity in mind. Those who lose sight of it run the risk of falling into the very trap they set for others. Not least among those who ought to keep this in mind are the more zealous among the national-religious settlers of the West Bank. In the 1970s they banded together to form *Gush Emunim*, the "block of the faithful", with the purpose of once more accelerating the "beginning of salvation" by founding Jewish settlements in the occupied territories: continuity in change and continuity in escalation. The arguments and instruments of these national-religious extremists may, however, boomerang, as they are based on the ambiguity of religion.

It is, of course, entirely understandable that (like the majority of non-religious Jewish Israelis) the national-religious prefer Jewish statehood to a minority status in an Arab environment. The plight of minorities in the Arab world today is anything but tempting. Who would voluntarily share the fate of the Palestinians of Kuwait, a large portion of whom at first jubilantly welcomed the Iraqi invaders in August 1990? Who would willingly trade places with the Christians of Lebanon or the Shiites or Kurds in Iraq? Who would want, as a Jew, to live in a state dominated by a group whose stated aim is to achieve a new "final solution" of the "Jewish question", this time in Palestine? Such a "final solution" is the aim of the Islamic-fundamentalist Palestinian Hamas movement.

Zionism in the Quran?

Most Islamic fundamentalists active today seek to establish their theocratic state with the help of the sword or, more exactly, the machine gun or the atomic bomb. Iran and Libya, for example, have nuclear weapons programs. Iran has received or is receiving assistance from China, India, Russia and—it is rumored—France. Libya employs Pakistani experts and—it is also rumored—is being supported by German companies.

Apparently even the Islamic theocrats do not leave the affairs of this world entirely to God's providence. Here and there they also lend Him a helping hand. As fundamentalist *activists* they see it as their duty to steer the course of salvation with a firm human hand. Despite all other differences, this view of history exhibits obvious similarities with that of national-religious Jews. As so often, the most bitter opponents display considerable similarities, more than they desire or are willing to acknowledge.

There is, however, one decisive difference. In contradistinction to the Palestinian fundamentalists of the Hamas movement, hardly any Jewish Israeli speaks in terms of a "final solution" to the Palestinian question. (Since there are also Muslim and Christian Israelis, we deliberately use the apparent redundancy "Jewish Israeli".) Neither religious nor non-religious Jewish Israelis have proclaimed such a monstrous ultimate goal. For lack of evidence, we cannot know whether or not they have contemplated the possibilities, but spoken or written statements to such effect do not exist.

Apart from this significant exception, the national-religious extremes of both sides share common ground in their admixture of (secular) history and the plan of salvation—and in conjuring up the diabolical in the name of the divine.

Paradoxically, it is even possible to cite the Quran as an historical-political atlas in support of the Jewish-Zionist cause. It is beyond question that the prophet Mohammed placed himself firmly in the Judaic tradition, that is in the tradition of the Hebrew Bible. And according to the Bible, God promised the Holy Land to the Jews.

A reading of the Quran thus brings no surprises. Sura 10,94 reads: "We had prepared a permanent home [in Canaan] for the Children of Israel." This text is by no means the only proof. Whether it is permissible to desirable to argue on religious grounds is an entirely different matter.

In the 14th Sura, Abraham (the progenitor of the Jews and thus also of Muslims) gives voice to a significant revelation to Mecca. In the verses 14–15 the Lord of the Jews confirms the right of the People of Israel (whose faith, as so often, was wavering) to the Promised Land: "We will wipe out the evildoers and give you the land as your dwelling. … And they [the Jews] called on Allah for aid and the rebels were undone." The invocation of violence here is certainly a matter for controversy, but the right of the Jews to the land is clearly expressed in the 14th Sura, which also says that this right can be forfeited in the case of sacrilegious acts which sever the link to Allah/God. This is entirely consistent with the tradition of the Jewish prophets.

Sura 17 tells how one night the Mohammed, accompanied by of the Archangel Gabriel, flew through the air from "the holy temple of Mecca to the distant temple of Jerusalem" (verse 2). The latter had, of course, been destroyed by the Roman army under Titus in the year 70. Verse 105 of Sura 17 reads: "We said to the Children of Israel: 'Dwell upon the Land, and when the promise of life to come is fulfilled, we will go with you to the judgment.'"

These verses from the Quran are bad news for anti-Zionist fundamentalists.

Sura 21, verse 72 and following are also of interest: "So we saved him [Abraham] and Lot and brought them into the Land in which … we blessed all creatures. We gave him Isaac and Jacob and made them all righteous men." Once again there is little room for doubt, as little as in Sura 24,56: "Allah promises to those among you who believe and perform good works that He will install you in the land as the successors of the infidels, just as He made them the successors of the infidels of their time." This means that the unbelieving Jews were the successors of those who had lived in unbelief before. These predecessors can be identified as the Canaanites. The exile of the Jews, whose can thus be succeeded by the Muslims, is to be attributed to their turning away from God (here Allah). Here, too, the Muslim prophet speaks the language of the Jewish prophets, who by no means excluded the possibility of the Jewish people returning to Zion. However, they postulated the religious purification of the Jews as a precondition. This would then permit the reestablishment of Jewish statehood in the form of a theocratic rule to be established by the Messiah, who would then extend His sovereignty to all mankind, thus erasing all religious distinctions between Jew and non-Jew. All would believe in God, whom the Muslims call Allah, and the Jews Elohim.

Against this background the convergence of the Muslim interpretation with that of Jewish fundamentalists is no surprise. Without this proximity of views there could be no basis of contact between Neturei Karta and Palestinian nationalists. Whatever we may think of this convergence, both Jewish and Muslim sources make it explicable.

Sura 26,58 also refers to Canaan, which the Jews inherited by Allah's will. The passage mentions gardens, springs and wonderful dwellings, all of which the Children of Israel inherited. Does this not remind us of the "Land of milk and honey" of the Old Testament?

The Islamic fundamentalists of the Hisbollah ought to first study the Quran before swearing to "liberate" Palestine from the Jews. They might thus avoid the embarrassment of violating the spirit of the same Quran upon which they base their appeal. Of course, as in any religion, there are differences of interpretation which can serve to transmute an unambiguous statement into its opposite. As so often, it is useful to return to the sources themselves—without the cosmetics of partisan commentators. One need not possess prophetic abilities in order to predict that such information will be met with intense criticism and protest. To many, a presentation of the facts is regarded as a provocation. This is true of Muslims, Jews, Christians and others.

The religious-spiritual and political ideal of the Islamic community was never Palestine or Jerusalem, but always the original community founded by Mohammed himself in the Islamic city-state of Medina. For true Muslims, the past represents the dream of the future. The Arabic peoples and Arabia are the chief pillars of Islam, which is thus an "Arab-centered" religion. For Muslims, the holiest sites of their religion are located in Arabia. Today's "Palestine-centered" orientation is a recent, politically motivated growth. Nevertheless, the International Conference for the Support of the Islamic

Revolution in Palestine, held in October 1991, appears to have overlooked this fact when it designated the "Palestinian question" as "the most important problem of the Islamic world" and labelled the "Zionist regime" as a "totally unjustifiable entity in the heart of Islamic countries". Fundamentalists ought to be measured on the basis of their own fundamentals—Islamic fundamentalists therefore by the Quran.

What the Arab language and Arabia with its holy sites represent to Muslims, that is Israel and the Hebrew language to Jews. We will return to the importance of the Jewish holy sites in connection with the question as to *where* the Holy Land is holy.

Part II

The Holy Land, Religions and Politics

What Is the Holy Land?—Biblical Borders?

"From the Euphrates to the Nile", it is claimed, is the expanse of territory to which a "Greater Israel" aspires. Yasir Arafat has frequently reiterated this charge and many of his followers have taken up the cry, citing the Bible, Israel's supposed political atlas, as their source. The Bible, it is claimed, identifies the area "from the Euphrates to the Nile" as the Promised land of the Jews, as the Holy Land.

Upon closer examination, Arafat and his followers prove to be not so much biblical experts as political propagandists.

The Hebrew Bible (the Christian Old Testament) actually refers to *three* geographical areas as the Promised Land, each of which is described differently:

1. The land of the forefathers
2. The land of the Children of Israel, who fled Egypt and conquered the territory of the Canaanites
3. The area of settlement of the Jews who returned from Babylonian exile after 538 B.C. (the period of the Second Temple).

The Land of the Forefathers: In the First Book of Moses (Genesis 15:18) we read "The Lord made a covenant with Abraham, saying: "... to your descendants I give this land, from the river of Egypt to the great river, the river Euphrates...." Isaac receives an indirect confirmation of these borders: "Do not go down to Egypt; dwell in the land of which I shall tell you. Sojourn in this land, and I will be with you, and will bless you; for to you and to your descendants I will give all these lands, and I will fulfill the oath which I swore to Abraham your father." (Genesis 26:2–3)

© The Author(s), under exclusive license to Springer Nature Switzerland AG 2021
M. Wolffsohn, *Whose Holy Land?*, https://doi.org/10.1007/978-3-030-74286-7_6

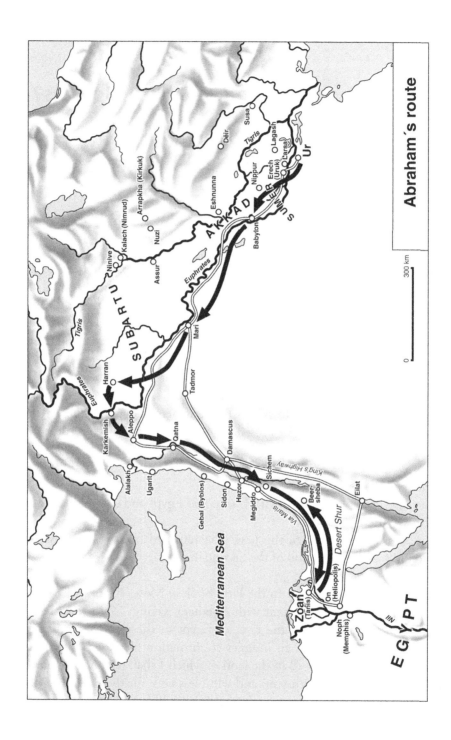

Abraham´s route

The Second Book of Moses (Exodus 23:31) delineates a similar region: "And I will set your bounds from the Red Sea to the sea of the Philistines, and from the wilderness to the Euphrates." The "sea of the Philistines" is the Mediterranean.

Arafat thus appears to be justified in his claim. The promise to one people becomes the curse for another. We must, however, examine the historical facts.

The forefathers Abraham, Isaac and Jacob were nomads or semi-nomads. The biblical stories make it quite clear that they moved with their animals from one grazing area or water hole to another. They knew no permanent place of residence.

Later parts of the Bible describe the gradual transition from nomadic wandering to permanent settlement, especially the story of the conquest of the land of the Canaanites, which did not take place until the thirteenth century B.C.E.

The passage from the Bible cited above thus merely delineates the territory in which the nomads wandered, but it does not define permanent borders, certainly not borders in the political sense. A closer look at the routes followed by the forefathers and the places where they sojourned reveals that they kept their distance from the larger towns and cities and thus from the political and economic centers. Abraham and his followers avoided the important trade routes—so as to not come into conflict with the established powers. As the map on p. 30 makes clear, one need not be an historian or an expert on the Bible to understand this basic context. It is quite sufficient to follow the relevant parts of the Hebrew Bible, a highly reliable source of information, with an atlas at hand.

When we also regard the geography of the Middle East in this context (see map on p. 33), we see that the heavily travelled trade routes generally followed the geographically most easily passable path, for example along the coastal plain, where we find Ugarit, Sidon and Gaza. But Abraham traversed the region through much more circuitous and difficult mountainous interior. Clearly, it is the weaker party whose wanderings do not follow the obviously more preferable route.

Even then, the wanderings of the forefathers were not entirely lacking in frictions, but no major conflicts, much less wars, developed. We will return to this aspect in connection with the history of the Holy Land.

The region through which the forefathers roamed can hardly be taken as an historical legitimation for the claims of a modern polity or state. This would be a poor joke, as Abraham was politically powerless and cautiously plotted his path to avoid to spheres of the powerful wherever possible. The prototypical conqueror he was not. This ought to be finally recognized by those who seek to explain Israel's supposedly innate "expansionism" in terms of the biblical borders from the Euphrates to the Nile.

The land of the Jewish conquerors of Canaan as described in the Bible is considerably more modest in size, encompassing mainly the areas east and west of the River Jordan. This much more moderate description not only sounds better to the present-day ear, it is also more in tune with the modern political tone. True, the Euphrates is once again mentioned in the Fifth Book of Moses (Deuteronomy 1:7–8), but not the Nile. The southern limits remain undefined. The Lebanon massif is given as the northern border. Comparable descriptions are to be found in Deuteronomy 11:24 and in Joshua 1:4: "From the wilderness [Sinai] and this Lebanon as far as the great river, the river Euphrates, all the land of the Hittites to the Great Sea toward the going down of the sun" [Mediterranean].

"I will myself drive them out from before the people of Israel" God says to Joshua (12:6) of the previously enumerated other peoples (Joshua 12:2–5). The land is essentially the same as that mentioned in the first chapter. The area of El-Arish is named as the southern demarcation to the Sinai dessert. In Exodus 23:31 the Jews led out of Egypt by Moses and then by Joshua had been promised considerably more: the whole sweep from the Red Sea to the Euphrates.

On the other hand, the land which Moses promises the Jews in Numbers 4:3–15 is almost as minuscule as that of the borders of Israel between 1948 and 1967. Although the exact areas can no longer be defined with certainty, the area encompassed at least parts of the northern Negev, the West Bank and Galilee.

At first glance it appears rather odd that God retracts one promise after another given to Moses, who is, after all, the greatest Jewish prophet and leader. We must recognize, however, that the biblical text shifts from a mode of religious promise to a concrete narration of how the land was taken into possession. We find ourselves in a zone between the realms of metaphysics and historical politics. As the promise became more binding, its dimensions diminished. In the fifth book of the Torah (Deuteronomy) Moses is able to view the entire land from a single vantage point with the unaided eye: "And Moses went up from the plains of Moab to Mount Nebo, to the top of Pisgah, which is opposite to Jericho. And the Lord showed him all the land, Gilead as far as Dan, all Naphtali, the land of Ephraim and Manasseh, all the land of Jodah as far as the Western Sea, the Negeb and the Plain, that is, the valley of Jericho the city of palm trees, as far as Zoar. And the Lord said to him, 'This is the land of which I swore to Abraham, to Isaac, and to Jacob. 'I will give it to your descendants.' I have let you see it with your eyes, but you shall not go over there.'" (Deuteronomy 34:1–4)

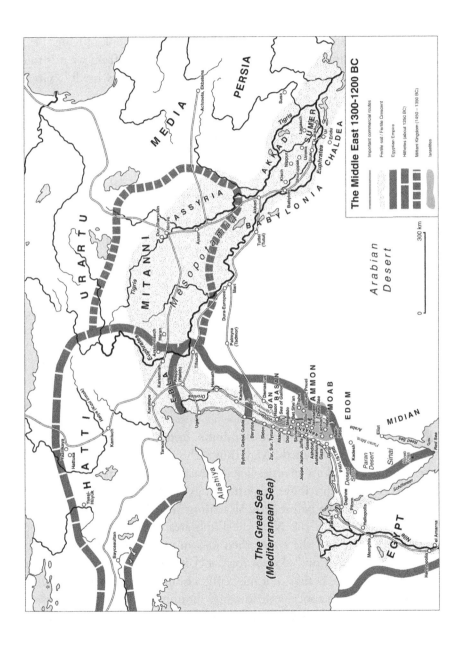

The Middle East 1300–1200 BC

Indeed, the land promised to Abraham was certainly much more extensive. Does the biblical narrative count on our forgetfulness? We choose not to speculate on this possibility, but do wish to point out the contradiction.

Both the Second Book of Samuel, which refers to "all the tribes of Israel, from Dan to Beer-sheba" (2 Samuel 24:2) and the First Book of Kings (4:25) reflect the narrow limits of the Promised Land, stretching from what is today northern Israel to the northern part of the Negev. This is hardly "Greater Israel".

The considerable expansion of territory through the conquests of the kings, especially David and Solomon, is simply not counted as part of the Holy Land, even if the area ruled over by these kings came considerably closer to the expanse promised to Abraham. The conquests were, in the final analysis, simply not part of the (varying) package declared by God as the Promised Land. Recent archeological proof contradicts the huge biblical geography of David's and Solomon's kingdom. In fact, it was much smaller than described in this "source". (See Finkelstein's books). No wonder, the Bible tells one religious story after the other rather than history, and its authors did not really pretend writing waterproof history. Only religious officials have.

The area "from Dan to Beer-sheba" is presented as the core region, even in the time of Solomon, who "ruled over all the kings west of the Euphrates from Tiphsah to Gaza, over all the kings west of the Euphrates; and he had peace on all sides round about him. And Judah and Israel dwelt in safety, from Dan even to Beer-sheba, every man under his vine and under his fig tree" (1 Kings 4:24–25).

The boundaries assigned to the land for the messianic age grow to enormous dimensions. Psalm 72 (8–11) speaks in terms of a huge empire under the Messiah-king: "May he have dominion from sea to sea, and from the River to the ends of the earth! May those who dwell in the wilderness bow down before him, and his enemies lick the dust! May the kings of Tarhish and of the isles render him tribute, may the kings of Sheba and Seba bring gifts! May all kings fall down before him, all nations serve him!"

The borders are thus the Nile, the Euphrates, the Persian Gulf and the Mediterranean—almost the entire then known world. But even the phrases "all kings" and "all nations" do not form a claim to Jewish world hegemony. Instead, the language is that of a messianic vision, a mixture of well-known geographic terms with apocalyptic longings for universal peace. But we should not be surprised that those whose anti-Semitic prejudices remain unshakable interpret this passage as evidence of the beginning of Jewish efforts to rule the world.

The period of the Second Temple lasted from 520 B.C.E to the year 70. The Jewish people formed a community that achieved full independence only for brief periods and otherwise enjoyed the advantages and disadvantages of semi-autonomy, i.e. internal self-rule without independence.

In this period the lands east and west of the Jordan formed the core of a Jewish community that varied considerably in its geographical dimensions. The Jews who returned from Babylonian exile under Ezra and Nehemiah could look down from the mountains of Jerusalem upon the fertile coastal plain (that was to form the heartland of the State of Israel from 1948 to 1967) but they were unable to attain dominance over these lands. The autonomous Jewish area did grow in size, but also included numerous non-Jewish populations. In turn, many Jews lived in non-Jewish areas. Today this is called "settlement policy".

As a religious and historical guidebook, the Hebrew Bible ends with the books of Ezra and Nehemiah, that is in the fifth century before the Christian era. What follows is purely historical writing and need not concern us in the present context.

No matter what angle of view we choose, we run into nothing but contradictions. We choose here not to attempt to deal with the root causes for this condition, as our concern is not biblical text analysis. In the search for biblical passages relevant to the status of the Holy Land, we find that the Holy Book is unsuitable for use as a political atlas, neither for believers, nor for the scholarly researcher, nor for Yasir Arafat, nor for Greater Israel advocates.

We speak here only of biblical, not of historical boundaries. The former are confusing enough. Thus, the Bible can serve as political atlas only for those who ignore its contradictions and whose approach is deliberately à la carte, be it pro or contra Israel and the Jewish people.

What is the Holy Land from the *Christian* perspective? Essentially, it is identical with the Jewish view, as it is undisputed that Jesus lived and taught as a Jew, among Jews and in the land of the Jewish people. Political borders played no role. For Christians, the land is holy because of the miracles Jesus performed there, because Jesus' life, death and resurrection took place there. The holy places in the Holy Land thus have more meaning for Christians than the land itself. From the Christian perspective, therefore, the key issues are access to as well as administration and control of the holy sites.

Until the Islamic conquest, the Christian Byzantine Empire held sway over the Holy Land and watched over its holy places. Between 1096 and 1291 the Crusaders attempted to re-establish a similar situation. Their efforts met with short-term success but proved a failure over the long term. As a result, the

Christian world effectively abandoned hope of controlling the Holy Land for a long period of history. With the insight born of necessity, Christians were satisfied with free access to the holy sites and strove to achieve the greatest possible latitude in self-administration.

Not until the nineteenth century were the European colonial powers in a position to demand more influence. For the brief period between 1917 and 1948 the British Empire became the successor of the Byzantines and the Crusaders, controlling both the Holy Land and its holy sites.

And the *Islamic* perspective? It, too, is much the same as the Jewish—'even if many fanatics refuse to acknowledge the fact. The Quran is based on Judaism and Mohammed indisputably stands in the tradition of the biblical prophets. The God's promise of the Holy Land is accepted as a given fact in the Quran, where it is nowhere called into question. Furthermore, the issue of political borders is irrelevant in the context of the plan of salvation.

Why Is the Land Holy?

The answer is readily at hand. In the first of the five books of Moses which comprise the Torah we read: "For to you and to your descendants I will give all these lands, and I will fill the oath which I swore to Abraham your father." (Genesis 26,3) Even in their most anti-Jewish manifestations, neither Christianity nor Islam could entirely ignore this fundamental religious touchstone. We therefore concentrate here on the Jewish perspective. As already mentioned, the Christian and Muslim viewpoints are closely tied to the holy places.

In their wonderful narrations, the authors of the 63 lengthy tracts which comprise the Talmud glorify the holiness of the Promised Land. In their view there was no greater good in this world. Frequently, the Talmudic sages utilize biblical quotations and references to back up their arguments:

> Our masters taught (Taanit 10a): "The Land of Israel was created first, and all of the rest of the world was created last, as it is written: 'Before he had made the earth with its fields' [Proverbs 8:26]. The Holy One, praise be to him, waters the Land of Israel himself and the rest of the world through a messenger, for it is written: 'He gives rain upon the earth and sends waters upon the fields.'" (Job 5:10)

> Our masters taught (Ketubbot 110b): "A man should always dwell in the Land of Israel, even in a city where the greater number are from other peoples. And he should not dwell outside the land, not even in a city where the greater number are of the people of Israel. Every man who lives in the Land of Israel is like a man who has a god. And every man who lives outside the land, is like a man who has no god. For it is written: 'to give you the land of Canaan, and to be

M. Wolffsohn, *Whose Holy Land?*, https://doi.org/10.1007/978-3-030-74286-7_7

your God' [Leviticus 25:38] Does every man who does not dwell in the Land of Israel no god? But no, it is only to say: Every man who lives outside the land is like a man who serves an idol. And so says David in Holy Book: '... for they have driven me out this day that I should have no share in the heritage of the Lord, saying, 'Go, serve other gods.''[1 Samuel 26:19] Who should have said to David; 'Go, serve other gods'? But no, it is only to say: Every man who lives outside the land is like a man who serves an idol."

And Rabbi Seira said: "The air of the Land of Israel makes one wise." (Bava Batra 158b)

And who would not want to become wise in this simple manner? The fulfillment of religious law—all of the laws—was, however, the precondition. And this is only possible in the Land of Israel:

And Rabbi Simlai explained: "Why did Moses, our master, desire to enter the Land of Israel? Was it necessary for him to eat of its fruits? Or was it necessary for him to satisfy himself from its goodness? But no, Moses said to himself: Many laws were given to Israel which can only be fulfilled in the Land of Israel. I desire to enter the Land of Israel so that they may all be fulfilled through me." (Sota 14a)

The Talmudic sages clearly recognized the weak points of religious argumentation, which they attempted to shore up by taking up the contradictions and their doubts with the purpose of gently but firmly removing them.

By rough estimation, the Talmud took on its definitive written form during the first five centuries of the Christian era, that is in the period following the destruction of the Second Temple and the Jewish polity by the Romans. The Talmud is thus also a response to the loss of Jewish statehood. The goal of the Talmudic sages was to preserve the Jewish religion in the absence of a geographically centralized Jewish political community or state. Their purpose was therefore to lay the foundations for a renewed Jewish statehood—in the Holy Land, of course. In contrast to their forefathers, whose all too frequent sacrileges provoked divine retribution, the renewed Jewish people was to base its future community or state on Jewish piety.

Another Talmud passage makes a further interesting point:

"'A land like a gazelle'—so it is written. Like the gazelle, whose hide [after skinning] can no longer contain its flesh, so it is with the Land of Israel: In the time in which it is inhabited, it is wide, and in the time in which it is not inhabited it shrinks." (Gittin 57a)

The authors of the Talmud register and allude to various forms of "shrinkage". Primarily, they recognize the neglect of the land. In their time, this neglect was all too obvious. The land had deteriorated under the rule of its (Christian) Byzantine masters. Of course, such descriptions were intended to further arouse the ire of Jewish readers, and the consequences of misrule were thus drastically portrayed. But should—we ask somewhat heretically—this "shrinkage" not also be interpreted as a reference to the considerable differences in the biblical descriptions of the extent of the Promised Land? Of course, many, including experts, will protest and insist upon a totally differing interpretation, but the phenomenon of "shrinkage" cannot be simply ignored.

We must also take into account the fact that the flow of "milk and honey" (Exodus 3:8) was by no means automatic. The precondition was always zealous, dedicated, hard work—and service to God. The land was "good and broad" (Exodus 3:8) when the people of Israel dwelt there—but only when they took the laws of their religion seriously, for this strip of earth, then as now, was by no means climatically favored. The largely infertile land could only be maintained as a fertile garden if its inhabitants' labor more than compensated for their negligence and lack of piety.

The holiness of the land remains relevant even beyond death, as it is the place where the resurrection of the dead will begin (Ketubbot 111a). And furthermore:

Rav Anan said (Ketubbot 111a): "For everyone who is buried in the Land of Israel it is like being buried under an altar. Here it is written: 'An altar of earth you shall make for me' [Exodus 20:24]. And there it is written: 'His land reconciles his people.'" (Deuteronomy 32:43)

Rabbi Elazer said: "The dead outside the land will not be raised." (Ketubbot 111a)

For religious Jews, the Holy Land is the real (or, in the Diaspora, the hoped-for) homeland whose language (Hebrew) they speak—but only while at prayer, religious services, Torah readings and other religious occasions. They otherwise speak Jiddish so as not to profane the holy.

For religious Jews, the Holy Land is thus not just their fatherland or mother country. It is, above all, God's land, the land which God promised and granted to the Jewish people—but only on condition. It thus depends upon the Jewish people whether God's land will belong to Jews or not. If Jews sin against God, they must leave the land—thus commands religious law. Of course, religious and non-religious Jews may argue over this furiously, and the differences of opinion are enormous even among the religious: Is the State of Israel the "beginning of salvation" (the national-religious view) or is it blasphemy (as the ultra-orthodox contend)? One may argue endlessly, but the knowledge of basic facts is the prerequisite for arriving at an informed opinion.

Why did the mass return of Jews to the Holy Land set in only at the end of the nineteenth century? This is a frequently posed question, bit it fails to address the heart of the problem. Again, it is necessary to know that the most religious jews were extremely skeptical of or rejected outright any politically motivated and secularly organized return to Zion, choosing instead to await an unambiguous sign from God as the prerequisite for the re-establishment of a Jewish community in the Holy Land.

In the past, more than a few false prophets proclaimed such a sign and forged plans for a return to Zion. All of them failed miserably. Sabbatai Zvi (1626–1676) was the most famous of the false messiahs. His attempt to wrest control of the Holy Land from the Turks proved a personal boomerang. In the end, this supposed Jewish messiah converted to Islam.

Why and how should the comparatively minuscule ranks of the scattered Jewish people have succeeded where the armies of the Crusaders had repeatedly failed? Until well into the twentieth century, any such effort on the part of the Jewish people appeared futile, even suicidal. No handful of Jews could have hoped to prevail against the might of the Turkish Ottoman Empire, the Euro-Asian great power which held sway over the Holy Land from the beginning of the sixteenth century until 1917. It was considered the better part of valor to forget about a patently foolish enterprise doomed to all but certain failure.

But this argument only leads us onto a sidetrack. Since an organized return to Zion was only conceivable on a religious basis, the only such possibility before the age of secularization existed in the form of a messianic movement. But the protagonists of such movements proved to be political failures and charlatans such as Sabbatai Zvi—or David Rëubeni, or Salomo Molcho in their time. Rëubeni was imprisoned by the Inquisition, which burned Moloch at the state in 1532. Their fates did not exactly invite imitation, even though messianic expectations continued in currency.

In 1453 Constantinople, the capital of the Byzantine Empire, was captured by the Islamic Turks, but its Christian rulers before had not distinguished themselves through tolerance toward their Jewish subjects.

In 1492 the Catholic majesties Isabella of Castile and Ferdinand of Aragón completed the Reconquista, the Christian re-conquest of Spain. The Muslim rulers were driven out of Grenada and with them the Jewish population throughout the kingdoms. Many of the Jewish exiles from Spain and Portugal found refuge in the Ottoman Empire, some in the Holy land. The Muslim rulers of the Ottoman Empire proved considerably more tolerant than the majority of their Christian contemporaries.

1492, it is well known, was also the date of an historical event of world-wide and long-term impact: the Spanish "discovery" of America. Although its significance was not immediately grasped by Columbus' contemporaries, it was soon realized that his discovery was an historical turning-point.

At the same time, dramatic events were also unfolding in Eastern Europe. Around 1500 Russia embarked upon its "gathering of the Russian earth", which entailed the gradual and irreversible conquest of the lands under the rule of the descendants of the medieval Mongolian invaders. This was soon followed by a rapid expansion of the Russian Empire to the Pacific Coast.

That the period around the year 1500 marked the dawn of a new era was registered by Jew and non-Jew alike. For many, however, it was a period of horrors. But was is messianic? The answer is yes, because Jewish tradition expects the advent of the Messiah to follow a period of intense trial and tribulation. The self-anointed messiah of that era could thus expect a ready audience, as the persecution of Jews in Christian Europe had been in high fashion since the fourteenth century. In the recurring phases of acute economic crisis it was often the poorest and thus most afflicted classes who clamored for their rulers to drive out the "evil Jews".

At the time of the false messiah Sabbatai Zvi—in the middle of the seventeenth century—the Ukraine was the scene of especially odious persecutions. Under the leadership of Bogdan Chmielnicki, the Cossacks sought to cast off the yoke of their Polish overlords. In the process, Chmielnicki instigated the greatest bloodbath in the entire history of the Jewish People previous to the Nazi Holocaust. It is estimated that a hundred thousand Jews were brutally murdered.

Those who ask why Jews did not seek to organize a return to Zion at an earlier date need to be reminded of the fact that Europe before the beginning of the nineteenth century was deeply and pervasively religious. This applied to Jews and non-Jews alike. We again must recall how controversial Zionism and the State of Israel remain even today among orthodox religious Jews, who condemn any attempt on the part of man to interfere with God's plan of salvation as the work of the devil. We consequently should not be surprised to learn of signs such as one spotted mounted to the house of a strict orthodox rabbi of the Neturei Kartha movement in Jerusalem: "A Jew is not a Zionist."

Of course, orthodox Jews do not believe that God has irrevocably abandoned the Jewish people and thus invalidated their claim to the Holy Land. Nor do enlightened Christians adhere to this dogma—at least no longer. But it also should come as no surprise that the political re-establishment of a Jewish State represents a problem not only for orthodox Jews, but also for religious Christians and Muslims.

The issue of God's abandonment of the Jewish people in fact presents a problem in the context of the Quran. The already mentioned Sura 24,56 can be read with an anti-Jewish interpretation: Accordingly, Allah has chosen the righteous believers (i.e. the Muslims) to be the "successors of the infidels" (i.e. the Jews) in the Holy Land. In the eyes of Muslims, Jews are to be classified as infidels because they refuse to recognize the Prophet Mohammed. In turn, Christians accuse the Jews of refusing to acknowledge Jesus as Christ, as Saviour and Messiah. Be it abandonment or a milder form of accusation, from both Muslim and Christian viewpoints the Jewish people can no longer assert an indisputable claim to the Holy Land—unless, of course, the foundation of the State of Israel is to be interpreted in the national-religious sense as the "beginning of salvation", an interpretation in fact shared by some "fundamentalist" Christian sects but vehemently rejected by orthodox religious Jews as blasphemous.

Just one question, but a multitude of answers. Where are we to find certainty in religious issues, where, as Hannah Arendt observed, fallible humans seek to interpret God's will?

Before the historical process of secularization began to affect the Jewish people in the course of the nineteenth century a politically motivated return to Zion was unthinkable. It is secularization which made political Zionism possible.

As paradoxical as the thesis may sound: Without secularization there would have been no Zionist movement and without Zionism no return to Zion would have been possible. As long as Jews remained deeply religious they could not seek to establish a Jewish political community in Zion. This, of course, does not mean that religious Jews had abandoned their ties to the Holy Land. To the contrary, the prayers and rituals of religious Jews daily emphasize their unbroken links to Zion.

Time was not a factor for religious Jews, nor did political history ultimately count. Only the plan of salvation mattered. Thus, the length of the Jewish exile from Zion was insignificant. It remained the Promised Land, no matter who lived there and who ruled the land.

The age of secularization began in earnest in the early years of the nineteenth century. The beginning of politically motivated, Zionist immigration to Palestine can be traced to the year 1881. It was one reaction to a series of horrible pogroms in Russia. In 1897 Theodor Herzl founded the World Zionist Organization - as a response to anti-Semitism in France. In less than a hundred years, the process of secularization led to Zionist results. The actions were by no means sanctioned and supported by a majority of the Jewish people but only by a relatively small number of highly motivated Jews who,—and this is decisive—were religious, non-religious and even anti-religious. The Zionists turned the spiritual-intellectual world of their pious forefathers upside-down. In their view, of course, they were only attempting to set aright a topsy-turvy Jewish world from its head back onto its feet, that is to give what they saw as an all too exclusively intellectual-spiritual Judaism a practical economic and political footing. Whatever the viewpoint, the Zionists began their new movement by tying into a very ancient phenomenon: the hope for salvation. Zionism, however, shifted the focus of these expectations from an uncertain messianic age to the immediate present.

Their sufferings in the Diaspora served to intensify Jewish hopes and wishes for an immediate and concrete form of salvation. Secularized Jews refused to be consoled with waiting for the Messiah. For them, Zion promised liberation, rescue and salvation not as a part of a distant divine plan of salvation but in the form of an historic locality and as part of a concrete political plan. For secularized, non-religious Jews, Zionism took over the role of the messianic expectations of religious Jews. The other-worldly, messianic longing for Zion became Zionism, a new, secularized plan of salvation intended to unfold in this world. Therefore, as the noted German-Jewish-Israeli scholar Gerschom Scholem noted, Zionism was always accompanied by "overtones of messianism". Scholem described Zionism as a form of "pseudo-messianism"—a label by no means meant as derogatory. What is most important is that the messianic core of Zionism is ancient, but its political raiments are new. Zionism is a secularized form of Jewish messianism.

Why is the Holy Land holy to Christians? The question is easily misunderstood, as Christianity—not even in the age of the Crusaders—has never raised the claim that the Holy Land was promised to the Christians. Very early on, under the leadership of the Apostle Paul, Christianity very deliberately dissolved the existing tie between religion and a specific people or nation. Anyone who became a Christian thus joined the new people of God, and Christianity became an inter-national community—in conscious contrast to the national Jewish community. A national community requires its specific territory, an international community does not.

The Holy Land was thus never the land of the life and history of the Christian people, as is the case with the Jewish people. But it was the location of the life, passion and resurrection of Jesus Christ and thus tied to the history of Christian salvation. For this reason, the Holy Land remains a special place for Christians. It was always painful for pious Christians to see the control of the Holy Land pass into non-Christian hands. For those whose responsibility it was to translate religion into concrete policy, the chief goals were the erection of churches at the holy sites and the administration of, or at least a say in the administration of these sites.

And why is the land holy to Muslims? In the first part of this book we permitted ourselves the heretical question as to whether the Quran cannot be read as a Zionist source book. For Muslims as well as Christians, the Holy Land is not the focus of national history, in this case of the Arab nation. However, as we will later examine more closely, there have always been close ties between the Holy Land and the Arabs as the founders and original bearers of Islam. As in the case of the Christians, the land is part of the Islamic history of salvation, More exactly put: It is the focus of one very small but important part of that history, namely Mohammed's night visit to Jerusalem.

It is well known that Mohammed neither lived nor taught in the Holy Land. But without any direct religious connection to this land (and thus to Judaism and Christianity) Islam would have been lacking in ties to the other revealed religions. Mohammed's nighttime journey to Jerusalem cemented this link.

Mohammed's journey brought him "from the holy temple in Mecca to the distant temple of Jerusalem" (Sura 17,2). Allah and the archangel Gabriel transported Mohammed through the air to Zion, thus establishing the link between Islam and Judaism, specifically between Islam, the Jewish temple and the rock located there, upon which Abraham was to have sacrificed his son Isaac. According to Islamic tradition (but not the Quran itself) it is from this rock that Mohammed ascended into heaven. It is not claimed that Mohammed was resurrected, but a connection to the nearby sites of Christ's resurrection and ascension appears obvious and is hardly pure coincidence. Islam, after all, recognizes Jesus as a prophet—but not as "Son of God": "Praise be to Allah, who has neither a son nor any other companion in his realm" (Sura 17,112) We recognize that Islam is characteristically close to and yet maintains a safe distance from both Judaism and Christianity.

We find additional evidence of this affinity in the further elaboration of the tradition of Mohammed's ascent to heaven, in the course of which, the tradition relates, the Prophet met Abraham, Moses and Jesus. Of course, according to Islamic tradition, this was by no means a meeting of equals, as Mohammed is ranked as first among the prophets and founders of the religions. Abraham, Moses and Jesus therefore recognized Mohammed as the greatest of the prophets. Who can seriously contend that it is only the Jewish religion which emphasizes its "chosen" status?

Only through and in the Holy Land can the links between the religions of Islam, Christianity and Judaism exist, the links between the religious founders Mohammed, Jesus, Moses and Abraham, the links between the nations and the peoples: Arabs, Christians and Jews, only in and through the "land in which we blessed all creatures" (Sura 21,72).

Let us turn again to Sura 24,56: "Allah promises all those among you who believe in him and do good works that he will make you the successors of the infidels in the land, just as he made them the successors of the infidels of their time." We have already interpreted this passage as saying that the Jews who had become "infidels" were the successors in the land of those who had become unbelievers before them, in other words of the Canaanite peoples. The exile of the Jews, whose successors in the land would then be the Muslims, could be interpreted as a sign that God/Allah had withdrawn his favor.

In this Sura, the prophet of Islam speaks the language of the Jewish prophets. The latter had never excluded the possibility of a return of the Jewish people to Zion, but always stipulated that religious renewal would be the precondition. This would then also permit the re-establishment of Jewish statehood in the form of divine rule instituted by the Messiah. This divine rule would be extended to all men, thus abolishing religious differences between Jews and non-Jews, as all men would believe in and serve God. "But they should all serve me alone and not in the company of any other being. Whoever becomes an infidel is an evildoer." This statement is not that of a Jewish prophet. Its author is Mohammed (Sura 24,56).

That the Quran also foresees a second chance for the Jewish people is indicated by Sura 17,9: "Perhaps your master will yet have mercy with you. But if you return to your sins, then we will return to our punishments; and moreover we have chosen hell as the prison for the infidels."

To Whom Is the Land Holy?

We have thus far examined the manner in which the Holy Land is sacred to Jews, Christians and Muslims, but other religions also have significant ties to the same land—for example, the Samaritans, Karaites, Druse and Bahai.

The Samaritans are familiar to readers of the Bible. Theirs is a mixed heritage, both in terms of origins and religion. The Samaritans are Jewish, and yet they are not Jews. Theirs is the unenviable fate of those who are caught up in the middle of an epic conflict.

In the year 722 B.C. the Assyrians destroyed the Kingdom of Israel. Part of the Jewish population, including the greater part of the Jewish leadership, was carried off into Mesopotamia. In their place the Assyrians settled other, non-Jewish peoples. In the course of time, however, the new inhabitants mixed with the remaining Jews, but the latter continued to regard the newcomers as "unclean".

In the Second Book of Kings (17,24) we read: "And the king of Assyria brought people from Babylon, Cuthah, Avva, Hamath and Sepharvaim, and placed them in the cities of Samaria instead of the people of Israel; and they took possession of Samaria, and dwelt in its cities."

The Jews did not take kindly to the Samaritans' refusal to convert to Judaism. In the language of the Bible: "And at the beginning of their dwelling there, they did not fear the Lord; therefore the Lord sent lions among them, which killed some of them. So the king of Assyria was told, 'The nations which you have carried away and placed in the cities of Samaria do not know the law of the god of the land; therefore he has sent lions among them, and behold, they are killing them, because they do not know the law of the god of the land.'" The argument must have been convincing, for "the king of Assyria commanded, 'Send there one of the priests whom you carried away thence [i.e. a Jewish priest]; and let him go and dwell there, and teach them the law of the god of the land.'" (2 Kings 25–27) Thus, by royal decree, did the Samaritans become Jews.

Although the Jewish priest residing in Bethel apparently did his best to teach the Samaritans "how they should fear the Lord" (2 Kings 17,28), his efforts proved not entirely successful, as "every nation still made gods of its own, and put them in the shrines of the high places which the Samaritans had made" (2 Kings 17:29). Thus, the Jews continued to regard the Samaritans as unclean (see also: 2 Kings 23:19ff.).

At the beginning of the sixth century before the Christian era the Jews were allowed to return from their Babylonian exile and to rebuild their temple. As recorded in the Book of Ezra, the Samaritans approached the ancient "Zionists" with the offer: "'Let us build with you; for we worship your God as you do, and we have been sacrificing to him ever since the days of Esarhaddon king of Assyria who brought us here.' But Zerubbabel, Jeshua, and the rest of the heads of fathers' houses in Israel said to them, 'You have nothing to do with us in building a house to our God; but we alone will build to the Lord, the God of Israel. ...' Then the people of the land discouraged the people of Judah, and made them afraid to build" (Ezra 4:2–4).

The returning Jews showed little tolerance and rejected religious community with the Samaritans. Jewish-Samaritan and other mixed marriages were viewed as transgressions. In the tenth chapter of the Book of Ezra we read: "Shecaniah ... addressed Ezra: 'We have broken faith with our God and have married foreign women from the peoples of the lands, but even now there is hope for Israel in spite of this. Therefore let us make a covenant with our God to put away all these wives and their children, according to the counsel of my lord and of those who tremble at the commandment of our God; and let it be done according to the law.'" (Ezra 10:2–3) The rigorous temperament and the decisive language did not fail to have an effect on Ezra, the political and spiritual-religious leader of the returned exiles, who subsequently summoned his entire people to Jerusalem: "Then all the men of Judah and Benjamin assembled.... And all the people sat in the open square before the house of God, trembling because of this matter and because of the heavy rain. And Ezra the priest stood up and said to them, 'You have trespassed and married foreign women, and so increased the guilt of Israel. Now then make confession to the Lord the God of your fathers, and do his will; separate yourselves from the peoples of the land, and from the foreign wives.'" (Ezra 10:9–11)

Whether deeply impressed or merely cowed by Ezra's words, the assembly of Jewish men which had gathered in Jerusalem (in about the year 430 B.C.E.), "all the assembly answered with a loud voice, 'It is so; we must do as you have said.'" (Ezra 10:12) Only four men dissented. In the Book of Nehemiah (chapters 9 and 10) we find comparable examples of Jewish intolerance.

The Samaritans, too, withdrew onto themselves. In the middle of the fourth century B.C.E. they founded their own religious community centered at Mount Garizim near Shechem, today's Nablus. It is reported that Alexander the Great gave the Samaritans his personal permission to do so while passing through on his conquest of the Middle East. The Samaritan temple was razed and their city demolished by the Maccabees under John Hyrcanus I in the year 129 B.C.E.—a further example of Jewish intolerance, particularly in view of the fact that we read in Deuteronomy (11:29): "And when the Lord your God brings you into the land which you are entering to take possession of you shall set the blessing on Mount Gerizim …", which is exactly what the Samaritans' temple was all about. The destruction of their temple was a traumatic experience for the Samaritans, who since then await the arrival of the Ta'eb, their Messiah.

Generations of Christian schoolchildren learned the parable of the merciful Samaritan in Luke (10:30–37). Repeatedly, the New Testament points to Samaritans—in contrast to the Jews—as shining examples of tolerance, humanity and mercy. Ten lepers are healed by Jesus; only one bothers to express his thanks—a Samaritan (Luke 17:11–19).

But the portrayals of the New Testament did not inspire the Byzantine Christian rulers of the Holy Land (until 634) to show any consideration towards the Samaritans. Nor did their Muslim successors after 634. In 1137 they carried out a bloodbath among the Samaritans of Nablus. Nor was there much improvement in their treatment under the Turkish Ottoman Empire from the sixteenth century on. The local Arabs forbid the traditional yearly procession to Mount Garizim, where the Samaritans' religious leaders dwelt—and still live. Only under British pressure were the Samaritans once again allowed access to their sacred mountain in 1820.

At nearly the same time a fundamental change in the Jewish-Samaritan relationship took place. Chief Rabbi Abraham Hajim proclaimed: "The Samaritan people is a branch of the Jewish people. It acknowledges the truth of the Torah."

This is correct, as—with the exception of some deviations—the five books of Moses (the Torah) have always formed the basis of Samaritan belief. But it took more than two thousand years for the Jewish side to arrive at this recognition.

After centuries of persecution under Jews, Christians and Muslims, only 146 members of the Samaritan religious community remained in Nablus when the Turks departed in 1917. Today about 400 live within the territory of Israel's 1967 borders, mainly in Holon (near Tel Aviv). About the same number live in the Nablus area.

Even if their historic and demographic weight is not great, the Samaritans must not be forgotten in the context of the question *to whom* the Holy Land is sacred. Their fate deserves attention for another reason as well. The Samaritans are a religious community that has repeatedly been subjected to the consequences of the shifts in power between majorities and minorities, especially the various reversals of the roles of victim and perpetrator. As long as the Christian community was itself a persecuted minority, it showed compassion towards the Samaritans. From this period dates the figure of the merciful Samaritan. Later, as the ruling majority in the Byzantine Empire, the Christians showed themselves to be as intolerant as the Jewish leaders Ezra, Nehemiah and company centuries before. The Muslims followed in their footsteps. One of the temptations of power is cruelty, especially when a former minority achieves dominance.

The history of the Jewish people also provides abundant instructional material of this sort. As a persecuted minority, the Jewish people reached the heights of moral achievement, but the rewards were often destruction and death. Having achieved dominance, Jews—of course not the entire collective, but many, all too many—also proved capable of turning into oppressors and persecutors. We find that the same applies to the Palestinians—suffering as victims when in the weaker position, turning into as persecutors when armed and strong. In the latter case we are reminded of the Palestinian killer squads in Jordan in 1969/70 and in Lebanon in the 1970s and 1980s, and of the manner in which Palestinian residents of Kuwait acted after the sheikdom was occupied by Saddam Hussein's troops in 1990.

Every nation, people or group relentlessly registers the moral weaknesses and the crimes of others, but none appear immune to the eternal cycle of changing roles.

The Karaites are actually a Jewish sect which recognizes exclusively the Hebrew Bible as the basis of religious law and rejects the rabbinical interpretations of the Talmud as well as other Jewish traditions. This makes the Karaites more "Jewish" than the Samaritans, who recognize only the Torah. Obviously, therefore, the Holy Land is sacred to the Karaites, whose numbers remain small. About 12,000 lived in Israel in 1990, the majority in the area of Ramlah, near the Ben Gurion international airport.

For the Druse, too, the Holy Land is sacred. In Hittim, in the north of Israel, lies the tomb of Jethro, who was Moses' father-in-law and who is an important figure in the Druse religion.

The Druse religious community was founded around the year 1000 of the Christian era. Its roots are Islamic, but the Druse religion is not counted as part of Islam. Although they speak Arabic, the Druse have traditionally kept themselves apart from Arabs and Muslims. Their centers of population are to be found in Lebanon, Syria, on the Golan and in Israel.

In 1990 the Druse of Israel numbered some 56,000. They are loyal citizens who also serve in the nation's armed forces. An additional 14,000 Druse live on the Golan, which was officially annexed by Israel in 1981.

Few details of dogma and practise can be reported about the Druse religion itself, as its adherents place the greatest emphasis on secrecy, but the connection via the Jewish prophet Moses to parts of the Jewish tradition and therefore to the Holy Land is undisputed.

This is not the place for an extensive examination of the Bahai religion, which was founded in Persia in the mid-nineteenth century. Especially since the Islamic revolution of 1979 the adherents of the Bahai religion—not least of all because of their reputation for tolerance—have been severely persecuted in Iran. The Bahai have chosen the Israeli city Practice as the world center for their faith. The golden-domed temple, which is the holiest Bahai site, is one of the dominant landmarks of this Israeli port city.

Where Is the Land Holy?
Or: To Whom Does Jerusalem Belong?

Where is the Holy Land sacred? Certainly not everywhere—nor is it holy to all who live there. Of course, to religious Jews, the *entire* land is holy, because it is the Promised Land pledged (with differing definitions of its borders!) to Abraham and his descendants. But we must recall that only about a third of all Jews consider themselves religious. Religious Christians also speak of the Holy Land, but these believers, too, are a minority today. And they do not claim that the Holy Land is their land. Nor do religious Muslims make this claim. For Christians and Muslims, *specific sites* make the Holy Land sacred. Their emotional ties are thus to various individual places within the land rather than to the land as a whole.

For Jews, too, there are certain sites in the Holy Land which are especially sacred. The sometimes perceived contradiction is more apparent than real.

Religious Jews, Muslims and Christians thus direct their vision primarily toward the holy places. The authenticity of their feelings and beliefs is certainly less subject to question than the authenticity of the holy sites themselves. Who today can actually authoritatively name and locate these holy places—especially in view of the competition? Where, for example, did Jesus' mother Mary die? In Jerusalem or in Ephesus (today in Turkey)? In both cities we are shown the site of this event.

The competition between religious communities is also keen, as is obvious to even the casual visitor to the Church of the Holy Sepulchre in Jerusalem,

M. Wolffsohn, *Whose Holy Land?*, https://doi.org/10.1007/978-3-030-74286-7_9

where Roman Catholic, Greek Orthodox and Armenian Christians represent the chief rivals, Syrian and Coptic Christians enjoy little better than a second-rate presence and Anglicans and Ethiopians are forced to maintain their chapels "outside" in the courtyard.

"You shall not make yourself a graven image" is the exhortation of the Commandments (Exodus 20:4). But are the holy sites not a substitute for the "graven image"? Are they not vestiges of the ancient cult of idols in religions which claim to acknowledge only the One God? Is the purpose of the holy place not that of a bridge to faith, an aid to religious understanding?

The image of God in Judaism, Christianity and Islam is extremely abstract. The holy sites thus serve as a kind of bridge for those in need of having something concrete in their religion, something they can "put their hands on" without falling into idolatry. They function as bridges for men and women on their way to a God who would otherwise be much less comprehensible, perhaps even unreachable for them.

These comments are not meant as heresy, but rather as virtually self-evident observations which question not the religions themselves but instead reflect the difficulties of many believers. When one's faith in God remains firm, despite the knowledge that the authenticity of many holy sites is doubtful, it is certainly a sign of a true and lasting faith.

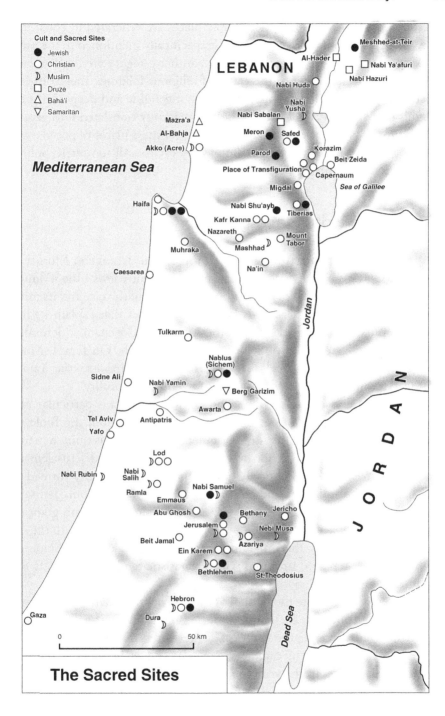

Cult and Sacred Sites

- ● Jewish
- ○ Christian
- ☽ Muslim
- ☐ Druze
- △ Bahá'í
- ▽ Samaritan

Meshhed-at-Teir

LEBANON

Al-Hader

Nabi Ya'afuri

Nabi Hazuri

Nabi Huda

Nabi Yusha

Mazra'a

Nabi Sabalan

Al-Bahja

Meron   Safed

Akko (Acre)

Mediterranean Sea

Parod

Korazim

Beit Zeida

Place of Transfiguration

Capernaum

Migdal

Sea of Galilee

Haifa

Nabi Shu'ayb   Tiberias

Kafr Kanna

Nazareth

Muhraka

Mashhad

Mount Tabor

Na'in

Caesarea

Tulkarm

Nablus (Sichem)

Sidne Ali

Nabi Yamin

▽ Berg Garizim

Awarta

Tel Aviv

Antipatris

Yafo

Lod

Nabi Rubin

Nabi Salih

Ramla

Nabi Samuel

Emmaus

Abu Ghosh

Bethany

Jericho

Jerusalem

Nebi Musa

Beit Jamal

Azariya

Ein Karem

Bethlehem

St. Theodosius

Hebron

Gaza

Dura

Jordan

J O R D A N

Dead Sea

0   50 km

The Sacred Sites

Not all of the actual or supposed holy places are venerated in equal measure. One type of holy site includes those specifically mentioned in the sacred books as part of the plan of salvation. In another category are the numerous places which belong more to the realm of religious folklore. They constitute aspects of popular belief and are the objects of genuine and deeply felt piety, but this piety in individuals cannot be automatically translated into genuine holiness for the locality which is its focus, even if these places of popular veneration are often presented as the site of holy events. All too often, political motives are also involved.

The Jewish Holy Places

Why is Jerusalem so sacred to Jews? "If I forget you, Jerusalem, I forget my right hand." is a popular formulation among religious Jews. The Talmudic and other sages never tired of describing the holiness of the city and its miraculous effect. Granted, Jerusalem is beautiful, but does that explain its holiness? Of course, King David brought the Ark of the Covenant to Jerusalem, and there his son and successor Solomon built the temple. On Temple Mount the *Schechina*, God's spiritual presence, remains eternal—so the Talmud instructs us, but offers no explanation for the choice of locality.

The original decision to ascribe a special holiness to this particular place was in all probability *politically* motivated. As we recall from the Bible, the twelve tribes of Israel were first united under King Saul. This unity remained fragile, even under King David. It was David who captured Jerusalem and made it the new capital. Politically and geographically, the city formed the link between the northern and southern parts of the kingdom. Jerusalem became a symbol of unity. The holy city stood for the unifiers' program of a centralized state. David's son Absalom rebelled against his father with the support of those opposed to this program of centralized power. During Solomon's reign there were repeated uprisings with separatistic tendencies, and after his death the kingdom was soon divided.

Jerusalem was therefore the symbol of the unity and solidarity of the Jewish people. At the same time its temple was the central of Jewish cultic practice. Jerusalem again became the political center after the destruction of the Kingdom of Israel (with its capital of Samaria) and again after the return of the Babylonian exiles in the year 538 B.C.E. to a part of their former homeland, namely to Zion, that is to Jerusalem and its vicinity.

This is a great deal of history and politics, interwoven with an equal amount of religion, so much so that it becomes virtually impossible to separate the sacred from the political. This is what makes any attempt at understanding confusing to the point of utter discouragement.

And once again we encounter a stumbling block, for in Judaism there are not really any holy places. As already stated, for religious Jews, the land in its entirety is holy. Nevertheless, there are individual places to which specific religious laws and precepts (Hebrew: *mitzwot*) apply. This would permit us to apply the rule of thumb: the greater the quantity of religious law, the holier the site.

This is most evident in the Mischna, the part of the Talmud which consists mainly of precepts and prescriptions but also contains many commentaries and, in addition, wonderful, deeply meaningful stories and anecdotes. Although the text may at first appear highly formalistic and long-winded, this first impression proves wrong. A closer look at the teachings of the Talmudic sages reveals highly political messages for the present. Their potential effect could be described as explosive, except for the fact that the conclusions support are a balsam for peace.

In the Mischna text Kelim 1:6 we read: "There are ten levels of holiness: The Land of Israel is holy before all other lands. Wherein does its holiness lie? It is in the Omer-Sacrifice, the firstborn and the two loaves of bread, which can be offered there but not in any other land."

The gist of this passage is more or less familiar to all: There are certain Jewish laws which can only be fulfilled in the Holy Land itself. There is no need to go into the details in this context. In Kelim 1:7 the Talmud becomes more specific about the holiness of certain places: "The cities surrounded by walls are holier because lepers must be cast out of them and a corpse may be carried within them until it is ready for burial; but once it has been carried outside the walls, it may not be brought back within." This passage not only sounds like the text of a law, it is indeed intended as such.

Kelim 1:8 continues: "Within the walls [of Jerusalem] the space is even more holy, for it is easier there to eat the holy and the second tenth." The reference is to the meat of specific animal sacrifices.

And further on: "The Temple Mount is even holier, for … none suffering from bleeding, no menstruating women or women about to give birth may set foot there."

Jerusalem is holy, the Temple Mount is more holy. And in direct relation to the holiness of the locality, higher levels of bodily cleanliness and spiritual purity are required for those allowed to enter.

Here we choose not to spare the reader with regard to detail and proceed on the assumption of the reader's interest in exploring a totally foreign world, in this case one almost as unfamiliar to the majority of Jewish as to non-Jewish readers. More importantly, if we propose to examine the holiness of the Jewish holy places, then we need to know exactly what is holy in Judaism. Kelim 1:8 continues: "The Temple Gate is even more holy, for no one who is not a Jew may enter there, and no one unpurified by the dead. The Women's Court is even more holy, for no unclean person may enter there, who was immersed the same day [in a ritual bath]. But a sacrificial offering is not required of that person. The Court of the Israelites [reserved to men who were neither priests nor Levites] is even more holy, for no one may enter there who is not free of sin and therefore has yet to bring a sacrificial offering. The Forecourt of the Priests is even more holy, for no one may enter here who is not a priest, unless it is necessary for him to lay on hands … in a sacrifice."

The description is continued in Kelim 1:9: "The room between the Forecourt of the Priests and the Altar is even more holy, for no priest with bodily defect or wild-grown hair may set foot here." Were there, we wonder, priests at the temple who appearance was that of an long-haired hippie? Whatever the case may have been, law and order were certainly demanded. "The Temple is even more holy, for no one may enter there who has not first washed his hands and his feet." (Kelim 1:9)

The perspective reader recognizes here another area of common ground between Judaism and Islam. In both religions ritual washing plays an important role. Once again, we see that for Jews (and Muslims) holiness is tied to cleanliness. Bodily cleanliness is both prerequisite and symbol for spiritual-religious purity.

All of this, of course, has little to do with the standard propagandistic arguments about the holiness of the holy places.

Kelim 1:9 also states: "The Holy of Holies is more holy than these other places, for only the High Priest may enter here at the time of service on the Day of Reconciliation."

The hierarchy of holiness is self-evident. It is a pattern of circles within circles, each circle representing a higher level of holiness. The widest circle is that of the Holy Land, the smallest is the Holy of Holies. The smaller the circle, the higher the requirements in terms of cleanliness and purity. The most holy place of all was open to only a single person, namely the high priest, and to him only once a year.

And where do we find the balsam for peace? Since the destruction of the temple by the army of Titus in 70 A.D. no truly religious Jew has set foot on Temple Mount, as he must fear accidentally treading upon the Holy of Holies, and this, of course, would be sacrilege. To be sure, the experts, as always, have examined and determined everything, but doubts remain, and because of these doubts, no pious Jew will risk the profanation of the Holy of Holies.

Since the destruction of the temple there have been no temple priests, much less a high priest, and thus there is effectively no Jew permitted to set foot upon this piece of holy ground.

So what? Have we not all seen the TV-footage of Jewish groups attempting over and over again (since Israel's takeover of the Old City in 1967) to forcibly occupy the Temple Mount? Were these Jews not wearing the *kippa* as a sign of their religiosity? Do not the members of most publicized of these groups refer to themselves as the "Temple Mount Faithful" Indeed, it is so. These zealots do regard themselves as intensely pious. The magnifying effect of television is also evident. Nevertheless, in the eyes of the truly strict, Talmud-oriented religious Jews, this public display of piety smacks more of sanctimony and cant, which no amount of public prayer can disguise. Although they intend no disrespect toward the Talmud, the "Temple Mount Faithful" certainly disregard it, probably for political reasons.

These "faithful" claim that they will at long last return the holy places to their rightful, namely Jewish, owners. But in presenting their political demands they at the same time strip Judaism of its religious content. This is the boomerang nature of zealotry. Not every interested party is always the best representative of the overall interests at stake.

The role of the Temple Mount is but another example for the coolness of relations between the strict believers of the extreme religious orthodoxy and the national-religious extremists. As an aside, we note that there is a more or less reliable method of distinguishing the two groups by outer their appearance: The national-religious tend to wear a knitted *kippa* whereas those worn by the extreme orthodox are usually of black cloth. Moreover, the latter tend to wear the *kaftan*, the black coat and the *streimel*, the large, round black hat. Of course, there are exceptions.

The national-religious (and here, too, the exceptions confirm the rule) are among the most rigorous of political hawks with regard to the Palestinians and the occupied territories. Because of their strict religiosity, the extreme orthodox tend to the camp of the doves, as they wish to scrupulously avoid any interference with God's unfolding of his plan of salvation in history and proceed on the assumption that to this end God does not depend upon the assistance of either religious-political fanatics or the Israeli armed forces. Instead of confronting the Palestinians, the orthodox desire is to await the coming of the Messiah.

The decisive point is this: The holiness of the Jewish holy places has no connection whatsoever with particular prophets, personalities or the performance of miracles. It has nothing to do with political claims or statehood.

Every reader will have noticed by now: The purity of dogma has long been lost. Since 1967 even Israeli pop music has besung the holiness of the Western Wall, but we search in vain for a reference to its sacredness in the Mishna! A pop evergreen dating from 1967 carries the refrain: "There are humans with a heart of stone and stones with human hearts." If we believe that man was created "in the image of God" then we may be permitted to dismiss the pop tune as blasphemous. Or we may choose to simply label it as sentimental *kitsch*.

The spectacle becomes grotesque and hypocritical—as well as an encouragement to political radicalism—because it decorates the political assertion of exclusive rights with religious window-dressing. The performance can never be truly religious as long as is produced and acted out by the non-religious, but this is exactly what is happening.

Although—or perhaps precisely because—the "God is dead" syndrome (also) prevails among a majority of Jews, many hold fast to a sort of idol—for example the stones of the so-called "Wailing Wall", the Western Wall of the ancient temple. But symbolic objects cannot substitute for religious content. "And the Lord said to [King Solomon], '… I have consecrated this house which you have built, and put my name there for ever; my eyes and my heart will be there for all time. … But if you turn aside from following me, you or your children, and do not keep my commandments, … then I will cut off Israel from the land which I have given them; and the house which I have consecrated for my name I will cast out of my sight." (1 Kings 9:3–7)

Another pop tune from 1967 which in the meantime has become a pop classic in Israel sings the praises of "golden Jerusalem", a formulation which originated with great Rabbi Akiva ben Joseph (ca. 50–135). One of the most important of the Talmudic sages, Akiva was one of the spiritual leaders of the Jewish revolt against the Romans (132–135). Brutally tortured and executed by the Romans, Akiva qualifies as a true martyr—except for the fact that this sort of sanctity and the type of holy site which goes with it are both foreign to Judaism. In a form of pseudo-Christianization of Judaism, however, Rabbi Akiva has become the secularized object of a sentimental cult.

This phenomenon of "Christianization" need not be seen as intrinsically negative, but the final product is certainly less Jewish and more a form of folklore which over the centuries has been absorbed by Jews and is now marketed as "Jewish".

Once again, we must attempt to understand that the more abstract the concept, especially when it comes to the nature of God, the more people have difficulty comprehending it. Besides, the Western (Wailing) Wall is undoubtedly both an historical and a political symbol. The Western Wall symbolizes both the religious and the political ties between the land and the people, between the Jewish people and its Promised Land.

The Temple was also a symbol of Jewish sovereignty. King Solomon's First Temple was destroyed by the Babylonians in 586 B.C.E. This event also marked an end to Jewish statehood. The erection of the Second Temple commenced in 538 (and then again in 520) B.C.E. At the same time, a new form of Jewish statehood also emerged. To be more exact, King Cyrus of Persia permitted the Jews to establish an autonomous community in Zion. The Jews were thus granted self-determination without full sovereignty. And so it remained, apart from the interlude of Jewish statehood under the Maccabees, which lasted for just a century before being ended by the soldiers of Caesar's rival Pompey in 63 B.C.E.

In the year 70 of the Christian era the Second Temple—and with it Jewish sovereignty—was destroyed. This condition lasted nearly 2000 years and the temple ruins became emblematic of Jewish diaspora existence.

Twice Jewish religious leaders accomplished the major feat of compensating for the loss of the religious center (the Temple of Jerusalem) with a renewed spiritual intensity. By their success in stabilizing the Jewish religion they saved Judaism itself. How? During the Babylonian exile, rabbis served as replacements for the priests and Levites and introduced the synagogue as a substitute for the Temple. Formerly centered on the Holy Land, Judaism became a "portable" religion, independent of a particular locality. Judaism, of course, continued to nurture its ties to the Holy Land, but a Jewish presence there was no long a prerequisite for Jewish existence.

From the time of the return from Babylonia until the destruction of the Second Temple, an open rivalry prevailed between the rabbis on the one hand and the priests and Levites on the other. The attentive reader of the New Testament cannot fail to register the tensions. The supposedly so sinister Pharisees were the rabbis. The Sadduceans were the priestly caste. History decided the spiritual and political battle in favor of the Pharisees. These grandiose Jewish scholars (who deserve far better than their reputation in the Christian world even today) completed the process of freeing the Jewish religion from dependence on a specific locality. Their instrument was the Talmud, which collected and commented on all the religious statutes and precepts and illustrated them with wonderful stories.

Today, the notebook or palmtop computer is the status symbol of mobility. The numerous thick volumes of the Talmud weigh a lot more than the modern laptop, but they were clearly easier to transport than the stones of the Temple or its ruins.

It is obvious that the Jewish people always maintained an especially close emotional relationship with the ruins of their Temple (the Western Wall) without ever raising it to the status of the "graven image". The Talmudic sages established once and for all time that for Judaism the spirit of God had become omnipresent and universal. God no longer required a headquarters.

During the centuries of Islamic rule over the Holy Land, Jews desired and were permitted to visit the Western Wall. Of course, this was also permitted under the British Mandate, but curiously, beginning in 1929, the supposedly so enlightened island Europeans imposed an extremely pedantic and restrictive set of regulations. From 1948 to 1967 the Kingdom of Jordan, in violation of international law, occupied and annexed the eastern parts of Jerusalem, including the Old City, which was rendered *judenrein*. Jews were not permitted to enter, not even to pray at the Western Wall. This state of affairs was ended by Israel's conquest of East Jerusalem during the Six Day War of 1967 and its subsequent annexation by the Jewish State—also in violation of international law.

In short: One needs to understand that even non-religious Jews have emotional ties to this symbol. What remains irrational and unfathomable is the fact that some non-religious Jews nevertheless attempt to make a religious spectacle out of it.

Are there other Jewish holy places in the Holy land? Of course. Of particular significance is the Mount of Olives. Here, according to Jewish tradition, is where God will stand when the resurrection of the dead commences: "On that day his feet shall stand on the Mount of Olives which lies before Jerusalem on the east" (Zechariah 14:4).

Ever since biblical times the Mount of Olives has been a Jewish burial place. The Jordanians set a particularly outstanding example of tolerance and respect for the dead when, after occupying East Jerusalem, they utilized the gravesites of the Mount of Olives as a quarry for building materials. It is understandable that even secularized, non-religious Jews have no desire to provide an opportunity for the repetition of such a desecration.

King David's tomb is located on Mount Zion in Jerusalem. It is more a place of popular veneration than an "official" holy site, as it has more to do with a "cult of personality". The "City of David" was neither the first nor the last such phenomenon. The "City of Lenin" (Leningrad), the "City of Stalin" (Stalingrad) … how transient is mortal fame! David's has lasted longer than most. But then, he wasn't such a bad character after all, even though some biblical accounts are anything but flattering.

To be sure, according to the Bible (not to contemporary archeology) David was a very successful ruler, probably the most powerful of all Jewish kings, and the Hebrew Bible, the Old Testament, proclaims that the Messiah will come from the House of David. The New Testament emphasizes Jesus' descent from the House of David. Politically, David was certainly a model, but not in terms of personal morals, and thus not from the religious standpoint. As the Bible reports, he did not even shrink from breaking the commandment against adultery. That David's son Absalom was no angel is also clear, but there are always two parties to a dispute. That alone Absalom's rebellious coveting of his father's throne is to blame is not convincing.

David's hands were covered with blood, and the Old Testament informs us that this was anything but pleasing to God, who therefore did not permit David to build His house, the Temple. This task was assigned to David's son and successor Solomon. David is thus venerated more as a symbol of former Jewish power rather than as a spiritual source of Jewish religion and tradition.

Another Jerusalem tomb which is the object of popular devotion is that of Simon the Just, who held the office of High Priest at the time of Alexander the Great. The Talmud tells us that this all-powerful ruler dismounted from his horse upon the approach of Simon the Just (Joma 69). The High Priest had been informed that the Samaritans intended to destroy the Jewish Temple and that Alexander had given them permission to do so. This Simon sought to prevent. The rest of the story comes as no surprise: Simon the Just convinced Alexander with his arguments, and it was the Samaritans who had to suffer in the end. Certainly, Simon's powers of persuasion were impressive, but was he also "just"? He was highly successful in asserting the interests of his people—at the cost of another.

By way of contrast, the memory and repute of Rabbi Simon Bar-Yochai appear unblemished. Religious Jews make an annual pilgrimage to the presumed site of his tomb at Meron (near Safed in Galilee) on the feast of Lag ba-Omer, which normally falls between Easter and Pentecost in the Christian calendar. This site, too, is primarily a place of popular veneration.

Although the experts are not in full agreement on its origins, the semi-holiday of Lag ba-Omer probably goes back to a (temporary) Jewish victory in the Bar-Kochba rebellion against Rome (between 132 and 135), after which the Jews still living in the Holy Land were (for the time being) allowed to remain.

Rabbi Simon Bar-Yochai, a pupil of the great Talmudist Rabbi Akiva, hid from the Romans for thirteen years in a cave. His determination to continue the struggle against Rome remained unbroken, despite the horrible execution of his teacher and the total defeat of the Jewish rebellion in 135. "Slay the best among the heathens", he advised his followers, meaning, of course, the

Romans, who brutally suppressed and massacred the few Jews still to be found in the Holy Land.

The passage Brachot 61b in the Talmud relates details of Rabbi Akiva's gruesome execution at the hands of the Romans: "The hour at which they led Rabbi Akiva to be executed was the time to pray the "Hear, Israel" [the most important Jewish prayer]. As they tore out his flesh with rakes of iron, he took the burden of the mater of heaven upon himself. His pupils [among them Rabbi Simon Bar-Yochai] said to him: 'Our master! This far?'" Akiva's followers were thus questioning whether martyrdom in the fulfillment of God's commandments was not going too far.

But Rabbi Akiva answered them: "All the days of my life this verse has troubled me: 'with all of your soul'—even if its fulfillment takes away the breath of life. I said to myself: When will it be your turn to fulfill the content of this verse? And now that it is my turn, should I not fulfill the commandment?"

In the passage Menachot 29b in the Talmud we discover that even Moses complained: "Master of the world! Such commands and such a reward?" To which God replied: "Silence! Such is my plan."

As we learn from Brachot 61b, the same excited question was put to God by his "servant angels". The answer to their query is more conciliatory. First, Psalm 17 (14) is paraphrased: "Their portion in life is of the world." Then, as so often occurs in the stories of the Talmudic sages, a voice from on high is heard saying: "You are fortunate, Rabbi Akiva, for you have been chosen for life in the world to come!"

The form of the argument take as pattern characteristic of the Talmud, where God, angels and men frequently echo passages from the Bible. Despite God's apparently harsh reply in the face of Akiva's suffering, the reader also notes the Talmudic sages' painful doubts concerning divine justice. This, of course, is going too far. Therefore the sages chastise themselves with a drastically curt retort to their penetrating questions: "Silence!" God's designs are inscrutable to man, but the Talmudic sages nevertheless try again and again. We shall examine another such example for this procedure in the story of how the Jewish people took possession of the land.

We thus find it easier to understand Rabbi Simon Bar-Yochai's all-too-human burning hatred of the Romans. Forgiveness would have been superhuman—a description which does apply to his legendary learnedness. Rabbi Akiva died in the middle of the second century of the Christian era. The "exact" identification of his tomb was made in the thirteenth and the tradition of the pilgrimage to this site began in the sixteenth century. Its symbolism is therefore more unambiguous than the locality's historical authenticity.

In times of renewed persecution it is logical for people to seek orientation from the example of a spiritual leader who was also a fighter, a pupil of the Rabbi Akiva, but also one who declared the leader of the rebellion against the Romans, Simon Bar-Kochba, to be the Messiah, the savior. Bar-Kochba, of course, was not, nor is it known that he proclaimed himself to be the Messiah, but he and his followers did struggle bravely and mightily. The name Rabbi Simon Bar Yochai came to stand for a program, at least in the hopes and dreams of the powerless and suppressed Jews of the sixteenth and seventeenth centuries, whose hopes in the coming of the Messiah, as we have already seen, stood at a high tide. Because the Jews of the time were in to position to assert a political claim to the Holy Land, the pilgrimage to Bar Yochai's tomb fit in well with the political and historical program.

The story of Rabbi Bar Yochai is also almost ideally tailored to the modern-day, Zionist Jewish State with its consequent emphasis of military preparedness. Israel seeks to cultivate ties to Jewish spiritual traditions without ever again being led like the proverbial lamb to the slaughter. Above all, Israel seeks to once again live in peace in its land. Its land? Here, we must examine all the perspectives.

There are many other tombs of biblical or Talmudic figures which we might mention. As with many of the Christian and Islamic holy places, the historical authenticity of these sites is open to question, but the religious emotions connected with them are undoubtedly genuine.

In the first of the books of Moses we read: "And Sarah died at Kiriatharba (that is, Hebron) in the land of Canaan; and Abraham went in to mourn for Sarah and to weep for her. And Abraham rose up from before his dead, and said to the Hittites, 'I am a stranger and a sojourner among you; give me property among you for a burying place, that I may bury my dead out of my sight.'" (Genesis 23:2–5) After some negotiation, Abraham secured "the cave of the field of Machpelah" (Genesis 23:19). The tomb of the ancestral fathers and mothers in Hebron is a (so-to-speak semi-official) goal of Jewish and Muslim pilgrims. To a certain extent, the patriarchal ancestors Abraham, Isaac, Jacob and their wives Sarah, Rebecca, Lea and Rachel are also holy figures for Christians.

The facts appear clear enough for most Jews, but for Muslims? Let us recall that Ismael was Abraham's son by Hagar (the maid whom the still childless Sarah "gave to Abraham her husband as a wife" (Genesis 16:3)). Hagar is identified as Egyptian, meaning she was not Jewish. After Sarah gave birth to Isaac, however, she showed no scruples in insisting that Abraham cast Hagar and her son Ismael out into the desert. "And the thing was very displeasing to Abraham on account of his son" (Genesis 21:11). Nevertheless, "she departed, and wandered in the wilderness of Beersheba. When the water in the skin was gone she cast the child under one of the bushes. Then she went, and sat down over against him a good way off, about the distance of a bowshot; for she said, 'Let me not look upon the death of the child.' And as she sat over against him, the child lifted up his voice and wept. And God heard the voice of the lad; and the angel of God called to Hagar from heaven, and said to her: '… Fear not; for God has heard the voice of the lad. … Arise, lift up the lad, and hold him fast with your hand; for I will make him a great nation.' Then God opened her eyes, and she saw a well of water; and she went, and filled the skin with water, and gave the lad a drink. And God was with the lad, and he grew up; he lived in the wilderness of Paran [in the Sinai]; and his mother took a wife for him from the land of Egypt." (Genesis 21:14–21) Ismael is regarded as the ancestor of several Arab tribes.

In this biblical episode, Abraham resembles the figure of the fisherman in the famous tale of the fisherman and his wife. Like the fisherman, Abraham's behavior displays not badness but weakness. This is clearly the source of his guilt, although the Bible contains no direct statement to this effect. More criticism of the progenitor of the Jewish people would not have been possible. In contrast, Sarah is strong and the author of her own guilt, but this, too, is implied rather than explicitly stated. This biblical story leaves us with mixed feelings. Like the reader, the author of this text must apparently had mixed feelings as well.

Such feelings are similar to those of the observer of the Jewish-Arab conflict to this day. Two closely related peoples remain locked in bitter struggle, despite (or perhaps because of?) the fact that they are very close, both in heritage and geography. One need not engage in the study of ethnology, the Bible or history to realize this. One also need not believe in the Bible, but the twenty-first chapter of Genesis brings the religious, moral, political and historical complex is brought into a focus of unequaled literary clarity and brevity at the point where God speaks to Abraham: "And I will make a nation of the son of the slave woman also, because he is your offspring." (Genesis 21:13) God makes the Jewish people "His nation", the Arabs are made "a nation". Both spring from the seed of Abraham. So close and yet so far.

This is also true of the tomb of the patriarchs. For a long time a mosque and a synagogue apparently stood next to each other at this site, as archeological excavations have uncovered the remains of a synagogue dating from the late middle ages. Since then, however, the "infidels", the Jews and the Christians, were not permitted to enter the tomb. As a sign of accommodation, Jews and Christians were allowed to approach the mosque, but only as far as the seventh step before the entry.

To whom does the tomb of the patriarchs belong? To the Jews, the Muslims, or both? The religious as well as non-religious will agree that both Jews and Muslims can advance clearly legitimate claims to this holy site. After the Israeli occupation of the West Bank in 1967 the only solution which made sense both in terms of organization and morality was put into effect, at least here: The site is opened to Muslims and non-Muslims at specific times. The model of differing times of access is certainly reasonable and laudable, but—unfortunately!—it cannot be extended to the Holy Land as a whole. Or would anyone propose that the Jews be allowed in from nine to twelve and non-Jews from twelve to three?

The tomb of Rachel, the favorite wife of the patriarch Jacob is mentioned in the Bible: "So Rachel died, and she was buried on the way to Ephrath (that is, Bethlehem), and Jacob set up a pillar upon her grave; it is the pillar of Rachel's tomb, which is there to this day." (Genesis 36:19–20, also 48:7) The holiness of this site would thus carry more weight than that of many places of popular veneration. But with all due respect to Rachel: She was a human being and not a saint, as Judaism knows no saints. Anyone who speaks in terms of the "holy ancestral mother Rachel" only demonstrates his ignorance of Judaism.

However: Rachel's story is part of the history of the Jewish people and of God's plan of salvation—and therefore another bridge between the human and the divine. In this sense, Rachel's tomb is to be counted among the holy places. In the Bible, the location is imprecisely given as somewhere between Jerusalem and Bethlehem. The Talmudic sages expressed their doubts, and today's experts follow in their footsteps. But popular piety believes to have precise knowledge. It does not really matter.

Somewhere between Jerusalem and Bethlehem, and somehow, this manifestation of religious history and popular devotion needed to be given concrete form. In the Byzantine period, Christians erected a holy site and Muslims built the still existing domed monument in the nineteenth century.

We of course cannot go on to list all of the Jewish holy sites and the places of popular Jewish piety here. Let us mention only in passing the presumed tomb of Joseph (Rachel's son) near Nablus, the cave of the prophet Elijah near Practice, the tomb of Jehuda Hanassi (the Prince) and other Talmudic sages in Shearim near Practice.

And this tomb and that tomb, and yet another tomb. Near the cities of Tiberias (on the Sea of Galilee) and Safed (also in Galilee) we find many tombs of Jewish greats. Popular piety, for example, has transferred the tomb of Rabbi Akiva to Tiberias. The experts emphatically reject the authenticity of this site as well as one nearby which is presumed to be the tomb of Rabbi

Jochanan Ben Saccai. Had it not been for this courageous man, who outwitted both the Jewish nationalists and the Romans, Judaism would probably have never survived.

The Jewish zealots in Jerusalem were determined to fight the Romans down to the last drop of Jewish blood. And this is exactly what they did. That they stood no chance against the power of the Roman Empire was easy enough to see—for anyone who would see. Among these was Rabbi Jochanan Ben Saccai. But the zealots had forbidden any and all contact, much less negotiations with the Roman besiegers—on pain of death. What did the clever Rabbi do? He played dead and had himself carried out of the city in a coffin—directly to the Roman commander. There he climbed out of the coffin, quite alive and quite in command of his senses. Rabbi Bar Saccai succeeded in convincing the Roman commander to grant him permission to erect a Jewish school in Javne after the war.

Javne lies to the southeast of Jaffo. It is in this tiny village that Rabbi Jochanan Ben Sacci and his pupils laid the foundations of the Talmud. Here the future of Judaism was secured, for it is there that the Jewish faith was transformed into a truly "portable" religion.

Let us return to the "holy places" of Tiberius. Here we also find the supposed tomb of Rabbi Moses ben Maimon (Maimonides). The authenticity of this site is at least the subject of an open debate. Maimonides (1135–1204) was the most important Jewish philosopher and legal scholar of the middle ages. He was also a physician, in fact the personal physician of the Sultan of Egypt. Maimonides personified the close relations between the Jewish and the Islamic worlds in the middle ages. This symbiosis reached its zenith in Spain, where it ended in a bloodbath in 1492. "From Moses to Moses [ben Maimon] there was no one like Moses [ben Maimon]" is a popular Jewish saying, and at least here the voice of the people is right.

In contrast to Ishmael and Israel, the example of Maimonides clearly demonstrates the existence of a Jewish-Arab-Islamic common ground. It belongs, unfortunately, to the past.

What is the reason for the concentration of tombs of important Jewish personages at Tiberias and Safed? After the destruction of the Second Temple, these cities became the centers of Jewish scholarship and piety. Rabbi Jochanan Ben Saccai himself proclaimed Tiberias a "clean city". It was in this center of Talmudic scholarship that the "Jerusalem Talmud" was written. Until the Muslim conquest of the Holy Land, Tiberias was the religious and spiritual center of the (few) Jews remaining in the Holy Land—another example for the distinction between quantity and quality. In the eighteenth and nineteenth centuries, Tiberias (together with Jerusalem, Hebron and Safed) once again was counted as one of the "four holy cities".

In the sixteenth century, Safed was the bastion of the *Kaballa*, of Jewish mysticism. These mystics were also the discoverer of the holy tombs, which they revealed one after the other—a feat convincing from the mystics', but less so from the scientific point of view. But who is to seriously claim that the scientific perspective is more right and more important for the well-being and the soul of mankind than deeply religious mysticism?

The more soberly rational believer, of course, finds it difficult to comprehend the mystics' approach. As early as the tenth century the Karaite Sahl ben Mahliah became incensed over the cult of the tombs: "How can I remain calm when some Jews behave like the servants of idols? They sit on the graves, sometimes remaining there overnight and call out to the dead: 'Oh Rabbi Jossi, heal me.' Or; 'Give me children.' They light candles and wave incense." No doubt, as a Karaite (who rejected the Talmud and recognized only the Hebrew Bible) Sahl ben Mahliah was caricaturizing what he saw and condemned as the Christianization of Judaism.

The Christian Holy Places

The birth, ministry, miracles and death of Jesus are the focal relationships of most of the Christian holy places. Some, however, are also associated with Mary or the apostles.

The early Christians were neither able nor willing to take charge of those places in the Roman province of Palestine associated with the foundation of their religion. They were not only a severely persecuted minority, but one which willingly submitted to its fate in this world because its orientation was to the world beyond. The early Christians lived in anticipation of the imminent return of the Messiah and the creation of the kingdom of God on earth.

Emperor Constantine the Great (ca. 280 to 337) converted to Christianity and put an end to the persecution of Christians in the Roman Empire. Since the time of Constantine, who granted Christianity a status akin to that of a state religion, secular history and salvation have been politically interwoven.

Under Constantine, four centuries after Jesus' passion, the exact locations of most of the holy places were determined.

Some three centuries later came the Muslims, who wrested control over the Holy Land from the Byzantine Empire. Although most of the holy places were destroyed, Christian pilgrimage still continued.

A mere century and a half later (for what are 150 years against the background of the history of the Holy Land?) Charlemagne found a religiously tolerant and politically farsighted partner in the legendary Harun al-Rashid (786–809), whose generosity was certainly related to his relative lack of interest in Jerusalem and Palestine. Harun al-Rashid is even said to have presented Charlemagne with the key to the Church of the Holy Sepulchre. In any case, the erection of a hostel for pilgrims was permitted.

Harun al-Rashid was both religiously tolerant and politically clever. His cultivation of good relations with Charlemagne had sound political reasons. The King of the Franks was at the time engaged in a struggle for the control of the Iberian peninsula with the Abbasid ruler's chief rivals, the Umayyads, who had invaded and conquered Spain from North Africa in the year 711.

But individual rulers were only able to reign in the tradition of intolerance for brief periods. In the year 1077, following the fall of the Fatimid dynasty, which had ruled Egypt, and with it Palestine, Christian pilgrimage was halted. The Christian world was not long in coming up with a response. "Liberation" might have been the catchword of the epoch which followed. To "free the Holy Sepulchre" was the mission of the Crusades, beginning in 1096 and initiating a further escalation of intolerance. Victorious for but a brief period, the Crusaders were forced out of the Holy Land in the year 1291. During their sojourn in the Holy Land, however, they did provide for a boom in the local construction industry, building or repairing church after church and numerous hostels for pilgrims.

Forty-two years later (in 1333) the Christian world discovered that it is sometimes possible to achieve more through diplomacy than through war. The Franciscans were given possession of the site of the Last Supper and they were once again allowed to celebrate Mass at the Church of the Holy Sepulchre, at Mary's tomb and at the Church of the Nativity in Bethlehem—privileges which lasted until the next turnover of civilizations. This took place in 1517, when the Turks conquered the Holy Land. A new set of rules was established in 1552, whereby the influence of the Greek Orthodox church grew massively—and, beginning in 1634, even violently—at the expense of other Christians. For centuries, the Latin Christians had had the upper hand. Now it was the turn of the Greek Orthodox. In 1757 they drove the Franciscans out of the Church of the Nativity (but not out of the grotto) as well as the Church of Mary and in part from the Church of the Holy Sepulchre.

The state of affairs which was thus established is largely identical with the present status quo at the holy sites—which is not to say that this historical explanation makes the complex relationships any more understandable. In any case, the Christians in the Holy Land found a formula for survival under the Turkish-Ottoman overlords.

A prime example for the lack of intra-Christian tolerance was the Crimean War of 1854 to 1856. The trigger (but not the cause) was a conflict over rights in the Church of the Nativity in Bethlehem in which Roman Catholics were pitted against Greek and Russian Orthodox. France, Great Britain and Turkey went to war against Russia. All four powers pursued their own political aims, but claimed religious motivations. As so often, sanctimonious bigotry and hypocrisy were sold as piety.

How can there be peace *between* the great religions laying claim to the Holy Land when it not even possible to achieve tolerance *within* a religious camp? Although the claims of Christianity with regard to the Holy Land are more religious than political in nature, it appears impossible to achieve peace even among the Christian churches. Those Christians who shake their heads over the inability of Jews and Muslims to reach agreement over the Holy Land need to be reminded that they are sitting in a glass house.

The advent of British rule in 1917 failed to bring about an era of sunshine in intra-Christian relations in the Holy Land, but as the new "masters of the house", the Christians there certainly found life easier. We mention only in passing that throughout the British Mandate Jews were denied access to King David's tomb. "Out with the Jews, in with the Muslims" was the operating principle. Why should the British overlords have proven more sovereign than their predecessors?

Despite all the fears and malicious rumors to the contrary, the Christians in the Holy Land were able to achieve much more than just a formula for survival under the new, Jewish rulers from 1948 on. This despite the fact that Christian leaders—for example the present Latin Patriarch (a Palestinian)—have not distinguished themselves in their practice of political restraint.

Were all the rumors merely malicious or was their more behind them? In the early 1950s, for example, the alarming "news" spread, first in Vatican circles, then to South America and finally to all parts of the Catholic world, making its way even to Bonn on the Rhine, that "the Jews" had converted numerous Christian holy sites into bars and other places of morally dubious entertainment. Investigation soon proved the rumors to be without basis. Their real foundation was a modern, somewhat more innocuous variation of the ages-old prejudice against "the Jews" as "the murders of Christ". The further purpose behind the rumors was clear enough: Had any evidence of profanation turned up, it would have been automatically blamed on the Jewish State.

To the present day, Christian-Jewish relations in the Holy Land and at the holy places are anything but cordial. One fairly recent example: On December

6, 1991, newspapers reported that the Armenian Christians, Franciscans and Greek Orthodox Christians were complaining of the failure of the Israeli civilian authorities in the occupied territories to repair the leaking roof of the Church of the Nativity in Bethlehem. They even indicated that this might force the cancellation of the Christmas services. This threat appears to have made a mighty impression on the Israeli civilian administrators, almost as though Christmas were a Jewish holiday. Only days later, surprised newspaper readers learned that the roof had already been repaired. Like repairmen elsewhere, those in Israel and the West Bank are not exactly famous for their prompt responses. But it is, after all, a land of wonders, this wonderful Holy Land.

A few weeks later, on January 14, 1992, to be exact, the Christian world was shook by alarming news from the Holy City: "Nine bishops of the most important churches in Jerusalem stated today that they may appeal to UNESCO for international protection for the Christian holy places if the Israeli government proves incapable of providing protection. This is not the first time that church leaders have raised the demand for United Nations' supervision of the Christian monuments in Jerusalem, after a Christian monastery disappeared under a new highway in Jerusalem. The representatives of the churches declared [in rare unanimity but with their usual presumption—MW] that Israel is responsible for the preservation of the holy places of all religions but that Israel was showing concern only for the Jewish holy sites." So far, so dramatic. What the church leaders apparently overlooked was the fact that orthodox Jews had also protested against the same road construction, as their interests were also directly affected. This either failed to impress the churchmen, or they preferred not to mention it, so as not to dilute the drama of their own protest. Problems involving holy places? Certainly, but the political background behind the pious presentation was all too obvious, since the churchmen simultaneously protested against Israel's settlement policy. Such protest is both understandable and legitimate, but it is political. Once again, the holy places were used as a political instrument.

In connection with the Christian holy places we hear nothing of the Temple Mount. Jesus' teachings and works were directed against the Temple establishment, and not merely against the misjudged Pharisees, who, as we have noted, deserve much better than their bad reputation in the Christian tradition.

The reader of the Gospel according to Matthew has no difficulty recognizing early Christianity's anti-Temple thrust: "And Jesus entered the temple of God and drove out all who sold and bought in the temple, and he overturned the tables of the money-changers and the seats of those who sold pigeons. He said to them, 'It is written, 'My house shall be called a house of prayer'; but you make it a den of robbers.'" (Matthew 21: 12–13) "But when the chief priests [i.e. the Temple establishment] and the scribes [i.e. the Pharisees] saw the wonderful things that he did ... they were indignant." (Matthew 21:15) This seemed to make little impression on Jesus: "And leaving them, he went out of the city to Bethany and lodged there." (Matthew 21:17)

In chapter 24 Matthew is even more dramatic: "Jesus left the temple and was going away, when his disciples came to point out to him the buildings of the temple. But he answered them, 'You see all these, do you not? Truly I say to you, there will not be left here one stone upon another, that will not be thrown down." (Matthew 24:1–2)

From the Christian perspective, the destruction of the Second Temple was the fulfillment of this prophecy and proof of God's rejection of the Jews for their refusal to recognize Jesus as the Christ, the Messiah.

Upon the site of the temple ruins the Romans erected a temple of their own: the cult of a contrary culture, a counter-religion—in human history an ancient but proven means of demonstrating victory over and suppression of an opponent.

For Christianity, however, the most visible sign of its overcoming Judaism could not be the establishment of a counter-cult on the Temple Mount but rather the permanent and visible state of ruin of this former "den of robbers".

Following the Christianization of the Roman Empire (under Constantine in the fourth century), numerous and elaborate structures were erected in Jerusalem. But the Temple Mount was deliberately neglected. It continued to deteriorate until, at the end of the Byzantine Empire (the successor to the Eastern Roman Empire in Palestine) the Temple Mount was little more than a rubbish dump. Both the Temple Mount and Judaism had ended up on the garbage heap of history—so the view of the early Christians.

The early Christians expended an astounding amount of energy in settling political accounts with Judaism. Once victory was achieved, the goal was to enjoy its fruits by making Jerusalem *judenrein*—free of Jews. *Judenrein* is a German word but not a Nazi invention. It has an ancient tradition. After the suppression of the Jewish uprising against the Romans (132–135) Jerusalem was, by imperial decree, renamed and repopulated—with loyal pagans.

Emperor Hadrian decreed that Jerusalem was henceforth to bear the name Aelia Capitolina. Jews were not even permitted access to the lands in the periphery of the city. Caesarea, not Jerusalem, was the provincial capital.

In the spirit of supposed Christian brotherly love, Emperor Constantine the Great confirmed and even sharpened the policy which had been watered down as a result of the weakness of Roman administration in the previous century.

Was Emperor Constantine truly "the Great"? Politically, he was certainly an outstanding character, but morally? In any case, he did permit the Jews access to Jerusalem—on one day in the year, namely on the ninth day of the Jewish month of Aw. It is on this day, according to Jewish tradition, that both the First and the Second Temples were destroyed. On this day of total humiliation the most-Christian emperor chose to permit Jews access to the Temple Mount in Jerusalem. Of course, some Jews continued to risk approaching or entering the Holy City illegally.

Constantine the Great described Judaism as a "pernicious" and "vile" sect. That Jews were "murders of the prophets" and "murderers of the Lord" was taken as self-evident. In his Easter message for the year 352 the emperor spoke of the "most hated Jewish rabble".

In short: Constantine was a most un-Christian Christian, his superficially assumed Christianity a hollow shell—something which unfortunately must be said of other Christians of his and other ages. Some experts (Günter Stemberger, for example) recognize in Constantine's anti-Jewish statements "the handwriting of his Christian advisors". This may be true. In any case, as one of the more powerful emperors, the political responsibility was indubitably his. That Constantine's more restrictive laws did not result in any real deterioration of the position of the Jews in the Holy Land (also Stemberger) has more the ring of a queer academic argument than historic reality—and overlooks the very dramatic worsening of the situation of Jews in other parts of the Roman Empire.

Much more important than the putative or real anti-Judaism of this emperor, whom Judaism survived, just as it survived so many others, is another thought: Where human beings (mis)interpret the spirit of religion, the fault is theirs, not the religion's.

Emperor Julian behaved differently than his cousin Constantine, but is not known as "the Great". Perhaps this is precisely because so many of the "Greats" of history achieved great political and military power, but were moral failures. In 362 Emperor Julian allowed the Jews to return to Jerusalem. Just a year later he granted them permission to rebuild their Temple. After a severe fire, however, work was abandoned, never again to resume. The Temple Mount once again became a Christian garbage dump.

Julian, of course, was anything but the typical Christian emperor. To the contrary, during his reign, Emperor Julian resisted the Christianization of the empire, striving instead for a re-hellenization, a revival of Greek-Roman "paganism".

The learned men of the Talmud, the rabbis, were anything but pleased at the prospect of rebuilding the Temple. They had every reason to fear a rebirth and re-empowerment of the priestly caste. Whether they were right or not, their priority was to secure their decentralized, "portable" form of Judaism. Each group worked towards its own ends, but history appears to confirm the political wisdom of the Talmudic sages, for the tolerant Emperor Julian's reign lasted a mere two years.

In 629 the Byzantine Emperor Heracleios launched a new effort to render Jerusalem *judenrein*. The joy over his success proved of short duration, however, as just five years later the Arab-Islamic conquest of the Holy Land began. By 638 the Holy City was in Muslim hands. The dream of a Christian Jerusalem was over—or so it appeared.

Some four centuries later it was revived—at least briefly. On July 15, 1099 the Crusaders captured the Holy City. Their conduct was anything but holy. In the El Aqsa Mosque, "the Franks killed more than 70,000 Muslims, among them many imams, religious scholars, pious persons and ascetics who had left their homes in other lands in order to live in this holy place" reported the Muslim historian Ibn al-Atir. Although the exaggeration in this report is evident, the central facts are indisputable. There is no doubt that the conquering Crusaders conducted themselves in a murderous fashion. The Israeli expert on the era of the Crusaders, Jehoshua Praver, estimates that the actual number of victims slaughtered in the conquest of the Holy City was approximately 40,000.

Archbishop William of Tyre (1130–1184), a generally reliable chronicler who drew on eyewitness reports, confirms the Islamic descriptions of July 15, 1099. No one can accuse the Archbishop of anti-Christian propaganda where he reports: "One could not view this mass of dead without horror, and the picture of the victory, covered with blood from their heads to their feet, was no less horrible."

It is thus not surprising that the Jewish residents of Jerusalem were also not spared. They thronged to the synagogues, where they barricaded themselves inside and prayed. Their prayers were not answered. The Crusaders set the synagogues afire. Some Jews managed to flee onto the Temple Mount, which they attempted to defend—together with the Muslims. It was all was in vain. Everyone was massacred. "No one has ever heard of or seen such a bloodbath among the heathens. Corpses were burning in fires as numerous as the cornerstones and no one except God knows their number." Thus reads the report of an anonymous Christian eyewitness.

Almost the entire Islamic and Jewish populations of Jerusalem were slaughtered by the un-Christian Christian Crusaders. Under the banner of religion, Jerusalem had been purged of both Muslims and Jews. The Holy City was virtually *muslimrein* and *judenrein*—also a "final solution." But the contemporary Christian world saw it as a kind of salvation. It is not known whether the reigning Pope Urban II, the author of the First Crusade, learned of the Christian capture of the Holy City before his death, but his passing brought no improvement for the surviving non-Christian inhabitants of Jerusalem.

Despite the gruesome conquest of the Holy City, the Crusaders did not establish a reign of terror over Jerusalem. But neither was the Holy City pervaded by the spirit of tolerance. Relations remained those of victor and vanquished. As ever, however, the millstone of history continued to grind and the wheel of fortune—here the everlasting shifting of roles—eventually completed another revolution. As the years passed, Muslims and the Jews returned and finally the Christians were forced to abandon the Holy City.

For a time, the El Aqsa Mosque was Christianized and renamed. Names are never mere "sound and fury". They are always a reflection of program or content. The Mosque of El Aqsa was christened the "Templum Salomonis"—as though it had been built by Solomon. The Dome of the Rock became the "Temple of the Lord"—and so on and so forth. For Muslims and Jews, Jerusalem was essentially a forbidden city, but, like any principle, this one also soon developed holes.

"Love thy neighbor as thyself" was an injunction the Crusaders quickly forgot. Before long, rivalries broke out between the French and the Germans, the Latin and the Orthodox Christians. Odo of Deuill, chaplain to the French King Louis VII reported angrily on "the Germans" who frequented the inns and, of course, got drunk: "The Germans are intolerable, even for us … (the) Germans do not want to tolerate our buying anything until they have amply taken for themselves whatever they want. The result was a brawl amidst a fearful clamor," wrote Odo.

Christian brotherly love was apparently such a difficult exercise that the Christian community in Jerusalem divided the city into separate quarters for each of the nations.

Following their defeat by Saladin (in the battle of Hattin in 1187) the Crusaders had to abandon Jerusalem. For the brief period between 1229 and 1244 they were allowed to return because of a politically sensible and religiously exemplary compromise between Emperor Frederick II and Egypt's Muslim ruler Malik al-Kamil. With the exception of the Temple Mount, Jerusalem was turned over to the Christians, who also were given control over a corridor from the port of Jaffo through Ramlah to Jerusalem. The city was demilitarized and the free exercise of religion agreed upon.

Not only time, but the human spirit itself appeared to have progressed. Emperor Frederick's reward was his coronation as "King of Jerusalem" in the Church of the Holy Sepulchre. As a diplomatic triumph, however, the compromise, did not prove to be very durable. Vehement protest was soon heard on both sides. The pope refused his blessing, as Frederick was under papal ban at the time. At the holiest of the Christian holy places, therefore, the Emperor's coronation took place without the participation of the clergy.

The compromise was rich in insight, its intentions were far-sighted, but is tenure was but brief. Once again, reasonable men proved able to contain the conflict for but a brief period of time.

The era of promise was followed by a deep setback. In 1244 the Ayyubi rulers of Egypt summoned the Charismiens, a Turkish people, to aid in their struggle against their Muslim (and also Ayyubi) rivals in Damascus. This provided the opportunity for a Muslim return to Jerusalem, the expulsion of the Christians and the destruction of the Church of the Holy Sepulchre as well as other Christian places of worship. So quickly did the political star of the King of Jerusalem fade.

The fate of the Ayyubi dynasty in Egypt was similar. The pace of history accelerated dramatically. By 1250 the Ayyubis had been dethroned by their own military caste, the Mamluks. Early in 1260 the Mongolian Horde captured Jerusalem, only to be driven out by the Mamluks in September of the same year. After this, the pace of history once again slowed until the arrival of the Turks in 1516/17. From then until 1917 the Holy City remained part of the Ottoman Empire.

The departure of the Christian rulers of Jerusalem in 1244 was, of course, involuntary. It was not until December 9, 1917, that a Christian conqueror again entered the Holy City. On that day the British General Allenby arrived in Jerusalem with his troops. Upon reaching the Old City at the Jaffa Gate, Allenby dismounted from his horse. He wanted to enter the city as a pilgrim, not as a conqueror. Theater—but the general was serious.

British rule was little more than a brief interlude which ended officially on May 14, 1948. The British Mandate brought few political or religious advantages for either the Jewish or the Muslim populations. The see-saw swings which occurred in the British attempt to balance between Muslims and Jews in Palestine actually served to escalate the conflict between the Zionists and the Arab Palestinians.

In 1947 the General Assembly of the United Nations determined that Jerusalem should be neither Arab-Palestinian nor Jewish-Israeli. Both sides paid attention to this resolution only when it was to their advantage. In 1948 the Kingdom of Jordan (which then still went by the name "Trans-Jordan") occupied the eastern parts of Jerusalem, including the Old City. In 1952 it officially annexed these areas, but this act was not accorded international recognition except by Great Britain (as Jordan's protector) and Pakistan.

In 1949 Israel reorganized the western parts of the city and made it the nation's capital. In June 1967 Israel followed Jordan's example of 1948, captured the whole of the city in the course of the Six Day War, annexed East Jerusalem and subsequently cemented this act by means of further legislation in 1981. But how long does political cement hold in the course of history? Does not the history of Jewish *and* Christian *and* Muslim rule over the Holy City show it to more resemble putty?

Bethlehem: The home of King David, also the place where Samuel anointed him King. Here Rachel, the wife of the patriarch Jacob, found her final resting place. Here is the birthplace of Jesus. To whom does Bethlehem belong? Without a doubt, both religions have legitimate claims.

No doubt, as well, that the (politically and religiously understandable) drive on the part of Christianity to overcome Judaism from within again becomes manifest in Bethlehem.

The Church of the Nativity: The exact location was discovered by Helena, the mother of Emperor Constantine. Helena was a pious woman and she had a magnificent church built at the site (which has since undergone a number of ravages and rebuildings). Although the manner in which Helena determined the location for her church may bear elements of the grotesque, it must also be remembered that a fairly firm tradition was already established in connection with the chosen location.

The pious Helena also determined the places of Jesus' crucifixion and resurrection. She further claimed to have discovered the relics of the true Holy Cross. The Church of the Holy Sepulchre was built at the site indicated by Helena (and underwent numerous subsequent reconstructions, especially by the Crusaders after 1099 and after a fire in 1808). The last five of the fourteen stations of the cross, the Via Dolorosa, are located within this structure.

In order to avoid misunderstandings, I wish to reiterate at this point as clearly and explicitly as possible: Religious feelings are to be taken seriously, very seriously, be they those of Jews, Christians, Muslims or any other religion. I consider myself a religious person. Untrustworthiness and lack of credibility, however, are always damaging to genuine religion, be it Jewish, Christian, Islamic or other. Those who find themselves in need of crutches on their way to heaven also need to be devilishly careful that these crutches do no collapse from under them. Their faith may also fall, and this, in my opinion, is tragic. Whoever can proceed without crutches will be able to cover more ground and will be on a firmer religious footing.

The role of the emperor's pious mother once again demonstrates that interweaving politics and religion is usually not healthy for religion over the long term. Religion becomes politicized and politics religiously inflated. Politics is opium for religion.

But a loss of religious content can also be effected by the self-appointed representatives of purest dogma—as a product of the resulting conflicts within a religious community. We refer for one example to the rivalries between the Christian denominations at the Church of the Holy Sepulchre, where the results are painfully visible.

The main concentration of Christian holy places is to be found in and near Jerusalem. We shall not attempt to list them all. Summaries can be found in any good guidebook. Among the most important are, of course, the Via Dolorosa, the Garden of Gethsemane, the Valley of the Cross and the church which carries the Latin name Dominus Flevit, where Jesus cried over the Holy City: "And when he drew near and saw the city he wept over it, saying, 'Would that even today you knew the things that make for peace! But now they are hid from your eyes.'" (Luke 19:41–42) This is true even today, for the inhabitants of Jerusalem have yet to recognize the things make for peace.

Another goal of Christian pilgrims in Jerusalem is the Chapel of the Ascension: "Then he led them out as far as Bethany, and lifting up his hands he blessed them. While he blessed them, he parted from them." (Luke 24:50–51). According to the Acts of the Apostles (Acts 1:12), however, the Mount of Olives is the site of the Ascension.

We ask again and again from different viewpoints: Whose Holy Land? In this context it is important to realize that in Jerusalem the Jewish-Christian rivalry can be felt, so to speak, with one's own hands. Mount Zion is a good example. King David's tomb, the Dormition Church (where Mary died) and the site of the Last Supper all immediately adjoin. This had to do with the Christian striving to overcome Judaism from within, but it also reflects the fact that the focus of the events of Jesus' passion is in Jerusalem because the city was the focus of the political and religious conflicts of the time.

The situation becomes totally different when we turn to the other Christian holy places. Galilee is "new" country in the sense that Nazareth, for example, as the site of the Annunciation and as Jesus' childhood home, first achieved historical and religious importance in this Christian context. The same applies to Cana, where Jesus transformed water into wine. "This, the first of his signs, Jesus did at Cana in Galilee, and manifested his glory; and his disciples believed in him." (John 2:11)

Taghba overlooks the Sea of Galilee from the northwest. This magnificent setting is the site of several New Testament events: the miracle of the loaves and fishes, through which Jesus fed a throng of 5000 with just five loaves of bread and two fish (Mark 6:30–44), the Sermon on the Mount and the conferral of apostolic leadership on Peter.

Jesus "own city", Capernaum, lay nearby on the shore of the Sea of Galilee: "And getting into a boat he crossed over and came to his own city." (Matthew 9:1) Capernaum was the center of Jesus' ministry in Galilee. He was highly successful here. Any pastor who takes up chapter 2 of the Gospel of Mark will grow pale with envy: "And when he returned to Capernaum after some days, it was reported that he was at home. And many were gathered together, so that there was no longer room for them, not even about the door." (Mark 2:1–2)

Galilee was, so to speak, *Jesus' country.*

An irony of history? Whereas Judea and Samaria, the ancient heartland of the Jewish people, were occupied by Jordan in 1948, it was Jesus' home country of Galilee—together with the coastal areas that in Old Testament times formed the homeland of the Philistines, against whom the ancient Jews fought so many battles—which became the core of the State of Israel.

To whom does the Holy Land in Galilee belong? To the Christians? Apparently not, as after Jesus' time it became the center of settlement and spiritual life for the Jewish community remaining in the Holy Land. Tiberias, the city which was declared "clean" according to ritual Jewish law in the second century became the birthplace of the "Jerusalem Talmud". Again, we discover the holiness of the land in a multitude of forms and on differing levels.

This by now familiar multiplicity becomes particularly evident with regard to Mount Tabor, which lies between Nazareth and the Sea of Galilee. Here the Canaanites worshiped their god Baal. Some unbelieving Jews also followed their example, which aroused the ire of the prophet Hosea, who thundered: "O Ephraim, you have played the harlot, Israel is defiled." (Hosea 5:3) Even earlier, it was here that the judge Deborah defeated the Canaanite commander Sisera (Judges 4 and 5). Canaanite, Jewish and Christian layers form the multifaceted religious tradition of Mount Tabor, which is also the site of the Transfiguration: "He took with him Peter and John and James, and went up on the mountain to pray. And as he was praying, the appearance of his countenance was altered, and his raiment became dazzling white. And behold, two men talked with him, Moses and Elijah, who appeared in glory and spoke of his departure, which he was to accomplish at Jerusalem." (Luke 9:28–31)

Once again, we encounter the systematic Christian-Jewish relationship here. On the one hand we have a conscious tie to Jewish tradition, which, on the other hand, is regarded as fulfilled and thereby overcome. The setting chosen for the Transfiguration is one of breath-taking natural beauty. The religious experience on Mount Tabor also becomes an encounter with nature. Is it not also God's creation in the eyes of people of religion?

So we ask not of the land, but of this individual natural elevation: To whom does Mount Tabor belong? The Canaanites have the earliest claim to ownership. But they do not appear to have any living heirs. Or perhaps they do? The Palestinians claim to be descendants of the Canaanites. We shall have to examine this hereditary claim—in the third part of this book.

The Muslim Holy Places

Since the twelfth century Moses' tomb, on the way from Jerusalem to Jericho, has been a goal of Muslim pilgrimages. In the Bible we find no reference to where the tomb of this greatest of the prophets might be found. It is a further example of how popular piety shapes sources and traditions according to its needs, even ignoring contradictory sources standing in its way. On one point the Bible is absolutely clear: "So Moses the servant of the Lord died there in the land of Moab, according to the word of the Lord, and he buried him in the valley in the land of Moab opposite Bethpeor; but no man knows the place of his burial to this day." (Deuteronomy 34:5–6)

Another goal of the Muslim faithful is the tomb of Sayyiduna Ali, who died in battle against the Crusaders. For a long time the Israeli authorities allowed this site to decay. Granted, Sayyiduna Ali was not a saint in the narrow sense of the word, but popular piety has its own significance, as we have seen in connection with the Jewish holy sites.

The tomb of the prophet Samuel near Jerusalem is a further goal of Islamic pilgrims, as is the Tomb of the Patriarchs in Hebron and the tomb of Ruben (Jacob's eldest son) in the south. The Cave of the Prophet Elijah near Practice is sacred to both Muslims and Jews.

According to Islamic mysticism, Jerusalem and the Holy Land purify the soul. This reminds us of the Talmudic tradition, which mentions the faculty of reason in addition to the soul: "The air of the Land of Israel makes one wise." (Bava batra 158b)

The chief goal of Islamic pilgrims is of course the Haram al-Scharif (the Temple Mount) in Jerusalem. We have already seen why this site is especially sacred to Muslims and also raised the heretical question as to whether the Quran cannot be (mis)interpreted as a Zionist source. On the Haram al-Scharif, Muslims have erected the El Aqsa Mosque and the Dome of the Rock (also known as the Omar Mosque). Islamic oral tradition (in continuation of Talmudic stories) also maintains that the sacred rock under the dome of the Omar Mosque lies directly beneath the Allah's Throne. Tradition holds that below this rock is located a cave in which the souls of the departed gather every fortnight. Before the creation of mankind, the angels are said to have visited this cave 2000 times and it is here that Noah's arc is said to have come to rest after the flood. No wonder, then, that this place is described as a part of Paradise, and as the place from which all the world's sources of fresh water spring. In view of the importance of water in this hot and dry part of the world, we may easily understand the connection between water and Paradise. What is more, it is here where the Angel of Death is to stand on Judgement Day and (following good Jewish custom) blow three times into the ram's horn to mark the beginning of the Resurrection of the Dead.

In the year 638, Omar, the successor (caliph) of the Prophet and conqueror of Jerusalem ordered the Temple Mount to be cleared of the rubble accumulated there over the centuries of neglect during the Byzantine era. Caliph Omar directed that a temporary mosque be built of wood. The erection of the present Dome of the Rock began in 691. Though it bears his name, Caliph Omar was not responsible for its construction. A decade or two later the building of the nearby El Aqsa Mosque was undertaken.

The original position of Muslims at prayer (*kibla*) was facing Jerusalem, as it was then the only city holy to monotheists, and Islam deliberately tied in to the traditions of the two other monotheistic religions. To face Jerusalem in prayer was thus a natural decision. But the more self-confident, independent and powerful Islam became, the more it sought to establish its distance from the other religions. What could have been more logical than to change the orientation of prayer to Mecca, the city of the prophet Mohammed and the place most holy to all Muslims?

Over and over again we run into the theory that the original intention was to win over the Jews, and that for this reason the early Muslims prayed toward Jerusalem. After the break with the Jews the decision was made to face Mecca, it is said. The theory has long been demolished, but that has not prevented its continued dissemination.

Jerusalem's political significance under Muslim rule was never commensurate with its religious status. This is reflected in the fact that the city's new Muslim rulers did not apply the name "El Quds", i.e. "The Holy", until some fifty years after their conquest. Furthermore, the new rulers chose not El Quds/Jerusalem as the provincial capital, but founded for this purpose a new city, Ramlah, between 715 and 717. Today, Ramlah is a small town between Jerusalem and Tel Aviv.

In the year 750 the Abbasids defeated the Umayyads. One consequence was that distant Baghdad replaced nearby Damascus as the capital city of the Arab-Islamic Empire. The greater distance to the center of power was not without its effects on Jerusalem. Its holiness remained, but its political significance sank even further. The process of "Arabification" and "Islamification" in Jerusalem was not really intensified until the late phase of Umayyad rule with a flurry of building activity and the settlement of tribesmen from the south of the Arabian peninsula. Most of the earlier Arab settlers in Jerusalem appear to have come from the city of Medina.

Despite its insignificant political status, the holiness of the city was emphasized in the Abbasid period with a number of building projects. Not only was the city's architectural beauty enhanced, but so was its tolerance, especially under the Caliph Harun al Rashid. We have already mentioned his generosity in connection with Charlemagne and the Christian holy places. This tolerance was also extended to the Jews. The center of Jewish activities subsequently shifted from Tiberias to Jerusalem.

For certain periods of time such figures of political and moral intelligence and integrity as Harun al Rashid succeed in stopping the endless succession of slaughter and sacrilege (often enough perpetrated in the name of the sacred). But again and again, the dams they erect eventually collapse, unfettering a renewed inundation.

For a long time, in fact, neither Jews nor Christians did badly under Arab-Islamic rule. That the Muslims allegedly denied the Jews access to Jerusalem (like the "tolerant" Christian-Byzantine Emperors before) is a legend to be found only in Christian sources and is a reflection of wishful thinking. The reality was different, and the Muslim tolerance applied to both Jews and Christians. Cyclical ups and downs did occur, whereby it is sometimes difficult to distinguish between actions and reactions. This is especially true after the Byzantine Empire initiated an attempt to reconquer the Holy Land in the tenth century. The Muslim response was to battle not only the enemy before the gate, but those within the walls as well. In an attack in which both Muslims and Jews participated in 966 a number of churches, including the Church of the Holy Sepulchre were set on fire. The Jewish activists were even more fired up than their Muslim compatriots—according to Islamic sources. Is this a sign of a bad conscience? If so, it is hardly dishonorable.

Three years later a dramatic change in power took place when the Shiite Fatimid dynasty, the new rulers of Egypt, captured Jerusalem from the Sunni Abbasids. The peace which followed was only of brief duration. Shortly, attacks by Bedouin tribesmen began, and a series of persecutions of Jews and Christians took place. The Caliph al Hakim (who ruled from 996 to 1021) achieved an especially sad fame in this regard. In the year 1009 the Church of the Holy Sepulchre was destroyed. It took forty years before the restoration could be completed, after the Christians had again received permission to maintain their holy places. Another period of better times set in, and Christian pilgrims once again streamed into the Holy Land, which was not theirs politically, but which was inseparable from their religious faith.

The better times were followed by sudden disaster. One is tempted to ask cynically how it could have been any different. And where was the disaster worst? Of course, where the land is the holiest, in Jerusalem, which, until the Crusaders raised its political status, remained in the political shadow of Ramlah.

Lacking in morals as the Crusades and the Crusaders may have been, they did serve to enhance the perception of the city's holiness. And, for the first time in over a thousand years, Jerusalem was once again a political capital, namely of the "Kingdom of Jerusalem."

But before the arrival of the Crusaders, it was first the Seljuks who invaded the Byzantine Empire in 1071, overwhelmed the Holy Land in 1075 and proceeded to forbid Christian pilgrimages in 1077. This is the action which provoked the well-known Christian response in the form of the First Crusade from 1096 to 1099. The Egyptian Fatimids did succeed in retaking Jerusalem in 1098, but the Crusaders were already underway. Their conquest of the Holy City we have already described.

In a "Holy War" the Muslims retook the Holy Land and the Holy City under the leadership of the legendary Kurdish Ayyubi commander Salah al-Din al-Ayyubi, better known in the West as Saladin. Even today, the Arab world fondly and proudly recalls his exemplary faithfulness to the Islamic religion. His Kurdish heritage, however, is rarely deemed worthy of mention. To put it euphemistically, these two Islamic peoples, Arabs and Kurds, have a few problems with each other. We recall Saddam Hussein's treatment of the Kurds after the Gulf War in 1991 as but one recent example.

Saladin is to be counted among the true "greats" because, after his victory, he found the courage to forgive and to plan for peace. His generosity was also a dictate of political reason, since no society can sustain war indefinitely. In any case, Imad al Din's description of Saladin's reconquest of the Holy City is both impressive and entirely credible:

"The Patriarch gathered up everything which lay about the [Holy] Sepulchre … and everything that was in the Church of the Resurrection. … I therefore said to the Sultan: 'These are great riches of apparent value. … Free passage is allowed for their goods, but not for those of the churches and monasteries; do not leave these in the hands of the shameless!' But he replied: 'If we interpret the agreement to their disadvantage, they in their ignorance of the true facts will accuse us of breaking our word. Therefore we shall treat them according to the letter of the agreement and not permit them to accuse the faithful of breaking our oath. Instead, they should tell of the kindness with which we have showered them.'"

Where there is bright light, we also find shadows. Imad al Din, an intimate of Saladin's also reports: "Women and children counting 8000 we divided among ourselves, and the face of the empire smiled over their crying. How many well-guarded women were dishonored, rulers overruled, young girls married, nobles given away … virgins deflowered." Imad al Din made a good reporter. Since he was not as noble as his lord, all of this did not seem to bother him. To the contrary, he relates that Jerusalem was thus "cleansed of the dirty Franks".

After its "liberation" from the Crusaders, Jerusalem was no longer a capital. The Ayyubids ruled their Empire, including the Holy Land, from Egypt. Jerusalem had to wait another eight centuries before again becoming a capital city—of the State of Israel. Even under Jordanian rule (1948–1967), Jerusalem had to take second place to Amman.

By the time the Mamluks took over the reigns of the empire, Jerusalem had been almost totally leveled. Great destruction was caused by the Charismians in 1244 and again by the Mongols in 1260. The Mamluks invested great energy in the rebuilding of the city. Monuments in today's Jerusalem continue to bear witness to their efforts. The self-confident opulence of the city's architecture was certainly also meant as a political signal directed at discouraging potential aggressors. The Islamic world certainly had no interest in tempting the Crusaders or other Christians to try to recapture the Holy City. In this respect, Jerusalem was very important—but not important enough for its Muslim Mamluk ruler to make it the seat of his government.

This dichotomy between the holiness of the city and its political significance in the Islamic world is not only noteworthy, it is something close to an historical constant. The gap between rhetorical claim and political reality has proven a long-term phenomenon. To recognize and describe this is not an issue of prejudicial propaganda but rather one of historical honesty.

Under the Mamluks, Jerusalem served more as a place of internal exile for political has-beens than as a center of politics or religion. Precisely because it was not a center of power, however, the city slowly but surely gave rise to a local Muslim leadership around a group of families whose position among the present Palestinian population remains both prominent and powerful. The emergence of this local elite represents a kind of historical irony, but proved a blessing in the history of the Palestinian people. Unlike the Mamluk overlords in distant Egypt, these local families identified with their home, with their city of Jerusalem and with the Holy Land.

For Christians and Jews, Mamluk rule was, to say the least, a mixed blessing. We will not delve into the details of the ups and downs of this period. For both groups, the general historical "weather pattern" was that of a permanent depression. Christians were the favorite targets of the Muslim leadership (and of the mob, which, as we know, can arise in any population, whatever the religion). The Church of the Holy Sepulchre was repeatedly desecrated and the Franciscans subjected to especially oppressive treatment.

The Jews of the city did not prosper much, either, but, apart from extremely high taxes and the occasional destruction of a synagogue, their existence was not particularly precarious. Their lot was bad enough, but, the cynic might add, relatively mild in comparison with many, many other histories of Jewish suffering.

Above all, one would have needed a special demographic magnifying glass to have observed the Jewish population in the Jerusalem of that time. Around 1500 it was unlikely that the total Jewish population of the city exceeded 200 families or about 1600 souls.

In 1516 or 1517 (the exact date is disputed) Selim I captured Jerusalem and ushered in the era of Turkish rule. From then until 1917 the Holy City remained part of the Turkish Ottoman Empire.

The Turkish rulers were Muslims, good Muslims, even Caliphs, i.e. "successors" of the prophet Mohammed. Jerusalem/Al Quds/the Holy City, was holy and dear to their hearts, but it was the Byzantine-Christian city of Constantinople, conquered in 1453 and renamed Istanbul, which remained their capital. A symbol of Turkish-Muslim superiority, Istanbul at the same time indicated the direction of the Ottoman Empire's imperial orientation and drive: Europe.

As almost everyone knows, the Turks are Muslims but they are not Arabs. These simple facts are of special significance in connection with Jerusalem. For the non-Arab but nonetheless Muslim Ottoman Turks, the Holy City could, if the occasion called for it, fulfill a highly political function—at least theoretically—in a certain degree of rivalry with the Arabian holy cities of Mecca and Medina. No Ottoman ruler could or would have disputed that in Islam the holiness of the Holy City, Al Quds, ranked behind Mecca and Medina. But at times it was to the Turks' advantage to have something of an antidote to the dominance of the holy cities of Arabia, and thus to counter the dominant Arab position within the world of Islam.

The importance of this relation should not be lightly dismissed. As non-Arabian Caliphs, as non-Arab successors to the Arabian prophet Mohammed, this was a valuable trump in the sultan's domestic political hand. As long as its Arabian subjects remained quiescent, Istanbul could rest its hand. But whenever the Arabs became restive for greater self-determination, it was a potentially useful card. On the other hand, a joker it was not.

From history, the Turks had also learned that to neglect Jerusalem was to provide the Christian world with an excuse to (perhaps literally) crusade for a forceful assertion of Christian interests in the Holy City. On multiple levels, building projects in Jerusalem served to guard against Christian initiatives. Here, again, the fabric of religion and politics with regard to the holy places is most tightly woven.

Sultan Suleiman the Magnificent (1494–1566) did honor to his own and the Holy City's repute. He was Jerusalem's greatest builder. Many of the monuments he caused to be erected can still be admired, including the imposing city wall (built between 1537 and 1541, mainly for protection against Bedouin raids), improvements in the Dome of the Rock and a number of admirable fountains, among them those on Temple Mount. Sacredness and architectural magnificence were achieved in singular combination.

Nevertheless, the Holy City remained a small community. At the beginning of Ottoman rule it did not count more than 4000 inhabitants. Under Suleiman, the population grew to about 12,000, but soon after the fireworks of the great builder faded, Jerusalem settled back into provinciality. Between the middle of the sixteenth and the beginning of the nineteenth century the city's population varied between 7000 and 10,000.

Arab uprisings were not to be feared, Turkish rule was endangered neither from within nor from without and the incessant Bedouin raids had been part of everyday life in the Middle East for centuries. These were a manifestation of the ancient conflict between the region's urban and nomadic populations. It was simply a fact of life that travelers, even pilgrims, were robbed. It made no difference if they were Muslims, Christians or Jews. Until well into the nineteenth century, the Bedouins, who controlled the access routes to Jerusalem, continued to make travel to the Holy City insecure. In the eyes of the Ottoman authorities, the raids were pinpricks. They did not represent a serious threat to the security of the Empire.

Jerusalem's provincial status was reflected by its subordinate position in the administrative structure of the Ottoman Empire. After an initial period under the governor of Egypt, the Holy City was, as a rule, subject to the authority of the governor of Damascus. For some periods, however, the administrative seat was Sidon or Acco. Damascus was, of course, a large and important Islamic city rich in tradition, but how could Sidon or Acco compare or compete with Jerusalem?

Apart from a rarified political-military elite established in Jerusalem, neither the city nor the Holy Land were "turkified". That is to say, the Ottoman authorities did little to encourage Turkish settlement in the province—a clear sign of disinterest, even neglect. For the native Palestinian population, this proved to be an immeasurable boon. As under the Mamluks, the local leadership continued to develop. The greatest beneficiaries were the dominant local families: the Husseini, Nashashibi, Dagani, Khalidis, Khatib, Alami, Nusseiba clans as well as others. To even the superficially informed newspaper reader or TV news viewer, some of these names will sound quite familiar. Most will recall the prominent role played by the Jerusalem Palestinian leader Faisal Husseini as the interlocutor of US Secretary of State James Baker in the process leading up to the Madrid Conference. Since then, Husseini has played an even more prominent role as spokesmen for the city's Palestinians. The more informed will also be aware that he had been repeatedly jailed by the Israelis in an attempt to limit his influence within the Palestinian political leadership.

In the nineteenth century, Europeans, especially in London and Paris, began to eye the Holy Land and the Holy City with a growing imperialistic appetite. But practical political considerations kept them from carving up the Ottoman Empire—for the time being. At the same time, the Arab world was awakening from its long Ottoman-Turkish dormancy. Both developments alarmed the Ottoman rulers in Istanbul: the unspoken but easily decipherable imperialistic designs of the Europeans and the increasing insolence of the Islamic brothers in the Arab world who began to strive for greater independence.

The Sultan and his advisors decided that it was time to play one of their reserve trumps. From ancient times, architecture has been an instrument of political policy. Demonstrative improvements to the holy sites in Jerusalem was one way to send a clear signals to many capitals. From the middle of the nineteenth century on, the renovation of Jerusalem, especially the Moslem quarter, became a priority.

At the same time, a renovation of the administrative structure was also undertaken. The Jerusalem region was separated from the province of Damascus and its political status raised. Thereafter known as the Independent Sanjaq of Jerusalem, the new administrative region was subject only to the central government in Istanbul. Hebron, Jaffo and Gaza were incorporated into the Sanjaq of Jerusalem.

With the keen vision of historical hindsight, we now know that Turkish rule in the Holy Land was slowing approaching its end. In a first significant defeat, the Ottoman Empire was forced to yield to the Greeks in their successful war for independence (1821–1829). London had been especially supportive of the Greek cause. Soon, Russian and France, followed by Italy, Greece and the peoples of the Balkan, began to assert claims to pieces of the weakened empire, but the time was not yet ripe for a general division of the spoils.

Under the leadership of Mohammed Ali and his stepson Ibrahim Pasha, Egypt made an attempt to break away from Istanbul in the 1830s. They succeeded in bringing Jerusalem and the Holy Land under their control in 1831. Both of these rulers were western-oriented modernizers. Among the first things they did in Jerusalem was to trim the privileges of the leading Muslim clans. The Christians and the Jews were freed from traditional forced contributions and the discriminatory laws directed against their religions abolished. The influential Palestinian families of the Holy City resisted. Together with the dissatisfied small farmers of the region, they spearheaded a revolt against Ibrahim Pasha in 1834–1835. The uprising failed and the process of modernization continued. In 1838 a British consulate was opened in Jerusalem.

The British, however, together with the other European powers, insisted that Ibrahim Pasha withdraw from both the Holy City and the Holy Land. The imperialist powers were still undecided as to how they wanted to carve up the Ottoman Empire but were not about to allow Mohammed Ali and Ibrahim Pasha to get the jump on them.

In the Crimean War (1854–1856) the Ottomans were saved from the Russians with British and French assistance. The Turks were thus the victors who lost.

The Ottomans undertook a last, desperate rescue attempt and embarked on a radical plan of modernization for the Empire's military, administration, economy and society. The Holy City was made the focus of a great construction effort. But modernization and building projects cost money, and Istanbul had little. Large sums had to be borrowed from the western powers, and these did not come without strings attached: The Westerners demanded an increased presence and greater influence in the affairs of the Holy City. The result was that the Ottomans inadvertently pulled the rug from under their own Islamic program for the Holy City. Given their dependence on European loans and good will, the Ottomans really had no other choice.

The intended anti-European and anti-Christian signal that was to come from the expanded program of construction at the Islamic holy sites in Jerusalem thus failed its mark. The more Christians and Jews who settled in the Holy City, the more clearly could the Arab population recognize the disintegration of Ottoman power.

By the middle of the nineteenth century, Jerusalem had become an increasingly multi-confessional city. An Anglican bishop arrived in 1841 and in the same year the local Jews were permitted to establish the office of a Chief

Rabbi. From 1847 on, a Roman Catholic Patriarch once again resided in the city and the Greek Patriarch moved from Istanbul to Jerusalem. New churches and synagogues were built, including an "American colony" and a "German colony".

Of the approximately 15,000 residents of the Holy City in 1845 about 6000 were Jewish. By 1890 the population rose to about 43,000, of which 28,000 were Jews and only 8000 Muslims. The other 7000 were Christians. Before the end of the nineteenth century, a clear majority of the city's population was thus Jewish.

In the final analysis, the position of the Ottomans as the Empire's overlords could not prevent their increasing political impotence, and in consequence a general decline in Islamic influence within the Holy City. But the Turkish *millet* system, which allowed the various religious communities self-determination and self-administration in their internal affairs, remains without peer to the present day. To a great extent, the system was continued under both British and Israeli rule. That the Turks, British and Israelis also used it to their own purposes and that the *millet* system had its problems and deficiencies cannot be denied, but it nevertheless served to prevent (even more) violence and killing and provided the framework for a more or less peaceful co-existence of the confessional communities in the Holy City. Therein it remains unequaled.

As the nineteenth century progressed, the fabric of Ottoman power in Jerusalem wore ever thinner. Was it impotence, tolerance or both? In any case, the end result is well-known. In December 1917 the interlude of British-Christian rule in Jerusalem began.

After 1948 only the eastern parts of the city remained Islamic, that is to say Jordanian-Islamic. From 1948 to 1967 the city was divided between Jordan (in the east) and Israel (in the west).

Until 1967 the Temple Mount and the Old City were in Jordanian hands. During this period the Christian holy sites were preserved and even improved. The entire Jewish population, however, had been driven out. Of the dozens of synagogues, not one escaped destruction. The Jewish holy sites were also thoroughly desecrated, but these did not disappear. We have already mentioned that the monuments of the Jewish cemeteries on the Mount of Olives were plundered for use as material for the construction of buildings, roads and even latrines.

In 1967 Israel won the Six Day War against Egypt, Syria and Jordan. Jerusalem was once again united—under Israeli rule. More exactly put, the eastern portions of the city were annexed and incorporated into the Jewish State. After its conquest, Israel deliberately refrained from acts of retribution or revenge, but it cannot be said that Israeli rule ushered in an era of justice for the city's Muslim population. Israel's occupation was anything but restrained and gentle, but on the other hand, the persistent rumors of Israeli "provocations" with regard to the Muslim holy sites must be seen for what they were: propagandistic ploys. The game is as old as it is unholy. To cite just one example: In 1969 a fire broke out in the Al Aqsa Mosque. It was immediately portrayed as another Jewish "provocation", although the arsonist was soon captured—a mentally disturbed Christian from Australia.

Because today's Palestinian population in the Holy City continues to live under Israeli occupation—In this context we may neglect the Israeli view of the "liberation" of the Holy City.—it has not had and does not have a political representation of its own. It is only natural that the city's Islamic religious leaders have partly filled this vacuum. This is one of the reasons (but not the only reason) why the influence of Islam has continuously grown over recent years in East Jerusalem, the West Bank and in Gaza.

To whom does Jerusalem belong? To whom do the holy places belong? First of all to the Canaanite Jesubites. It was about 3000 years ago that King David took the city away from them by force of arms. And, of course, it was also a holy place to the Jesubites. This was nothing unusual, for at that time any larger settlement in the Orient had its local god or goddess, including ancient Jerusalem, and the ruler of the city was this god's earthly representative. The problem begins with the fact that today there are no legal heirs to the Jesubites, who have long disappeared into the historical tomb of the tribes and nations that grew and died in and around and because of Jerusalem. To be sure, the Palestinians claim to be the heirs of the Canaanites, and thus of the Jesubites, but this claim, as we shall see, rests on feet of clay. With all due piety and respect, we therefore turn from the Jesubites to the Jews and the other parties to the conflict.

To whom does Jerusalem belong? To whom do the holy places belong? In some instances the answer is simple: The holy sites which are claimed by only one of the religions do not present a problem. But to whom does the Tomb of the Patriarchs in Hebron "belong"? To the Jews, the Muslims or both? To whom does the Temple Mount "belong"? To the Jews, the Muslims or both? To whom does Mount Zion "belong"? To the Jews because David's tomb is there? Or to the Muslims because in 1524 it became the site of the Mosque of the Prophet David? Or to the Christians because it is the place Jesus selected to hold the Last Supper and because the Dormition Church is also there? As we have already seen, the list can be continued almost without end. To whom, then, do all of this multiple-religion holy places "belong"? To one religion, to all, to none?

The core problem lies, as usual, both in political history and in the various concepts of religious salvation. It is highly complex and nevertheless quite simple: Both Christianity and Islam sought to overcome Judaism. Both religions did so, each in their own way. Both triumphed, at least politically, over Judaism. Until 1948, that is, when, to the surprise and chagrin not only of the Christians and Muslims but also of strict orthodox Jews, in a politically and religiously unexpected turn of events, the Jewish State came into being.

For Christians and Muslims it was both necessary and desirable to establish visible evidence of their having overcome the Jewish heritage. One way was to impose new religious content on ancient religious sites, thus visibly demonstrating the political victory of the "church militant" and the "sword of Islam" over Judaism.

But: "As you sow, so shall you reap". After Christianity's triumph over Judaism, Islam set about overcoming Christianity. The Christians struck back with the Crusades, until their final defeat at the hands of the Muslims—or so it seemed. In the nineteenth and the twentieth centuries the Christians returned—for good, or so it seemed. And then the Jews returned. In final victory? How final?

Nothing in history appears as permanent as the constancy change, the cycle of rises and falls. Each of the victors in the Holy Land considered its triumph final—a foolish and dangerous delusion. Today's victors should always keep in mind that they may well—almost certainly will—be tomorrow's losers. Might we not hope that this realization could lead to greater tolerance?

To definitively "overcome" Judaism it was necessary to accomplish this at its very center, namely in the Holy Land and, best of all, in Jerusalem. The counter-religion needed to demonstrate its claims and its presence at the holy sites it selected. This may sound like an accusation, but is not intended as such. It is not our aim to argue the legitimacy of one or the other religion or its practices. These we accept as given. What we want to make clear is, once again, the multiple levels at which the sacredness of the holy sites becomes visible—in the most literal sense—and also the extreme difficulty of peaceful coexistence. Conflict is pre-programmed as long as Christians and Muslims persist in proceeding from the perspective of having "overcome" Judaism. If all three religions in fact believe in the same God, then it ought to be possible for all three to accept the concept that different paths can lead to the same goal.

In summation, we recognize that the conflicts were pre-programmed and deliberately sought. Throughout the many revolutions of power the goals remained high-minded but the conduct of the victors was frequently the opposite. Peace-minded were usually only the vanquished, who, upon regaining dominance, quickly forgot their previous weakness—and their earlier tolerance. On the scale of tolerance and intolerance, the Jewish side, for lack of opportunity in the exercise of power, generally deserve a favorable rating—at least until 1967. Since then, Israel's conduct has hardly been exemplary. Yet, in comparison with the Crusaders or the desecrations under Jordanian rule from 1948 to 1967, Israel's occupation begins to look like a model of tolerance. To be sure, the Turkish *millet* system had manifest advantages, and Israel adopted many of its principles.

Wherever we turn, we find that tolerance is only relative, the shifting of power and roles constant. Throughout history, the possession of the holy places by one power has only presented those not in possession with a religious and political challenge. Political motives appear to have been dominant, particularly in Islamic history. Interest in the Holy Land and in the holy places grew especially among those who did not have them under their political and military control.

Today, Christians and Muslims undoubtedly have cause to cast verbal stones at the Jewish Israelis. At the same time they should not forget that they, too, are sitting in glass houses. In countless works of art of the middle ages the "church militant" could cheer the victory of the Church, represented as the figure "Ecclesia", over "Synagogue", another symbolic figure whose eyes are always covered by a blind and who holds a broken staff (broken, of course, by the Church). The symbolism leaves little to doubt and represents a Christian perspective on Judaism that did not change significantly until after the Holocaust.

Under Islamic rule, Jews were not persecuted as often and as brutally as in the Christian occident, but the atmosphere of the Muslim orient was not generally one of personal and religious tolerance. Judaism (as well as Christianity) was at best suffered to exist in second-class status. As we have noted, Jews and Christians were permitted to climb to the seventh step before the entrance of the Mosque of the Tomb of the Patriarchs. But they were allowed to climb no higher.

Revenge and retribution always been bad advice. The Israelis have largely recognized this, even though we cannot report that they have always successfully avoided dispensing pinpricks, provocations and even blows.

What, therefore, is the "lesson of history" here? Someone, better all together, must sever the Gordian knot, must break the vicious cycle once and for all. The task is as daunting as ever, but at least some are trying.

How Is the Land Holy?
Or: Holiness and Statehood

Can the sacredness of the land only be secured by means of the establishment of a community's statehood in the Holy Land? The answer is clearly no. We can even go so far as to say: Holiness and statehood are mutually exclusive. In order to arrive at this conclusion one must not necessarily adopt extreme orthodox, especially extreme Jewish orthodox, positions. The same conclusion is suggested by a study of history. Let us look first at the Jewish side.

Only for shortest of periods in their history have the Jewish people lived under a sovereign Jewish state in the Holy Land. And only for a brief era in their history have the majority of Jews even lived in the Holy Land.

Let us take a brief look at the chronology. In the middle of the thirteenth century B.C.E. the Jewish people took possession of the land, says traditional history. Presently dominant archeologists deny the conquest theory and describe a process of rather organically growing quasi pre-Jewish communities in the Judaen hills. They were not fully secured and organized into a unified (but very small!) state until the period of the Kings Saul and David, about 1000 years before the Christian era. In the middle of the tenth century, David's kingdom was divided into "Israel" and "Judea". In 722 Israel was defeated by the Assyrians, the kingdom destroyed and a large part its population carried off into exile. Under Nebuchadnezzar, the Babylonians completed the destruction of Jewish statehood in 586.

Beginning in 538, Jews were permitted to return to Zion. The Persians had, in the meantime defeated the Assyrians, and King Cyrus allowed the creation of an *autonomous* (but not a sovereign) Jewish community. Zion remained part of the Persian Empire, but was allowed a large measure of self-administration in its internal (particularly religious and cultural) affairs. This autonomous Jewish community was much more Jewish in character than the preceding Jewish kingdoms of Israel and Judea. It was, in essence, a Jewish theocracy. How intolerant it could be we have already seen in the example of it relations with the Samaritans.

Internal self-determination without external sovereignty was the basic formula of this autonomous Jewish community. It was not a bad arrangement, although this question has been and continues to be the focus of intense debate.

The Persians were displaced by Alexander the Great and the Hellenistic rulers who followed him. The Jewish community, however, was able to maintain its autonomy until the founding of the Hasmonean (Maccabee) kingdom in the middle of the second century B.C.E. initiated another brief period of independence. In the year 63 B.C.E. the Romans arrived under Pompey. A short time later, King Herod ruled a nominally Jewish kingdom under Roman tutelage. After the rebellion of 132–135 even the name disappeared. Later, the Roman Empire was Christianized and the center of power passed from Rome to East Rome, to the Byzantine Empire. An independent Jewish State did not reemerge until 1948. In an irony of history, the main geographic centers of the new Jewish state, Israel, were precisely in those areas of the Holy Land which had traditionally been in the hands of the Jews' opponents: the "Philistine" coastal plain and Galilee, "Jesus country".

In round numbers, we count 3500 years of Jewish history. In how many of these years did the Jewish people enjoy independent statehood? For quick reference:

From 1000 to just before 600 B.C.E.   about 400 years
Hasmonean kingdom   about 100 years
State of Israel   about 50 years

By simple addition we arrive at the sum of 550 years of independent statehood in a total span of history nearly seven times as long. It is apparent that Jewish holiness was not dependent upon Jewish statehood for its survival.

Because almost nothing in history is as unambiguous as it may seem, we must note that, although the Jewish holiness of the Holy Land did survive despite the lack of Jewish statehood, the survival of Jews outside the Holy Land and in times of non-Jewish rule in the Holy Land was anything but guaranteed. This statement is, to put it mildly, a massive understatement. Almost everyone is aware of the fact that the lack of Jewish statehood was an significant contributing factor in making Jews the most convenient scapegoats available. Even in the periods of statehood the Jewish people rarely enjoyed a comfortable political existence, but their prospects for survival were considerably better than under non-Jewish rule, when Jewish existence was always dependent upon an act of domestic political grace on the part of the host majority. The importance of this context must not be underestimated.

Nevertheless, the continuation of the holiness of the Holy Land despite the lack of Jewish statehood is an undeniable fact. It was made possible by the Jewish religion itself, especially by the rabbinical tradition and the Talmudic sages (the "evil" Pharisees of the New Testament). They transformed Judaism into an international, "portable" religion, thus enabling the survival of Jews and Judaism in the diaspora. *Dina demalchuta dina*, "the law of the land is the law", they taught, meaning that, while always striving to strengthen Judaism from within, one must also accept integration with the host community as a requirement. This did not imply integration through assimilation (assumption of the host people's total culture and value system) but rather integration through co-existence on an everyday basis.

The rabbinical tradition transferred this pattern of thought to the Holy Land itself. We recall that nearly two thousand years ago Rabbi Jochanan Ben Saccai chose to oppose the nationalist Jewish Zealots (the *original* zealots) and to recognize Roman supremacy in order to strengthen the internal structure of the Jewish community and of Judaism itself. Following the defeat in the "Jewish War" against the Roman occupiers (66–70), Rabbi Ben Saccai began his work of religious reconstruction. The lack of worldly power became an inner strength of Judaism and the Jewish people—despite the zealots of all ages.

The antecedents of this rabbinical tradition reach at least as far back as the great prophet Jeremiah in the sixth century B.C.E. As Nebuchadnezzar and the Babylonians were advancing on Judea, Jeremiah cautioned his people against going to battle against them. He even went so far as to encourage the people of Jerusalem to switch sides: "And to this people you shall say: 'Thus says the Lord: Behold, I set before you the way of life and the way of death. He who stays in this city shall die by the sword, by famine, and by pestilence; but he who goes out and surrenders to the Chaldeans who are besieging you shall live." (Jeremiah 21:8–9)

That the future was to lie in "holiness without statehood" is made dramatically clear a few chapters later: "But any nation which will bring its neck under the yoke of the king of Babylon and serve him, I will leave on its own land, to till it and dwell there, says the Lord." (Jeremiah 27:11)

While extreme Jewish nationalists will tend to view these words of the prophet as more likely inspired by Lucifer than the Lord, the humanist will agree that inner values (holiness) are more important than external power (statehood).

Jeremiah's idea was very clear: The defeat of the Jewish people and its exile in Babylon were preconditions to a spiritual purification, a return to Judaism. In an apparent paradox, the Jews in the Holy Land had become unclean, had strayed from Judaism, but in exile from the Holy Land they would purify themselves and once again become Jews. Only after this "inward" return to Judaism was an "outward" return of the Jewish people to the Holy Land thinkable.

Therefore, the prophet Jeremiah advised the Babylonian exiles: "Multiply there, and do not decrease. But seek the welfare of the city where I have sent you into exile, and pray to the Lord on its behalf, for in its welfare you will find your welfare." (Jeremiah 29:6–7)

Jeremiah's real goal was thus the holiness of the people. The prerequisite for such holiness was a spiritual renewal from within. In other words: Holiness was the precondition to statehood. This has always been and still is the religious and political guideline of Jewish orthodoxy. One may criticize or reject their way of thinking, but one at least ought to understand its roots.

Unsurprisingly, we also learn from the Bible that the representatives of Jewish statehood and authority (including the religious establishment) have not always been happy with this line of literally "prophetic" argument. Moreover, we learn that they, and not the prophets, usually enjoyed the support of the majority of the Jewish people—much like today: "Now Pashhur the priest, the son of Immer, who was chief officer in the house of the Lord, heard Jeremiah prophesying these things. Then Pashhur beat Jeremiah the prophet, and put him in the stocks that were in the upper Benjamin Gate of the house of the Lord." (Jeremiah 20:1–2) It did not stop there: "And when Jeremiah had finished speaking all that the Lord had commanded him to speak to all the people, then the priests and the prophets and all the people laid hold of him, saying, 'You shall die!' … And all the people gathered about Jeremiah in the house of the Lord."

That Jeremiah escaped his threatened murder had in this instance to do with his eloquence and the moderating influence of the cautious leadership. For the rest of the story, we refer the reader to the Bible. The book of Jeremiah is of interest both for its content and its incomparable style.

We recall the already cited passage Ketubbot 110b from the Talmud: "A man should always dwell in the Land of Israel, even in a city where the greater number are from other peoples. And he should not dwell outside the land, not even in a city where the greater number are of the people of Israel. …" Clearly, the message of the Talmud is also that Jewish life in the Holy Land is possible without Jewish statehood. Whether this view is historically and politically correct and whether such a state of affairs is desirable remain matters of controversy. In these matters there is no law or binding guideline.

For the Christians of the West, holiness and statehood were conjoined in the Holy Land for but a very brief time, namely for two periods between 1099 and 1291, a total of less than two hundred years. To this we may also add the interlude of the British Mandate for Palestine from 1917 to 1948, another thirty years. Two-hundred-plus years are barely more than the blink of an eye in the long history of the Middle East.

More important for the Christian world is the conclusion it thus drew: The holiness of the Holy Land was and is not dependent on Christian statehood there. This can be no surprise, since for Christians the sacredness of the Holy Land is an aspect of God's plan of salvation but not an essential element of Christian political history.

And the Muslims? Apart from the brief period of the Crusader state, Islamic holiness and Islamic statehood held sway in the Holy Land from the first conquest in 638 until the founding of the State of Israel in 1948 and the Six Day War of 1967 (the Israeli conquest of East Jerusalem and the ancient Jewish homelands of Judea and Samaria—otherwise known as the West Bank).

But the holiness of the Holy Land as a whole was not a central religious or political concern in the Islamic world, which logically focused on the prophet Mohammed, his Arabian homeland and the Arab language.

For their survival, Muslims therefore do not require statehood in the Holy Land. Naturally, this statement has to be relativized when it comes to the Palestinians.

Both the Crusader kingdom and the disintegrating Ottoman Empire of the nineteenth century prove that sovereignty and statehood alone cannot guarantee the continuation of access to and the security of the Holy Land. In the terminal phase of Ottoman rule, as we know, the Holy City was rapidly becoming a city with a large Jewish majority and a Christian population that was as numerous as the Muslims.

By What Means Is the Land Acquired?

By what means did the actual or the presumed "owners" acquire the Holy Land? The answer is as simple as it is depressing: by conquest. The legitimations proffered were always of religious derivation, but the fact remains that violence was employed in every instance, no matter whether acquisition way accomplished by Jews, Christians or Muslims—or, for that matter, by their historic predecessors stretching back to the dawn of human history in the ancient world.

We should not assume, however, that this violent acquisition of the land was therefore not controversial. Quite to the contrary, we find abundant references to the problem in the Bible. Numbers relates the story of the spies Moses sent out (at the Lord's command) to discover out the strength and disposition of the Canaanites. Upon returning they reported: "We came to the land to which you sent us; it flows with milk and honey, and this is its fruit. Yet the people who dwell in the land are strong, and the cities are fortified and very large; and besides, we saw the descendants of Anak there." (Numbers 13:27–28) The descendants of Anak were considered giants. Caleb then sought to quiet the people by saying: "Let us go up at once, and occupy it; for we are well able to overcome it." But the spies disagreed: "We are not able to go up against the people; for they are stronger than we. … The land, through which we have gone, to spy it out, is a land that devours its inhabitants; and all the people that we saw in it are men of great stature. And there we saw the Nephalim (the sons of Anak, who come from the Nephilim); and we seemed to ourselves like grasshoppers, and so we seemed to them." (Numbers 13:30–33)

M. Wolffsohn, *Whose Holy Land?*, https://doi.org/10.1007/978-3-030-74286-7_11

The emotions felt by Moses' spies were all too familiar to the early Zionists and the founders of the modern state of Israel. Theirs were the words of those who despair at the daunting military (and also moral) obstacles looming before them.

"The people wept that night", we read in Numbers (14:1): "Would that we had died in the land of Egypt! Or would that we had died in this wilderness! Why does the Lord bring us into this land, to fall by the sword? Our wives and our little ones will become a prey; would it not be better for us to go back to Egypt?" (Numbers 14:2–3) How very current. We need only substitute "Europe" or "the US" for "Egypt".

And Moses replied in much the same vein as the Zionist founding fathers some 3200 years later: "Do not fear ..." (Numbers 14:9). "If you only want, it is not a fairy-tale" were the words of Theodor Herzl.

Of course, the ten pessimistic spies who "made all the congregation to murmur against [Moses] by bringing up an evil report against the land ... died by plague before the Lord." (Numbers 14:36–38) Only the optimists, Caleb and Joshua were spared.

Again and again, the Jewish conquerors were forced to gather up their courage, and to encourage each other, as in Joshua (1:6): "Be strong and of good courage." Neither the driving out of the non-Jewish population (Joshua 3:10) nor the massacres involved (Joshua 8:24 or 11:21, for example) are ignored in the Bible. It is a thoroughly honest book, but also a very contradictory document.

In connection with expulsions and killing, we are also reminded of King Saul, who was punished for refusing to carry out the command to slaughter the defeated Amelekites together with their wives, children and cattle (1 Samuel 15). The Talmudic sages also questioned the moral of this story until, we are told, a voice from heaven forbid them to question any further. This happens fairly often in the Talmud. Whenever the sages begin to formulate heretical thoughts, a commanding voice is heard from on high. But the questions are nevertheless raised.

This upright and candid struggle for the truth is a tradition which, after surmounting considerable initial obstacles, the majority of present-day Israeli historians seek to uphold. Not only among intellectuals but also among politicians and military officers there have always been those willing to raise their voice in objection to what they saw as excessively harsh measures taken against the Palestinians—in 1947/48, after 1967 and especially after the outbreak of the Intifada in late 1987. These inner-Jewish voices are now more numerous than ever before. On the other hand, there are still many among the non-Jewish "professional" friends of Israel who think it their duty to hide the spots on Israel's vest, fearing that they might otherwise be seen as "anti-Semitic". Their nonsense is well-meaning, but nonsense nevertheless.

In November of 1991 Israel's President, Chaim Herzog, admitted that in 1967, as a general of the Israeli army, he had participated in "channeling" some 200,000 Palestinians from the West Bank into Jordan. Busses and trucks were made available so that the Palestinians could "voluntarily" leave the West Bank for Jordan in order to join their relatives there—"voluntary" family reunification, a beneficial humanitarian program. Before leaving, the departees were given a paper to sign confirming the voluntary nature of their departure. Without a doubt it was an expulsion, but the procedure was, to say the least, considerably more humanitarian than that demanded of King Saul by the prophet Samuel.

Did Israel, did the Jews have any other choice? This is an important question. In the Egypt of biblical times as well as in the Europe of the mid-twentieth century they were being brutally persecuted, oppressed and murdered. In Canaan/Palestine, the native population resisted the Jewish conquest/return. They quite understandably saw no reason why they should be made to pay for the sins of others. Whether the native population (be they the Canaanite tribes or the Palestinians and the Arab nations of the twentieth century) employed morally suitable countermeasures is yet another important question.

Who can afford to cast the first stone? Was Rome, was Constantinople peace-loving and tolerant? The Crusaders? How did the British take Palestine?

And the Islamic world? Almost everywhere, Muslims first established themselves with the aid of the sword: Caliph Omar, Saladin, the Mamluks, the Ottomans …

Yes, yes, they were all "holy warriors". But so were the Jewish conquerors of the Bible. At least until after the Second World War, the methods of the modern Zionist were different. And orthodox Jews not only would not take part, they threw every possible stone onto the Zionists' path.

On November 29, 1947, the General Assembly of the United Nations voted to divide the British Mandate of Palestine and to thus enable the establishment of a Jewish and a Palestinian state. The Kingdom of Transjordan prevented the creation of a Palestinian state by its occupation of East Jerusalem and the West Bank in 1948. Peaceful? Voluntary? A highly unrepresentative assembly of pro-Jordanian Palestinian notables voted their approval in December 1948. The voice of the people?

In 1972 a summit conference of Islamic heads of state approved the "Islamic Charter" which called for a *jihad*, Islamic holy war, to "liberate" Palestine and the holy places in Al Quds. Almost 20 years later, in Dakar, the capital of

Senegal, in December of 1991, another Islamic summit conference decided to forgo *jihad*. The leaders of the Muslim world were not about to assume the risks inherent in a "holy war" over Palestine. Yet at the same time they promised that the struggle for the "liberation of Jerusalem" would continue "with all means". PLO chief Yasir Arafat professed his disappointment, despite—or perhaps because of?—the fact that his representatives were at the same time involved in negotiating an arrangement with Israel under American (later, secretly, under Norwegian) auspices. Is this what we call consistent and convincing behavior? At the beginning of the discussion, Arafat declared to the assembled leaders of the Islamic summit conference: "I was with you in Mecca as we stood before the *Kaaba* and prayed to Allah for the *jihad*." Arafat went on to explain that he had dedicated his entire life to holy war and asked: "What am I now to tell the Palestinian fighter who faces the Israeli enemy? Should I tell him that I was betraying him the whole time?"

We can only conclude that all the parties to the conflict sit in glass houses—but take all too much delight in casting stones at the others.

Whoever wants peace must be honest, upright and self-critical. We have seen that there are traditions to hearken back to, Jewish traditions and Christian traditions, for (out of historical necessity) Christianity has put aside the notion that it needs to conquer and hold the Holy Land. There are Islamic traditions as well, and there are other Muslim voices than those who equate an Islamic "solution" with a "final solution" for Israel. Unfortunately, even with today's improved political atmosphere, their position remains uneasy. If anything, it has become even more precarious.

What we do not need are any more examples such as the one set by Germany's Foreign Minister Hans Dietrich Genscher during his 1991 visit to Teheran. While Genscher sat next to him in utter silence, Iran's President Rafsanjani once again reiterated that his country will never accept Israel's right to exist. For a politician from the Christian West (not to mention from Germany) the limit of polite diplomacy and deference to economic interests should have been reached, especially in view of Iran's continuing efforts to acquire a nuclear arsenal. In any case, the limits of morality were clearly exceeded. Or did Genscher perhaps intend to repeat his performance earlier in the same year [during the Gulf War against Iraq) and fly to Tel Aviv to hand over a check after the first Iranian rocket delivered its nuclear payload?

Part III

The History of Changing Ownership

Whose Possession? Whose Property?

Whose Holy Land? or "Who owns the Holy Land?" is a question that has been asked time and again. Let us turn our attention to the history of the various possessors and the issue of property. But what do these terms mean? To whom do they refer? What is *possession* as opposed to *property*? This is an important distinction, as it is entirely possible that the possessors have frequently changed while the owners have not. The terms "possession" and "property" are often used interchangeably in everyday language. This use is not always accurate however. A quick look at the origins of the Latin, English and French terms will help us here. "Property" is something that is one's own, something that one owns, while "possession" comes from the Latin verb "to sit". One can sit on a chair that is not one's own. Sitting simply expresses physical presence. But sitting on or possessing something is not the same as ownership or property.

"Property" is "propriété" in French and "proprietas" in Latin. The Latin word expresses the characteristics of a person, i.e. his or her own particular identity.

"Possession" is "possessio" in Latin and "possession" in French, both of which come from the word "to sit" (Latin "sedere").

A dictionary can help us here. Possession is "the power or control over something". Property, by contrast, is "the right to the possession, use or disposal of something; ownership".

Possession is therefore closely connected to physical control, while property refers more to legal rights. There is of course the possibility that ownership can legally change, and with it possession. The crucial question is thus always "Is

M. Wolffsohn, *Whose Holy Land?*, https://doi.org/10.1007/978-3-030-74286-7_12

possession—the actual control over something—justified?" Are control and legal rights the same or do they contradict one another?

Who owns the Holy Land? We are looking for the *owners* of the Holy Land and not the possessors. Whose property is it?

The Jews were driven off their land by the Assyrians in 722 BCE, by the Babylonians in 586 BCE and by the Romans in 70 CE without ever having relinquished the claims and rights to their property (the Holy Land). The land remained their property, but there have since been a great many peoples who have possessed it. Did the possessors become owners?

Careful! We are treading on controversial ground in terms of history, politics and international law. If we adopt this way of thinking, then almost no people are living in a state that is their lawful property and almost no possessor is a lawful owner. We could begin with the indigenous peoples of the Americas, continue on to the displaced eastern Germans and Sudeten Germans, and then proceed to Jews and Palestinians without ever arriving at an end.

And if we are seeking peace, we cannot "make good" past injustices by displacing even more people. Even with good intentions, the results of our actions would be bad. We would only achieve the exact opposite of what we were trying to do.

We also have to think about the following question: Were the Jews the actual owners of this land? The land that is holy to them but also to Christians and Muslims? No.

The Jews first took possession of the Holy Land in the mid-thirteenth century BCE. The Bible provides a detailed description of this conquest in the Book of Joshua and in the Book of Judges.

But was this conquest lawful? The Bible says it was, since God promised the land to Abraham (and thus to the Jews). This is why it is called the Promised Land. This may be the case but we are no longer in the realm of earthly law, earthly politics or political history. This is the realm of salvation history, to which the categories of international law do not apply.

Salvation history is connected to religion, and religion is a question of faith. As we thankfully live in a society that guarantees freedom of faith, in which people are allowed to believe in different things, there is no definitive answer to this question. Jews may believe in their salvation history, others can or will not. How would we discuss this? This is not a theological debate. We want to give concrete answers to political questions. So let us turn back to earthly laws and earthly history.

Names and Power
(Canaanites, Philistines and Hebrews)

Our purpose here is not to conduct genealogical research. That was fashionable in Germany between 1933 and 1945, but it is neither good nor worth imitating. The slippery slope of history is dangerous enough as it is.

Some people are of course convinced that they know the answer—Mohammed Adib Aamiry, for example. In the very first sentence of his book "Jerusalem: Arab Origin and Heritage", which was published in London in 1978, he mentions the "continuity of the Arab race". The author was a government minister—among other things a minister of education—in Jordan. One can only imagine what the schoolbooks were like. Incidentally, if a German were to use the word "race" to refer to the inhabitants of a particular region that is contested by nations but not races, the most likely response would be, "Typical." But that is another matter.

What and whom does it actually help to insist on historical rights, be they real or alleged? The dead will not be brought back to life, unfortunately. And life is often neither easier nor more worthwhile for the living. Eliminating past injustices normally does not make things right or create justice but simply leads to more suffering. Insisting on historical truth sustains a never-ending history of suffering. I find this unsettling—partly because history is my profession.

If history teaches us anything, it is that history is highly unsuitable as an ultimate instance of appeal. Historians are even more unsuitable. Many of them—far too many of them in fact—are too susceptible to the spirit of the times. We can safely say that they are neither detached from their time nor objective. At times, historians act more like dutiful court poets than independent judges.

The Canaanites lived on a cemetery of nations on the baleful, blood-drenched soil of the Holy Land. It was above all the Canaanites from whom the Jews wrested this land more than three thousand years ago. This was done in an earthly manner, albeit with a religious justification. Sometime later, the Jews took land away from the Philistines as well. They took land from other peoples too, but mainly from these two.

Today, the Palestinians claim to be descendants of these peoples. What they are attempting to say is, "We are the legal successors of the Canaanites and the Philistines. We demand our property back from the Jewish occupiers."

As we are looking for the owners of the Holy Land, let us examine this assertion. It leads us to the field of genealogical research and, yes, even racial science. These are delicate disciplines not only in Germany but—understandably—especially in Germany. But it is no use. We must not shy away from controversial issues. To deny that they exist will solve nothing.

We will see that the Palestinians are *not* the legal successors of the Canaanites and the Philistines—at least not if they also claim to be Arabs. Some might ask why this is. Who would seriously want to deny that the Palestinians are Arabs? No one.

To begin with, the Canaanites were not a people or a tribe, Arab or Jewish, Mesopotamian or Egyptian.

The natives of (what is today) the Holy Land are referred to in the oldest archaeological sources as "Retenu" and later as "Hurru". An Egyptian monument from the fifteenth century BCE provides more details. It tells about a campaign carried out by the pharaoh Amenhotep II in the year 1429 BCE. The natives are called "Hurrians" (or "Hurru"). The "maryannu" were their ruling nobility. In addition to the maryannu, there were traders from the coastal cities. And these traders are referred to as "Canaanites" on this monument. The name "Canaanite" was thus originally a term that referred to a social class or occupation.

The monument also mentions the "Apiru-Habiru". These were foreign semi-nomadic people who had no land and mainly lived in the hills west of the Jordan. Some lived in cities as dependents of the natives. Habiru—Hebrew? They certainly sound similar, don't they? We are on the right track, because a century later in Egyptian documents all groups descending on or immigrating into (what is today) the Holy Land from the desert and other regions are referred to as "Hebrews".

The Israelites were "Hebrews"—but not the only ones. The Israelites, tribes from the Arabian Peninsula, the Ammonites, the Edomites, as well as the Moabites were also "Hebrews". They were all related, in other words, enemies included.

The close relationship and tense relations between the Ammonites and the Moabites is illustrated by the story of their ancestors. Lot's daughters "made their father drink wine that night: and the firstborn went in, and lay with her father; and he perceived not when she lay down, nor when she arose." (Genesis 19:33) The following night, the younger daughter slept with her drunk father. "Thus were both the daughters of Lot with child by their father. And the first-born bare a son, and called his name Moab: the same is the father of the Moabites unto this day. And the younger, she also bare a son, and called his name Benammi: the same is the father of the children of Ammon unto this day." (Genesis 19:36–38)

And so there we have them—the black sheep of the family. The Edomites, who were named after the Hebrew word for red, were also considered black sheep by the Bible and the Jews. The progenitor of the Edomites was Esau, the rough twin brother of the progenitor Jacob.

Egyptian sources also mention raiding nomads, the Bedouins, as a further group of people. In the fourteenth century BCE, the sources of the then ruling Egyptians named the entire region (now a province) "Canaan".

Thus far we can say

- The term "Canaan" was originally used to denote an occupational group (traders) but later came to be the name of a province.
- Accordingly, the inhabitants of this province were called "Canaanites", and these Canaanites were a mixture of peoples. They were in no way homogenous. They were multicultural, multiconfessional, "multinational" (although one cannot really speak of nations here), and "multi-racial".
- Both the traders (Canaanites) and the Hebrews (including the Israelites later on) were part of the native population—despite the fact that the Hebrews were immigrants.
- Later on, a part of the various Hebrew groups and tribes conquered the entire province of Canaan. These were the Israelites.
- The non-Israelite inhabitants of Canaan died out. Direct successors cannot be identified, not even with the microscope of history—unless you create them in a test tube. There are no legal successors to their property. They no longer exist. That is the distressing truth. Unfortunately, history is often cruel.

Who were the Philistines? Are they the real ancestors of the Palestinians? The assumption is likely, if only for linguistic reasons: Palestine—Philistine. The Romans not only annihilated the Jewish community; they also wiped out the name Judah. By doing so, the Roman occupants hoped to obliterate all memory of the earlier Jewish owners. Names and power are closely related. This has nothing to do with justice. It is the law of the strongest, a highly questionable type of law. The Romans changed Judah to the "Land of the Philistines", i.e. "Palestine".

But were the Philistines Arabs? Were, as modern-day Palestinians claim, the Philistines really the ancestors of today's Palestinians?

If the Philistines were Arabs, then they chose a strange route from their homeland to (what is today) the Holy Land. They originally came from the Greek mainland, the Peloponnese, from the Aegean Islands, Crete and Asia Minor. As we know, Arabia is located elsewhere.

The Philistines came to (what is today) the Holy Land as the Sea Peoples in the mid-twelfth century BCE. In Canaan, the rule of the Egyptians, which was already weak, began to falter, not least because of the invasion of the children of Israel about one hundred years earlier.

In 1168 BCE, the Sea Peoples attempted to invade the Egyptian heartland but were defeated by Pharaoh Ramesses III. His victory, however, was only partial. The Sea Peoples seized the southern coastal strip of the Egyptian province of Canaan and also captured its capital city, Gaza. These peoples had been fleeing from the Doric Greeks since the thirteenth century BCE, and they were Indo-Europeans, in other words they were not Semites. The Palestinians are both Semites and Arabs, and they rightly attach great importance to this. However, if they are Semites and Arabs, the Indo-European Philistines cannot be their ancestors.

The triumph of having their country named after them by the Romans was at the same time their historical downfall. They easily and fully adapted to the Roman world, and nothing more was heard of them—until the Palestinians discovered them as their ancestors. The Tel Aviv biologist Bat-Scheva Bonna Tamir discovered by means of DNA analyses that there is one people who are—genetically—closest to the Jews: the Palestinians (Tamara Traubmann and Ruthi Sinai, Haaretz, 9 May 2000).

Of course the Arabs also tried to penetrate (what is today) the Holy Land, which bordered on the Arabian Peninsula. As expected, the (pre-Islamic) Arab Bedouins also expanded into this neighbouring region. Such an attempt was made during the lifetime of the judge Gideon, in the twelfth century

BCE. They likely came more often, both previously and afterwards. In general, however, they conducted raids, did not settle, and therefore left no archaeological records.

The Canaanites and the Philistines were thus not the earliest inhabitants of the Holy Land. Let us therefore look back even further to clarify the issue of ownership and property. Adam and Eve are too far back, but we may have to begin with Abraham, Isaac and Jacob, the progenitors of the Jews, and perhaps even earlier.

The Patriarch Fathers
(The First Half of the Second Millennium BCE)

The Sea of Galilee is truly full of wonders. For example, when the water level dropped in the summer of 1991, a skeleton was found which was estimated to be around 19,000 years old. Was this the first Jew? The first Arab? It doesn't matter. It was a person. There is no point in measuring a skull to determine a person's race. The shape of a Jewish skull is the same as an Arab skull. Besides, we should avoid racial science and racial mysticism. We will not discuss in detail the life of cave dwellers either. They did indeed exist. Their dwellings can be found, for example, at Mount Carmel and around Haifa. But these caves were inhabited by Stone-Age people, not Jews or Arabs. They cannot be interpreted as ancestors of a nation or a people, which is why they are ill-suited as a means for justifying the historical and political claims of people today.

Many peoples had preceded the Jews when—as the children of Israel—they began to conquer (Bible) or rather settle (archeology) the Holy Land in the middle of the thirteenth century BCE or somewhat later But not surprisingly, these peoples had ancestors too. Their origins are unknown. Genealogists, of course, believe they are better informed. But we can safely doubt the accuracy of such research, although the aforementioned education minister of Jordan seems entirely convinced that the original inhabitants of the Holy Land were the Canaanites and the Amorites. And he believes these peoples came from the interior of the Arabian Peninsula and that they were therefore Arabs. However, even non-Zionistic accounts (in the Bible too, incidentally) include other reports of the various migrations to Palestine. These started in the land of the two rivers, i.e. Mesopotamia. As is generally known, the progenitor

© The Author(s), under exclusive license to Springer Nature Switzerland AG 2021
M. Wolffsohn, *Whose Holy Land?*, https://doi.org/10.1007/978-3-030-74286-7_14

Abraham came from the West Semitic area of Mesopotamia. This was also the origin of the first documented inhabitants of (what is today) the Holy Land.

In order to understand how the various peoples lived and fought in the Holy Land, we need to clarify the fundamental geographical background. Only then will we understand the various migration movements and, in turn, how different peoples inhabited this area.

The Holy Land was always a transit region for migration from the land of the Euphrates and the Tigris, namely Mesopotamia, to the country on the Nile, namely Egypt. It was a link between two old and advanced civilisations. These two civilisations initially developed independently of one another. At least politically, there were no points of contact and thus no sources of conflict. This changed, however, and anyone wishing to travel from one centre to the other had to go through the Holy Land. A look at a map tells us why. Very few were willing or able to travel over mountains or through deserts. The route along the coast and along the foot of the mountains was less arduous and less dangerous.

If we consider geography together with the region's political history, we come to the following conclusion. The Holy Land was almost invariably either part of the stronger of these two powers or an independent buffer between them. The latter was only true when neither Mesopotamia nor Egypt was strong enough to assert political or military control over this transit region. The Jews were thus politically independent only when there was a power vacuum or an equilibrium between Egypt and Mesopotamia.

The various peoples came to (what is today) the Holy Land not only from the north and south but also from the west and east (including the southeast). I have already mentioned the Sea Peoples from the west as well as the clash between Gideon and the tribes from the Arabian Peninsula (from the southeast).

"Germany's location is Germany's fate." This phrase reflects Germany's situation. It expresses the close interconnection between Germany's location in the heart of Europe and the country's historical development. The central historical and political role played by a country does not always coincide with a central geographical location. Korea is a good example of this. Despite its location on the eastern edge of Asia, the Korean Peninsula has, in political terms, always occupied a central position between China and Japan.

The same is true of the Holy Land. Its central position is clear, since peoples from the east and west and from the north and south met one another here. Given this mix of peoples, who would think of tracing precise ancestral lines from this cemetery of nations?

The Bible tells of this clash of peoples and divides them (always from the perspective of the Holy Land) into three groups:

- Semites from Mesopotamia and from the Arabian Peninsula,
- Hamites from Egypt, Sudan, etc. and
- Japhetites from the north and west.

The first advanced civilisation developed in Mesopotamia in the third millennium BCE. Shortly afterwards, a second such civilisation developed in Egypt. In demographic, military and cultural terms, both civilisations spread into (what is today) the Holy Land. City states developed there. Tourists are familiar with Megiddo and Hazor in Galilee. But we lack precise ethnological information. We do know with relative certainty, however, that around the year 2350 BCE the Egyptian pharaoh Pepi I increased his control over Palestine's insurgent city-states.

Around 2000 BCE, both Mesopotamia and the Holy Land were overrun by an invasion of west-Semitic nomads, i.e. people from the region west of the Euphrates. They are referred to in Akkadian documents as "Amurru". The Bible mentions Amorites, who apparently created settlements soon afterwards but ceded power to Egypt shortly thereafter (around 1900 BCE). They gradually adapted their way of life to that of the native inhabitants of the city-states. Trickling into the region rather than attacking it, the Amorites steered clear of major trade routes and cities in order to avoid conflicts. This is why they moved from one place to another in the thinly populated foothills west of the Jordan. They also crossed the Jordan to the east (Transjordan) or wandered south to the Negev Desert.

Most experts date Abraham's journey to the first half of the second millennium BCE. Nobody other than believers can confirm whether Abraham actually existed or not. It would certainly be difficult to disprove. The story of Abraham, Isaac and Jacob certainly tallies with historical developments confirmed by archaeological findings, i.e. the West Semitic migration that started in 2000 BCE. And it is believed that this West Semitic region is where Abraham came from, i.e. the city of Ur in Chaldea.

Abraham's journeys as related in the Bible correspond with information we have about the semi-nomadic Amorites. Since they were weaker than the native populations, they avoided large centres and trade routes—as well as the military bases of the Egyptians.

The Amorites as well as Abraham and his descendants were warriors. Whenever they could strike, they did. The Bible makes no secret of this. Jacob's sons regarded offence as the best form of defence. Their revenge on Shechem, who had raped their sister Dinah, was gruesome (Genesis 34). But Shechem clearly loved Jacob's daughter, Dinah. To marry her, he had himself circumcised, and his subjects had to follow this example. Weakened by this surgical procedure, the men were then overpowered and murdered by Jacob's sons.

As we can see, while the seminomads were generally the weaker party, they did indeed attack the natives—if circumstances allowed. The Bible makes no attempt to whitewash the actions of the Jews, neither here nor anywhere else. The Bible is an honest book. Some "professional" philosemites should follow this example. They could learn that is in no way anti-Semitic to point out problems with actions taken by Jews. Truth is always the best foundation of human interaction.

The historical and geographical summary is as follows:

- The story of the progenitors corresponds to the history of the first half of the second millennium BCE.
- This history also shows us that the "Land of the Fathers" was not the coastal strip but the land east and west of the Jordan River and the northern Negev.
- We cannot identify the Israelites as a clearly definable tribe or even as a people in this period. That is prehistory, perhaps even a legend, albeit a legend that tallies with the general historical picture. This is what makes it historically significant. It cannot, however, serve as a justification for taking possession of land or even for regarding it as legally acquired property.

Jewish Settlement as "Conquest"
(From the Middle of the Thirteenth Century BCE)

Let us skip the history of the children of Israel in Egypt and the fate of the direct descendants of Jacob.

We know that the power struggles and shifts of power between Egypt and its northern neighbours reached a new high as well as a turning point in the middle of the thirteenth century (around 1250 BCE). The Egyptians and the Hittites, whose empire stretched across parts of modern-day Turkey (Anatolia), fought, blocked and weakened one another. With the Egyptians and the Hittites thus occupied, third parties were able to use the resulting power vacuum to shake off the southern and the northern yoke.

The third parties who benefited from these disputes included Israelite tribes—if tribe they were rather than scattered settlers in the Judaen Hills The most important (and almost the only) thing they had in common was that they became a religious community. The earliest archaeological evidence of Israelites in the Holy Land date back to around 1220 BCE. Other third parties who benefited from this situation were the Canaanite city-states. They had a major problem, however, as they themselves were divided—again to the benefit of third parties including the Ammonites, Moabites and Edomites. They were advancing into the Holy Land from the east and southeast. From the southwest (Sinai Peninsula) came the Israelites and ultimately, as of 1200 BCE, the Sea Peoples, the Philistines.

The power vacuum was used by groups and peoples who were ready to immigrate and conquer. It attracted people like a magnet. The debilitated external major powers and the long-established Canaanites lost their influence. The Israelites were not the only ones to come on strong. The latecomers

M. Wolffsohn, *Whose Holy Land?*, https://doi.org/10.1007/978-3-030-74286-7_15

initially established themselves in the area east of the Jordan River. We know this not only from the Bible but also because we have archaeological evidence.

The territory was conquered gradually rather than suddenly. The Israelites had a particularly hard time pushing forwards because they were moving towards the interior and the east coast of the Mediterranean, where resistance was greater. Many people had been living there for centuries, and the more inhabitants, the greater the military presence and the greater the institutionalised power. Even in the areas seized by the Israelites, purely Canaanite enclaves continued to exist for a long time. Only very slowly—after the issue of power had been clarified—did the peoples start to mix.

The areas occupied and settled by the Jews were mainly to the east and west of the Jordan River. They were not Israel proper, which from 1948 to 1967 was located on the coast. We need to know this if we are to understand the modern-day political claims of those who speak of Greater Israel and mean at least the area west of the Jordan River and only grudgingly "renounce" the area east of it. But by the same token, we can see here that land was taken and occupied; this was not a lawful transfer of ownership. And of course there is again an argument to the contrary: *today*, none of the legal successors of the formerly legal owners are alive.

Did this make the occupier the owner? The only people who can answer yes to this question are believers, followers of the Bible, who believe it is a legal basis not only for Jews. This legal basis, however, involves so many ifs and buts that it is highly controversial, and will continue to be so in future.

Shortly after the Israelites, the Sea Peoples (the Philistines) arrived in the Holy Land and occupied the coast. Now the Israelites had the Canaanites (in the north of the coastal strip) and the Philistines (in the south around Gaza, Ashdod and Ashkelon, in the interior around Gath and Ekron) to overcome if they hoped to reach the coast. And they intended to do just that. The Philistines thus came even later than the Jews, which means they are not the owners of the Holy Land. What is more, the Philistines were not Arabs.

The conflict between the Jews and the Philistines continued for centuries. Many stories about this conflict are in the Bible, e.g. the fate of Samson, who was seduced and deceived by Delilah, the fight between David and Goliath, and so on. The Philistines did not, however, achieve great power. They did, however, triumph after the defeat of the Jews by the Romans, because the land was from then on called "Palestine". The Roman occupiers named it after a dependent but not exiled people in order to humiliate the conquered and displaced Jewish people even more.

When the Israelites came as conquerors, they were not a sedentary people who had only changed location once. Only after they occupied the land did the children of Israel become settled and abandon their nomadic or semi-nomadic lifestyle. These Jews did indeed have certain things in common with the nomads from the Arabian Peninsula. In terms of both civilisation and culture, the urban Philistines appeared much further developed. Their pagan religious practises, however, were on a much simpler level.

Despite their underdeveloped civilisation, the Jews had made an important cultural accomplishment: they had created a religion they could take with them, one that was independent of location. The Ark of the Covenant could be moved from place to place. This mobile shrine only became stationary when it was transferred to Jerusalem (around 1000 BCE). The era of the temple (up to 586 BCE) followed. The Babylonian exile resulted in the development of Rabbinic Judaism, which was also mobile. Between the rebuilding of the temple (at the end of the sixth century BCE) and its destruction by the Romans (in 70 CE), there developed a rivalry between mobile Rabbinic Judaism and a stationary Judaism based on temples and priests. History (i.e. the Romans) ensured that the mobile movement prevailed.

As a tribe held together only by religion, the Jews were weaker than the Canaanites and the Philistines in the early years. A northern and a southern group formed within the Jewish tribe. The northern group had its political base in Silo, the southern one in Hebron.

It was now necessary to concentrate forces and streamline the leadership. Although not necessarily holy, this strategy was necessary for political and military reasons: in the middle of the eleventh century BCE, the Philistines were the territorial rulers and the Israelites were dependent on then. We know from the Bible how this story continues. It is the era of the Judges.

Kingdom and Kingdoms Come and Go
(From 1000 to 722/586 BCE)

This, too, was only a transitional phase, and this time the Jews even fought one another. It was not until the united monarchy under Saul (from around 1025 to around 1006 BCE) that military success was achieved. Jewish rule was stabilised, and their territory expanded beyond the heartland west and east of the Jordan River. The Canaanites were gradually encircled. David seized their land and made it a "royal domain". The population was too weak to resist; they adapted and abandoned their independence. As "foreigners", most were neither free citizens nor slaves. We know such "foreigners" from the Bible. We also know "slaves" from the Bible. Among them were certainly Canaanites and their descendants.

Who are the descendants of the Canaanites? Are they the mixed Canaanite-Jewish population? And who are their descendants? Racial science once again leads us to a dead end. Whatever the case may be, it does not lead us to the Palestinians. This does not, however, weaken the "cause of the Palestinians", because genealogy and racial science are among the most questionable approaches to politics.

David annexed the cities of the Philistines and made them part of his kingdom. The Philistines, however, remained defiant subjects who were eager to regain their independence.

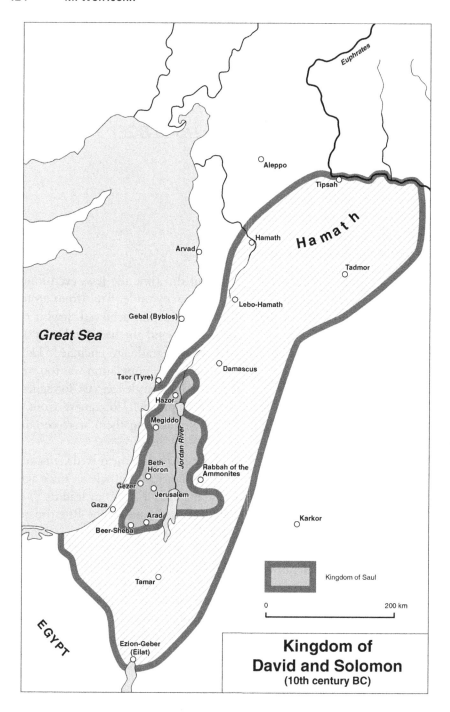

EGYPT

Great Sea

Euphrates

Aleppo

Tipsah

Hamath

Hamath

Arvad

Tadmor

Lebo-Hamath

Gebal (Byblos)

Damascus

Tsor (Tyre)

Hazor

Megiddo

Jordan River

Beth-Horon

Gezer

Rabbah of the Ammonites

Jerusalem

Gaza

Arad

Beer-Sheba

Tamar

Karkor

Kingdom of Saul

0   200 km

Ezion-Geber (Eilat)

Kingdom of David and Solomon
(10th century BC)

As a result of the power vacuum in both the north and the south, According to the Bible David's territory (990–968 BCE) was able to expand and became a multi-confessional empire. In fact, in was miniscule, according to archeology (Finkelstein et al.). It was already a mixture of peoples. Under David, non-Jews, too, reached top-level military and political positions. Uriah, for example, the husband of the beautiful Bathsheba, was not only a high-ranking general but also a Hittite.

David, the great Jewish king, also adopted the Egyptian model of administration. It was not designed with the needs of people in mind but was more of a type of "oriental despotism". It was controversial to copy Egypt, for both political and psychological reasons. About 250 years earlier, the exodus of the children of Israel from Egypt had taken place. Egypt signified a traumatic event in Jewish history, in much the same way that Germany became a symbol for the Holocaust. Every year, Passover (celebrated each spring around Easter) is a reminder of the slavery of the Jews in Egypt. At that time, Egypt was the epitome of Jewish persecution. And it was this of all countries that the most Jewish of all Jewish kings (at least in terms of his subsequent symbolic power) copied now and then.

By becoming "multinational" and multi-confessional on the one hand and a kingdom on the other hand, the Jews became more and more like other peoples. They became "like all the other peoples", which contradicted the need for distinction and thus also the essence of Judaism. Between those willing to adapt and those eager to distance themselves there arose a conflict that extends into the present (and will probably continue in future). These have remained the poles of Jewish identity.

Small wonder that domestic tensions have remained an abiding Jewish and Israeli issue. In those early days of the kingdom, it was mostly those tribal chieftains who had been deprived of power who rebelled. While they were happy to be rid of the Philistines, they were not happy to lose power. For this reason, they rebelled against David together with others, including David's son Absalom.

Jewish unity was and remained extremely unstable. Had not David himself, rebelling against Saul, ultimately acted as a splitter, as a separatist? He convinced the oldest, most influential men to crown him rival king in Hebron. On his way to power, southern Judaea joined forces with the Philistines. That was a degree of Jewish-Gentile cooperation in the Middle East that is no longer found (regardless of how kosher the objective was).

Under Solomon, too (who reigned from 968 to 928 BCE), there were intra-Jewish riots that are mentioned in the Bible. Again, the Jewish north-south conflict played a central role. This contrast is also reflected in the way

Solomon built up his administration. Solomon seems to have maintained good relations with the Arab world. Trade flourished, as did Jewish-Arab marriages, although they had no far-reaching historical impact (at least in the Middle East). But we must not forget that the smart and beautiful Queen of Sheba came from the southwest corner of the Arabian Peninsula. Solomon had even married a daughter of the pharaoh. The marriage took place after an obviously failed attempt by Egypt to invade the Holy Land. From a historical perspective, it is remarkable that this marriage occurred at all. Let us recall the slavery of the Jews in Egypt and their escape from that country—if, in fact, it did happen.

In the end, King Solomon's domestic policies were not beyond reproach, as the Bible makes quite clear. The Bible praises his wisdom, the temples he built, and several other things. Today, we would call him tolerant. But he was too indulgent of idolaters, says the Bible, and the idolatry of his wives went too far. The "punishment" (as the Bible quite clearly puts it) followed swiftly. Although not before Solomon died. It must be said, however, that he downright squeezed his subjects—despite his willingness for political reconciliation.

After Solomon's death in 928 BCE, the Jewish kingdom again collapsed. This was due to the old north-south conflict. The oppressed and conquered non-Jewish peoples, above all the Philistines, the Moabites, and the Ammonites, rose up against Jewish rule. The Edomites and other Arab tribes once again showed a willingness to attack. They blocked trade routes, raided and pillaged.

Egypt's ambitions had been growing since the tenth century BCE, and a new major power came into existence in the north about 100 years later: Assyria.

Science is sometimes able to present new findings on old issues. The archaeologists Israel Finkelstein and Neil A. Silberman (David und Salomo. Archäologen entschlüsseln einen Mythos, Munich, 2006) have consigned the conquests and the kingdoms of David and Solomon to the realm of mythology. Their findings and their brilliant books are convincing but do not alter the political question we face today—and its answer.

Exile, Return and Autonomy

(Assyrians, Babylonians, Persians, Greeks from 722/586 to 167 BCE)

Despite phases of political and military stability, the loss of Jewish independence was (in retrospect) only a matter of time. Irreconcilable, Israel (the Northern Kingdom) and Judah (the Southern Kingdom) abandoned themselves to fraternal conflict.

Around the year 800 BCE, Israel, a small nation, yet again became a tributary, this time to the great power Assyria. Internally as well, a large part of the Jewish population in the north and in the south was indeed willing to adapt to the non-Jews. The prophets responded to these developments with severe warnings and threats. Occasionally they succeeded, but their success never lasted. For a short period in the ninth century BCE, Israel even experienced an increase in political strength. This power, however, had no impact on Assyria but only on the less influential neighbouring peoples. We can see here the political games that are commonly played in a power vacuum.

Soon after came "God's punishment" for the renunciation of Jewish rites and customs (as the prophets saw it). In the year 722 BCE, Assyria destroyed the Israelite Northern Kingdom. The victorious major power wanted more than just tributes. It displaced the Jewish population, in particular the upper class. The Samaritans established themselves. Arabs were also introduced into the country. Not all Arabs appreciated this. Again and again, tribes on the Arabian Peninsula rebelled against Assyria and attacked Transjordan in particular. This was an ancient conflict in the Middle East, the rivalry between Bedouins and townspeople. It was not a national conflict.

Judah continued to exist. It was dependent, however; a tributary to Assyria. Judah became a vassal state. Jewish statehood had no real sovereignty, i.e. it was in no position to use and exercise power outwardly.

© The Author(s), under exclusive license to Springer Nature Switzerland AG 2021
M. Wolffsohn, *Whose Holy Land?*, https://doi.org/10.1007/978-3-030-74286-7_17

The Judean king Hezekiah, who ruled from 727 to 698 BCE, attempted to compensate for this outward weakness with internal strength and thus initiated religious reforms. Once again, Jewish attributes were cultivated and nurtured and the Temple was restored. Symbols are always an external sign of internal intentions. King Josiah followed this example during his rule (639–609 BCE). Pagan cults were banned, and Judaism was glorified. And lo and behold, a hitherto unknown Torah scroll was discovered, containing the fifth book of Moses (Deuteronomy).

It was a sensational discovery—and most importantly a political event. It was meant to strengthen Jewish morals. After all, it was the words of none other than the great prophet Moses. "These *be* the words which Moses spake unto all Israel." This is how this book begins. It is the legacy of Moses, his magnificent narrative. The book is politically motivating, galvanising, and an obligation for his descendants. It ends with Moses' death: "And there arose not a prophet since in Israel like unto Moses, whom the LORD knew face to face." (Deuteronomy 34:10). In the long term, however, none of this helped.

The Philistines had it no easier under the Assyrians than the Jews. At least the Assyrians did not attack the Jews for "anti-Semitic" reasons. The Assyrians (who were likewise Semites) pursued purely political objectives.

The Jews (or at least some of them) still lived on their land, but they were not the rulers of this land. The Jewish owners stayed (at least some of them did), but they lost possession of their land.

The next change in possession of and in the Holy Land happened for two reasons. Firstly, Babylon was the new major power around the year 620 BCE. Secondly, Babylon under Nebuchadnezzar conquered and destroyed the Kingdom of Judah and the Temple in Jerusalem in 586 BCE. Tributes were no longer enough for him because the Jews (as well as other peoples enslaved under the Babylonians) had rebelled repeatedly.

Cautionary voices had made themselves heard amongst the Jewish people, e.g. the prophet Jeremiah. He considered military resistance futile and demanded that the Jews live up to higher moral and religious standards. According to Jeremiah, internal strength was more important than outward independence. As we know, this approach, or this conviction, was a guiding force for the Talmudists approximately 500 years later. Their goal was internal stability too as well as mobility due to the lack of state sovereignty.

Unlike the Assyrians, the Babylonians did not introduce new population groups into the region. It was neglected until the Arab Edomites moved in from the south east of the Dead Sea, avoiding other advancing Arabs as they did so. And they too entered the deserted region, as did the Philistines.

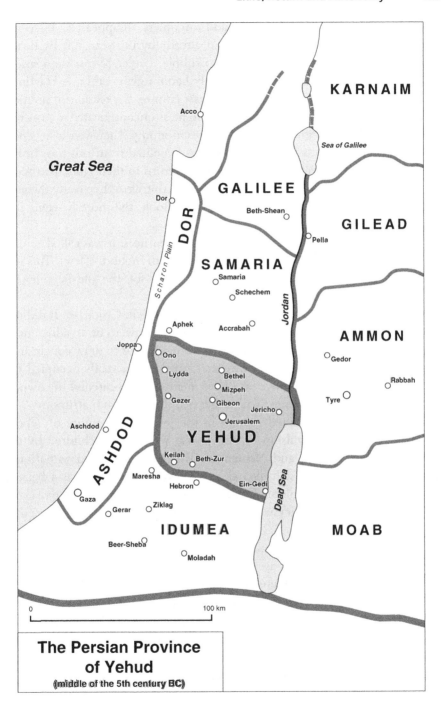

The Persian Province
of Yehud
(middle of the 5th century BC)

Occupiers came, occupiers left, and occupiers disappeared. First the Assyrians and then the Babylonians. But already by the year 500 BCE, the Babylonian Empire had been reduced to rubble. Under Kyros, the *Persians* were the new rulers of the region: the Holy Land, Egypt, Libya, Asia Minor, and the region extending to the Indus. A vast empire. For reasons of political necessity, control over foreign peoples had to be as uncomplicated as possible. The Persian rulers thus guaranteed extensive autonomy. They were also generous in granting religious freedoms. The Jews benefited from this too. In the year 538 BCE, they were given permission to return to their land. The occupier stayed while the displaced owner returned. But were they really owners? Or rather just previous occupiers? The closer I look, the more it seems this is true.

A tiny province was inhabited by the Jewish returnees. It was called Yehud. People tend to immediately associate this name with "Yehudi" (Jew). This was intended. And it was important—and allowed—for the old-new Jewish occupier.

Yehud also had its geographical and political centre in Cisjordan. It did not touch the Mediterranean coast at all. One does not have to be an adherent of Greater Israel to emphasise this fact. It does not allow us to draw conclusions about legal ownership. We can, however, clarify who actually occupied the land back then—especially since (as I have mentioned repeatedly) the owners had passed away or had merged with other peoples through matrimony.

Racist developments gained ground in the Jewish community of Yehud. We should recall the expulsion of non-Jewish women and children by the allegedly great men Esra and Nehemiah. This mainly affected Samaritans, Ammonites, and Moabites. It also affected Egyptians, which was a belated slap in the face for King Solomon, who had married an Egyptian wife.

The purpose of this policy was to preserve the purity of the "holy seed of the Jews".

The actions of Esra, Nehemiah and their helpers are celebrated in the Old Testament, but the authors are honest enough to present the voices and actions of the opposition. Opposition grew against this form of "cleansing" as it did against policies in general, not least economic policy—this was the beginning and the price of Jewish theocracy (circa 440 BCE). Esra came to the region around 458 BCE. Nehemiah was the Jewish governor in the service of the Persian Empire from 445 to 433 BCE.

Yehud was not a state but only an autonomous province (538–332 BCE) within the Persian Empire, with a governor as its political chief (and executive authority) and a high priest as its religious chief. It stayed this way under the successors of the Persians until a Jewish state was re-established (middle of the second century BCE). In other words, Alexander the Great and his successors (Diadochi) also adhered to it. The arrangement proved to be stable and effective.

Yehud was highly intolerant, outwardly weak, and internally inflexible (and therefore very narrow minded). In the year 515 BCE, the Second Temple was re-erected, albeit imperfectly. It therefore comes as no surprise that others with claims to the land, including the Arabs, did not exactly welcome Jewish returnees with open arms but instead with closed fists. The book Nehemiah (4:7–8) precisely describes the conflict: "And it came to pass, *that* when Sanballat [the Honorite], and Tobiah [the Ammonite servant], and the Arabians, and the Ammonites, and the Ashdodites [the Philistines], heard that the walls of Jerusalem were made up, *and* that the breaches began to be stopped, then they were very wroth. And conspired all of them together to come *and* to fight against Jerusalem…"

The Jews continued to build—as do their descendants in the twentieth century. For both, conquest is a birth defect. Both "with one of his hands wrought in the work, and with the other *hand* held a weapon." (Nehemiah 4:17) Then as now, the threat from outside had an integrating, motivating and galvanising effect on the inside.

But what else could the Jews have done? This question needs to be asked with regard to the sixth and fifth centuries before Christ and for the present. Every coin has two sides. Those concerned and affected only ever judge from their own perspective. This is understandable but at the same time one sided.

Persian rule did not last forever either. Only the change in occupiers was permanent. The Battle of Marathon (490 BCE) and the naval Battle of Salamis (480 BCE) were part of the Persian-Greek conflict. In the fifth century BCE, the Persians attempted to invade Greece, but failed. The Greeks (or more precisely, the Macedonians) struck back, and this dealt the Persian Empire a severe blow.

The Europeanization of the Holy Land
(Greeks, Romans and the Jewish Interlude, 332 BCE to 70)

Like the Battles of Marathon and Salamis, Alexander the Great's victory over the Persian King at Issus in 333 BCE shook civilisations and cultures. The Orient and the Occident collided in the wars between Persians and Greeks which had been fought since the fifth century BCE. We experience history not as an ever-revolving wheel but as a series of waves. One wave surges from the Orient to the Occident, and the next wave heads from the Occident towards the Orient. Strictly speaking, this pattern already applies to the time around the year 1200 BCE, when the "Sea Peoples" (such as the Philistines) advanced from Europe into the Orient.

Let me provide a few examples. Until the Arabic-Muslim conquest, the wave originated more or less from the Occident and affected the Orient. In 711 CE, Arabs crossed the Mediterranean to Spain. They were driven away in 1492. The Occident began its counteroffensive in the eleventh century (crusades and the Reconquista in Spain). In the thirteenth century, the crusaders were ousted from the Orient and, in the fifteenth century, the Orient came to Europe: the Ottomans started their conquest in the southeast. In 1683, the tide turned. The Turks were defeated near Vienna and their empire was slowly dismantled. This process lasted until 1918/1919. Europe (England and France) tried to defend its interests in the Orient until it was expelled after World War II. Particularly since the 1960s, the demographic interconnection between Europe and the Middle East has continued without military conquests. This political and economic dependence had negative effects on Europe in 1973 and again in 1979/1980. The key words in this context are the oil crisis after the Yom Kippur War in 1973 and the Iranian Revolution in

© The Author(s), under exclusive license to Springer Nature Switzerland AG 2021
M. Wolffsohn, *Whose Holy Land?*, https://doi.org/10.1007/978-3-030-74286-7_18

1979. This oil crisis (and Saddam Hussein's actions) was an oriental counter-attack. The occidental counter-attack followed with the Gulf War of 1991.

We have jumped far ahead in the course of history to outline the pattern of historical waves. So let us now return to pre-Christian times.

During the time of the First Temple, the Jews had time and again succumbed to the temptation of being "like all other peoples". Despite all prophetic warnings, they copied the social and religious customs of their non-Jewish neighbours. They often preferred to pray to the visible idol, Baal, instead of to their invisible god.

During the time of the Second Temple, the power and magnificence of Hellenistic culture represented a non-Jewish temptation for the Jews. It consisted primarily, but not exclusively, of Greek elements. Hellenistic culture was very cosmopolitan, even polytheistic. Since the late fourth century BCE, it had been admired in particular by the Jewish upper class, which evidently was fed up with a closed-off, strict, prudish and Jewish-centred theocracy that was racist by definition.

But not only the Jewish upper class succumbed to the Hellenistic temptation. Philistines living in coastal towns were also receptive to Hellenism. And the new Greek settlers were active.

Jewish traditionalists closed themselves off from these new influences, however, and an intra-Jewish conflict loomed. This is yet another example of conflict between open-minded Jewish universalists and their particularistic opponents who clung to Jewish tradition (and sometimes petrified in it). This is true both of those days and today. But who knows the right way? And which way is the right one?

On a side note, who can identify and name the ancestors of the Palestinians in this mixed population? Not to mention the other difficulties of "genealogical research" which we have already discussed.

The Jewish cultural struggle was a class struggle, but it was also a regional conflict. What is noteworthy with regard to this cultural struggle is also its political geography. The towns along the coast were open-minded towards Hellenism, while those further inland closed themselves off from it. It is certainly no coincidence that the Hasmoneans, the militantly Jewish, anti-Hellenistic rebels of the second century, originated from inland areas.

The first Greek visitor was Alexander, called "the Great". Incidentally, the town of Gaza, with the help of Arab mercenaries, stubbornly resisted Alexander's army in 332 BCE. This approach did not benefit the Samaritans— the city of Samaria was destroyed by the Greeks.

Alexander's life was short, and after his death his empire broke into three parts. The Holy Land was under the control of the Ptolemaic Kingdom, which

ruled Egypt (Alexandria) and was in constant conflict with the second suc-
ceeding empire, the Seleucid Empire. The Seleucids ruled from Syrian
Antioch, became more powerful over time, and conquered the Holy Land in
200 BCE, led by Antiochus III.

The Jews did not fare badly under Ptolemaic rule and initially under
Seleucid rule. They retained their autonomy. The high priest was at the top of
Jewish society. He was now considered both its spiritual and secular leader,
which resulted in increased power and prestige. At the time of the Persians, a
governor was the secular leader. The high priest was assisted by a council of
elders, of which he was also the chairman.

The triumph of the Seleucids under Antiochus III did not last long. Soon
after their victory over the Ptolemaic Kingdom in Egypt, Antiochus became
overconfident. He advanced into Greece, where he was confronted by the new
world power Rome. He was driven from Greece in 191 BCE and one year
later suffered a devastating defeat at Magnesia in Asia Minor.

Not only the outer walls of the Seleucid empire but also its foundations
began to collapse. Antiochus IV Epiphanes, son of Antiochus III, hoped to
stabilise them. "Unity is strength", he thought. This strategy weakened his
rule, however, because he was unable to achieve unity. Antiochus strove primarily for religious unity. This was not a problem for non-Jewish people,
apart from their wish to self-govern. Jewish traditionalists, however, were outraged and the Jewish Hellenists, notably Menelaus, a Hellenised high priest,
fought against them. The Jews experienced turmoil similar to civil war because
Antiochus IV wanted to eradicate Judaism. The Book of the Maccabees (and
thus the story of the Hanukkah) describes this ruler as an out-and-out villain.
He may have well been, but he acted not for anti-Jewish but for political reasons. He was up to his neck in trouble, and he drowned in it because he chose
the wrong political strategy.

The Hasmoneans ensured his downfall. They rebelled against "Greek idolatry" in the land, in Jerusalem, and in the Temple. Antiochus IV had dedicated
the Temple of the Jews to idols. From the point of view of devout Jews, this
was a defilement of the temple. The fact that it was politically motivated did
not excuse this act of sacrilege.

The decision taken by Antiochus IV was immoral, but even worse it was a
mistake. He had miscalculated and not expected the resistance of the Jews. He
thought the majority of Jews would be prepared to be Hellenised. Perhaps he
confused those living in cities with the Jewish population as a whole and
focused in particular on Jerusalem, the stronghold of the Hellenists.

The Holy City (which at the time was only holy to the Jews) was heavily
influenced by Hellenistic life and philosophy. At sporting events, for example,

athletes competed in the nude. They disregarded the fact that exhibiting nudity and looking at nudity are considered great sins in the Bible.

The Book of the Maccabees is a book written by victors, the purely Jewish-oriented victors over the Hellenistic Jews (1 Macc. 1:11–15): "It was then that there emerged from Israel a set of renegades who led many people astray. 'Come,' they said, 'let us ally ourselves with the gentiles surrounding us, for since we separated ourselves from them many misfortunes have overtaken us.'" These words may sound convincing but the Book of Maccabees continues with outrage: "This proposal proved acceptable." Even worse for the biblical commentator is the fact that these Jews obtained the king's approval to build a gymnasium in Jerusalem "such as the gentiles have, disguised their circumcision [since Jewish men are circumcised], and abandoned the holy covenant, submitting to gentile rule as willing slaves of impiety."

Needless to say, these Hellenised, urban Jews did not revolt. Surprisingly, however, resistance also did not originate in the Judean heartland. The rebellion started in Modein, a small town close to present-day Tel Aviv.

The Hasmonean or Maccabean Revolt started in 167 BCE. The Maccabees waged a guerrilla war of sorts and were relatively successful. Their spiritual leader was Mattathias, whose five sons led the revolt one after the other. They were as intolerant and as harsh as their father was. When Mattathias saw how a Jew offered sacrifice to idols at the altar, "he was fired with zeal; stirred to the depth of his being, he gave vent to his legitimate anger, threw himself on the man and slaughtered him on the altar [...] and tore down the altar" (1 Macc. 2:24). This set off the rebellion.

In 164 BCE, the Maccabees conquered the Temple Mount (not the whole city of Jerusalem). As we have already established, this is commemorated every year by the celebration of Hanukkah.

The Maccabees took advantage of the situation in 142 BCE to transform the autonomous Jewish community back into an independent, sovereign Jewish state, or rather, a kingdom. The situation was favourable in that the Seleucids were much too weak to defeat the Jewish rebels. Once again, a power vacuum was exploited. The Romans and the Parthians were on the doorstep, and the Seleucids were distracted by this threat. But they did not resign themselves to their fate without resistance and without a fight, not even in the Holy Land, where they were assisted by Arab forces. Still, there were other Arab tribes (such as the Nabataeans) who supported the Jews.

Aristobulus was the first Hasmonean regent (104–103 BCE) who assumed the title of king. This was not entirely unproblematic since, just as French Legitimists have wanted the Bourbons restored to the throne after the revolution, Jewish traditionalists at that time wanted to see power back in the hands of the House of David.

It is no wonder that a witch-hunt of sorts began against the Hellenistic Jews in this Jewish state. In the words of the victors, this happened as follows: Jonathan the Maccabee "rid Israel of the godless" (1 Macc. 9:73). They appear to have massacred the Jewish-Hellenistic defenders of Jerusalem, as the Book of Maccabees reports that "a great enemy had been crushed and thrown out of Israel" (1 Macc. 13:51). These merciless avengers likely saw themselves as "holy warriors".

The victors took harsh measures against non-Jewish adversaries too. Some surviving peoples were "allowed" to become Jewish, such as the (Arab) Edomites in 125 BCE and the (Arab) Itureans in Galilee—where Jesus of Nazareth would soon begin his mission—in 104 BCE. It is not surprising that Jesus was successful preaching in Galilee, which had been forcibly Judaised. Jesus provided local residents with an opportunity to overcome Judaism in a peaceful way. What they were unable to achieve by military force, they achieved through religion and faith with the help of Jesus and his followers.

The Edomites took revenge in their own way. In 47 BCE, Gaius Julius Caesar installed the Edomite Antipater as procurator in Judea. Antipater's son was King Herod. However, the historical truth and reality are once again much more complicated, since the Edomites fought with the Jewish rebels against the Romans in the First Jewish-Roman War (66–70 CE).

The Samaritans resisted efforts to convert them to Judaism. To punish them, the Hasmoneans destroyed Nablus and the Samaritan temple on Mount Gerizim. Samaria in the territory west of the Jordan River was destroyed and the local population was displaced and "relocated". The inhabitants of the port of Jaffa were "relocated" by force (an incident that reoccurred in 1947/1948 CE) as were the inhabitants of Gezer, an old Philistine city between present-day Tel Aviv and Jerusalem. Only a few decades later, however, the Jews were displaced and relocated by the Romans.

But the zeal of the Hasmoneans slowly lessened. The luxury and the carefree lifestyle of Hellenism, which had only been outwardly defeated (and only temporarily), increasingly influenced the Hasmoneans as well. Their former allies, the Pharisees, now called for a return to Jewish virtues. There ensued another struggle within Judaism about the true meaning of Jewishness and about Jewish statehood.

The Hasmonean empire reached its greatest extension under Alexander Jannaeus. But the tides always turn. Alexander Jannaeus ruled for a long time (from 103 to 76 BCE) but not forever. The power vacuum in the region was not permanent either. Regardless of the differences within the Jewish community, it was only a matter of time before new powers would come marching in. The Romans had been at the gates of the Holy Land since the time of Antiochus III. Only because Rome delayed its conquest was it possible for Jewish statehood to be restored.

But its end drew near in 63 BCE, when Pompey the Great conquered the Holy Land and the Holy City. He even entered the inner sanctum of the Jewish Temple but was respectful enough to leave it untouched. Once again, the victor had only a short time to enjoy his victory. Pompey was soon defeated by Caesar, who was then able to rule at will in Judea. Antipater acted as his extended arm here from 47 BCE.

However, even the Romans were unable to stay in the Holy Land for long. In 40 BCE, the Parthians came from the North and Herod, Antipater's son and successor, had to flee. He tried in vain to seek help from the Arab Nabataeans (on whom he later took bloody revenge) and finally received support from Rome.

The Roman Senate appointed Herod as king. In 37 BCE, he had finished his conquests with Roman help. Herod's Jewish kingdom covered a considerably large area. It was not fully Jewish, however, but rather multinational, multiconfessional and multi-ethnic—i.e. a state consisting of many peoples. This is how we must see and call it, even if some won't like it.

In any case, Herod's territory was vast. But can we call Herod "the Great"? Once again, doubts are justified, as even his rule was only "loaned" to him by the Romans.

The Arab Edomites now ruled over Judea, which at the time was Rome's *possession*, but not its *property*. And the Jews developed into a sort of "mixture" between inhabitants and those who used to possess the land. They were residents who now lived in a multi-ethnic state. Had they not always been like that? Such a question calls for an answer. Yes, the Holy Land was a multiethnic state with a variety of possessors. One of whom was the Jews.

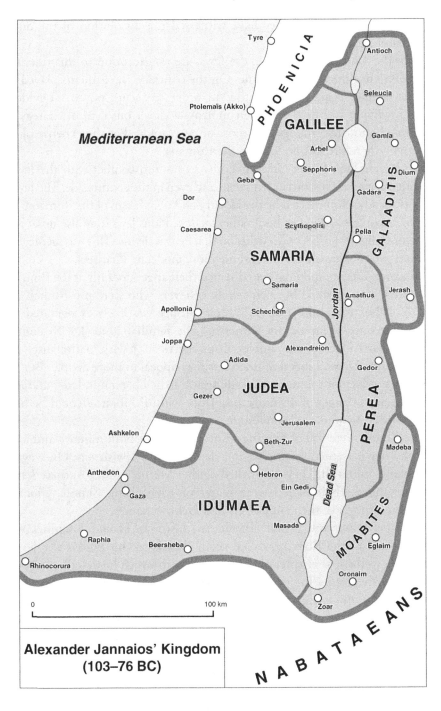

Alexander Jannaios' Kingdom
(103–76 BC)

Multi-ethnic, multinational, multiconfessional and multicultural societies are part of the dream of peace on Earth. Unfortunately, history has shown them to be a nightmare rather than a dream. This will come as no surprise to contemporary readers, as they have witnessed the dissolution of the Soviet Union and Yugoslavia.

Even the "chosen people", i.e. the Jews, are no exception to this rule, neither before nor during Roman rule. On the contrary, the Romans played the various peoples against one another in order to secure power. "Divide et impera" (divide and rule) was their motto—a clever but cynical strategy. In the Holy Land, this strategy was most often employed at the expense of the Jews, who therefore lost no love on the Romans.

In Caesarea, the Syrian-Greek majority came into conflict with the Jewish minority. There was discord in Jerusalem and even in the countryside. The Jewish Zealots already felt provoked by the idolatry and polytheism of the Romans. The Roman occupiers had in fact been rather tactless. Pious Jews were also upset with emperor Caligula's (37–41 CE) delusion that he was divine. This was sacrilegious in the eyes of the Jewish Zealots and the more moderate Pharisees.

However, Zealots and Pharisees directed their anger not only at the Romans. They were also appalled by their fellow believers who were pro-Roman and thus "collaborators" and "traitors". Their outrage was likely exaggerated and unfair but once again we are witnessing the familiar inner-Jewish conflict between particularism and universalism, between Jewish nationalists and liberal-minded Jews. Liberal mindedness may appeal to more people. But can a society survive if it promotes the willingness to be liberal minded—and thus places itself in danger of disintegrating from within? Libraries could be filled with possible answers to this question.

The Zealots were full of fighting spirit and resolve, both military and ideological. They presented themselves in a demonstrably Jewish way. Once again, their names said it all. They were called neither Marius, Gaius, Antipas, Levias nor Alexander. Their names were Elasar or Menachem, Simon, Giora or Jochanan—they and their supporters had Hebrew names.

Their behaviour was brutal. The Jewish historian Flavius Josephus, who had defected to the Romans, called them "beasts" in his book "The Jewish War" (e.g. in the first chapter of the fifth book, in which he described the different Jewish groups in Jerusalem). Admittedly, Josephus was not only a chronicler. He also engaged in politics, history and his own process of coming to terms with the past, for he was after all a collaborator and deserter. The Zealots certainly did not handle their adversaries with kid gloves. And did not exactly treat other Jews gently, let alone Romans.

In the first chapter of the fifth book of his history of the Jewish War, Flavius Josephus described this situation as follows: "O most wretched city [Jerusalem], …For thou couldst be no longer a place fit for God, nor couldst thou long continue in being, after thou hadst been a sepulcher for the bodies of thy own people, and hadst made the holy house itself a burying-place in this [Jewish] civil war of thine."

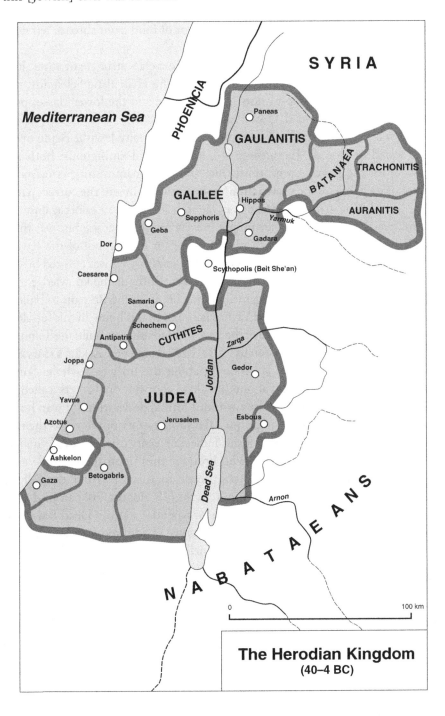

The Herodian Kingdom
(40–4 BC)

Josephus, the Jewish defector, naturally had to portray the Zealots as blood-thirsty in order to make his hands appear clean. However, his assessment of the political consequences of the Zealot rebellion is likely accurate. He called them "a wild beast grown mad, which, for want of food from abroad, fell now upon eating its own flesh".

The ideological struggle was at the same time a class struggle of sorts. Just as at the time of the Maccabean Revolt against the Hellenistic Seleucids, the upper class opened itself up to non-Jewish culture and the lower classes persisted in their self-contained, closed off Judaism.

What was (or still is and will be again and again) really Jewish? Being open to the world or closed? The answer is both clear and ambiguous: both are Jewish. Since the Jewish community, like any other community, consists of the sum of its parts, nobody has a monopoly on the truth and the correct path.

The "Jewish War" (66–70 CE), i.e. the war of the nationalist Zealots against the Romans, was bound to fail. They fought bravely and like heroes, but was their struggle worthwhile? Were their deaths the price for the survival of the Jewish people? No, no and no again. The survival of the Jews as Jews was ensured by the Talmudists, by men such as Yohanan ben Zakkai. Without the knowledge and against the will of the Zealots, he gained permission from the Romans to build a Jewish school in a small town called Yavne (Jamnia). In this house in this forsaken little town, the new spiritual palace of the Jews and Judaism was built: the Talmud.

Like many other things, the details of Rabbi Yohanan ben Zakkai's story are not entirely certain, but there is no doubt about the story as a whole. Some (even Talmudists) felt uneasy about his close cooperation (others called it ingratiation) with the Romans. Even without formal declarations of war, however, the Jews were masters of infighting. Ten Jews, twenty opinions, as the not exactly amiable stereotype goes. But this radical diversity often ensured vitality.

The Zealots were wild warriors who brought ruin upon their people and themselves. Their policies did not contribute to survival. After the fall of Jerusalem and the destruction of the Temple (28 August 70), around one thousand Zealots retreated to the fortress of Masada near the Dead Sea until 1 May 73. In present-day Israel, their resistance is admired and even glamourised. "Masada will not fall a second time!" is a popular slogan. Hopefully not. But Masada was an act of collective suicide that had no political purpose.

Politically, it would have made sense to seek some sort of autonomy. This would have secured both the physical and the spiritual survival of the Jews. Examples of this strategy can be seen during the time of the Second Temple.

Christianity, which was growing ever stronger at the time, benefited from the weakness of Judaism. The apostles taught the new gospel and one of the most successful ones was Paul, a former student of the Pharisees.

Visitors to Rome know the Arch of Titus and have surely seen its depiction of the Jews who were brought to Rome at the beginning of the European diaspora.

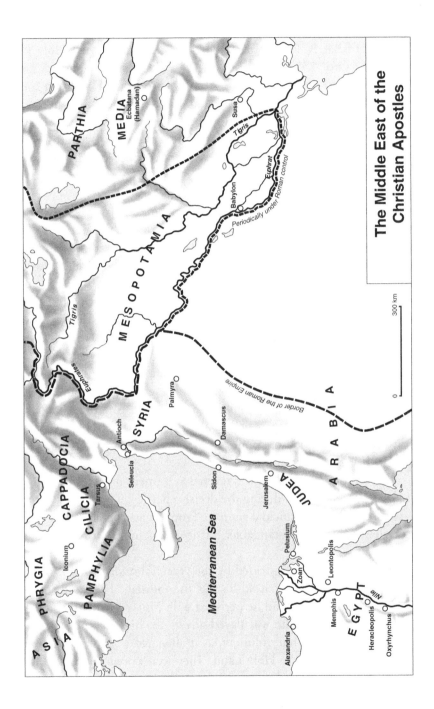

The Middle East of the Christian Apostles

But let us not forget that a large number of Jews were allowed to stay in the Holy Land. Those who were taken away were the Jewish ruling classes. The Jewish revolt of Bar Kokhba proves that Jews remained in the Holy Land. From 131/132 until 135 CE, Jews in the Holy Land made a last, desperate attempt to throw off the Roman yoke. According to Roman historian Cassius Dio, legionaries killed more than half a million people in this conflict. This number is probably a gross exaggeration, but it nevertheless reveals reality on the ground. Above all, it shows that it was more than just a handful of Jews who confronted the Romans, and that Jewish life continued in the Holy Land even after the Jewish War.

Until just a few years ago, this revolt, and Simon Bar Kokhba, was a sacred cow of sorts in Israel. This has not changed fundamentally in the official politics of memory but it has changed in historical scholarship, political science and journalism. One author has made a significant contribution to this development: the former chief of the Israeli military intelligence service, Yehoshafat Harkabi. In his book "The Bar Kokhba Syndrome" (Chappaqua, New York 1983), he called the revolt a prime example of irrational politics. In his opinion, Bar Kokhba led himself and those around him to their deaths, just like Samson, who had been seduced and fooled by Delilah (Book of Judges in the Old Testament).

Harkabi's book concerns ancient history to some extent but is really about present-day politics. His message is that we must learn today from yesterday's irrational mistakes in order not to fail again tomorrow. A nation that changes its interpretation of its own past will also change its future. History becomes a political argument and also a political instrument. History has an effect on the present. It is even part of the present.

The rebel Simon Bar Kokhba was revered as a "messiah". He was supposed to initiate the messianic era during the decisive battle—a politically and militarily foolish, deadly and suicidal venture. From a national and psychological point of view, it was understandable, but it was as foolish as the war of the Zealots from 66 to 70/73.

The spiritual protection provided by the great Talmudist Rabbi Akiva was clever. (He also thought Bar Kokhba was the messiah. He campaigned for him. He perished for him, and he perished with him. As I mentioned above, he was tortured horribly: he was flayed alive.) Yet his cleverness was also a colossal political and military blunder, as it alienated possible allies, namely the Jewish Christians in the Holy Land. They were convinced that the messiah, the "Christ", their saviour, namely Jesus Christ, had already come. Even among the Talmudists, Rabbi Akiva was not supported by the majority, despite the admiration his contemporaries and future generations had and have for him (which is completely justified in other respects).

"When will the Messiah come?" was a question that was contemplated repeatedly and intensely by Talmudic scholars. With their answers, they distanced themselves from Rabbi Akiva, as can be seen in Sanhedrin 97b: "… not in accordance with the opinion of Rabbi Akiva…". In Sanhedrin 93b, Bar Kokhba is clearly called a "false messiah": "Bar Koziva [another name for Bar Kokhba, which is discriminatory in Hebrew as it is related to the word "lie"], i.e., bar Kokheva, ruled for two and a half years. He said to the Sages: I am the Messiah. They said to him: With regard to the Messiah it is written that he is able to smell and judge, so let us see ourselves whether he, bar Kokheva, is able to smell and judge. Once they saw that he was not able to smell and judge, the gentiles killed him." The ending here is distorted, since Bar Kokhba fell in the struggle against the Romans in 135. The tenor of this statement, however, is clear: we want nothing to do with this false messiah—even if that means we have to distance ourselves from our beloved, great Rabbi Akiva (who died a martyr's death for Bar Kokhba).

The Talmudists were not wild warriors. They wanted to survive. They were convinced that, since they were Jews, the Holy Land was their property, but they resigned themselves to the different occupiers. They accepted the loss of outward power to ensure the inner strength and stability of Judaism and thus the survival of the Jews.

The Zealots and Bar Kokhba chose outward power. Is this how the modern-day state of Israel acts? One cannot help but gain this impression if we consider the fact that, from a religious perspective, around 70% of Jewish Israelis lead distinctly non-Jewish lives. This is exactly what orthodox believers accuse them of.

Like the Zealots, Bar Kokhba's men did not handle their inner-Jewish critics and opponents with kid gloves. "Purity of arms"? How and where would that be possible? Blood is always an impure substance when it runs off swords.

The land was ravaged and deserted, but parts of it were settled by Roman veterans. Now even citizens of the Roman Empire became part of the ethnic and cultural mixture. Jews at this time were neither possessors nor owners of the Holy Land. But there *were* Jews, if only in isolated pockets.

These few Jews made great economic and cultural achievements (working with the Romans and not against them) that have been all but ignored, even in academic literature. Israeli historian Seew Sifrai pointed out this fact in 1995. In fact, this should always have been known and said, since without this framework, Talmudists would not have been able to study, discuss and write.

In principle, the Roman emperor Hadrian wanted to take revenge and have a Holy Land "free of the Jews". Jews were driven from the mountainous area west of the River Jordan as they were from Galilee. If they survived their expulsion, they were mostly sold as slaves.

Even their name was to be erased from the map of the Holy Land. Judea was renamed "Syria Palaestina". In the fourth and fifth centuries, the area was divided into three administrative divisions. This did not, however, change anything with regard to the fundamental facts.

In spite of these efforts, the land was not entirely "free of the Jews". In the North, in Galilee, the Talmudists studied the Bible and the laws and prescribed commandments. They were both critical thinkers and forward thinkers. The Roman emperors no longer had to fear Jewish uprisings because there were so few Jews. The Roman emperors had changing attitudes towards the Jews, but they were always their masters, those who occupied the Holy Land. They saw themselves as occupiers but also as conquerors, which was not necessarily a new way of thinking in this region. This statement is of course not limited to the Holy Land.

We have discussed the question of ownership on multiple occasions. There was also no question of Jews possessing the land in those times. The few Jews who remained in the Holy Land had instead become residents, a mixture of inhabitants and those who (formerly) possessed the land.

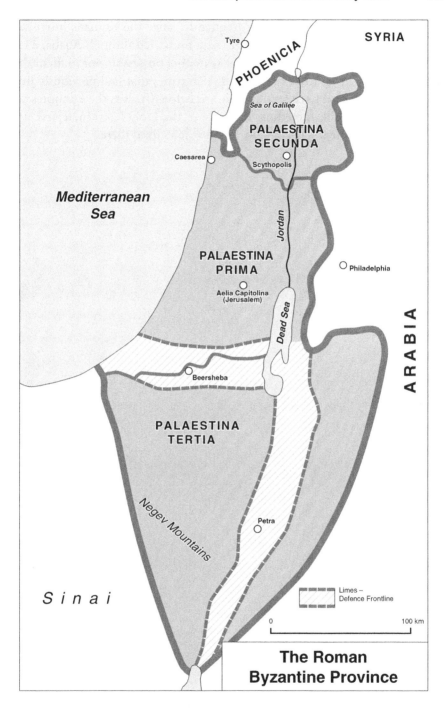

The Roman Byzantine Province

Arabs came to this region more frequently, since the Romans intensified trade with Arabia and India and their trade routes led through Aqaba, a city on the Red Sea. The Arabs, however, were neither possessors nor residents but rather migrants, apart from the various Arab tribes that had previously lived in this region and that have been mentioned before (such as the Edomites and the Itureans). Overall, the ethnic diversity of the Holy Land increased even though fewer people in general and very few Jews lived there.

Christians as Heirs and Owners
(Fourth to the Seventh Century)

From the third century CE onward, the Roman Empire descended into chaos. Even attempts to temporarily stabilise the empire did not alter the course of events. Rise was followed by decline as in many world empires both before and after. The weakening of the state, however, led to the rise of Christianity in the fourth century. It became the state religion. The reader will remember the section on holy places in which the significance of Emperor Constantine the Great was mentioned.

The Christians were lucky. They *inherited*, as it were, a great empire. They did not have to conquer it. Or did they? They did, in fact, but it was not an outward conquest—there was no occupation of land. It was more or less an inward conquest.

What is also remarkable in this context is the tide of historical events. Since Alexander the Great, the wave had swept from the Occident to the Orient. With Christianity, the wave swept from the Orient to the Occident, and then as an occidental Christian wave back to the Orient. However, the Christian wave from the Orient increasingly expanded throughout Europe.

Christianity thus came into an "inheritance" in the Holy Land. This appeared to be both legal (i.e. permitted by law) and legitimate (i.e. justified). Strictly speaking this was not true, because the inheritance came from the former possessor—who was not the owner. The fact that the (Roman) possessor considered itself to be the owner does not make any difference. Inheritance does not turn wrong into right.

Starting in the fourth century, Christianity was able to literally build and develop positions and bastions in the Holy Land, namely the holy sites as well as many churches and monasteries. Building programmes have always and everywhere had economic benefits. For this reason, people in the Holy Land were doing moderately well. The Christian religion boosted the economy. This thriving economy in turn attracted people, most of whom were Christians.

In 395, the Roman Empire was divided and Christianity became the *only* state religion. From then on, the Holy Land belonged to East Rome, to Byzantium. (There is, of course, a controversy among experts about when the Byzantine Empire actually began and when the Roman Empire ended, but that is not of interest here.) In the Byzantine era, there was no large-scale migration from or to the Holy Land. The question of owners, possessors, residents and migrants is confusing at this point and adds little to the discussion.

The Arab question, however, should not be left unmentioned. But there is little to be added. Byzantium too served as a bulwark against immigration and conquest by the inhabitants of the Arabian Peninsula. It was a bulwark because the military strength of the empire meant that Arabs had for the longest time little chance of conquering it. They did not want to conquer it either. Nevertheless, they still made repeated forays. But that has long been known.

In a way, the bulwark was permeable, but nevertheless effective. Byzantium continued to trade with Arabia.

Under Byzantine rule, the Jews had it neither good nor bad, although the basic attitude of triumphant Christianity was unmistakably discriminatory. There was absolutely no doubt as to who was the "master of the house". And like many other masters or possessors before and after, the Christian Byzantines regarded themselves as the true owners although they were not.

The Jewish wise men in the Holy Land continued to work on their undisputed intellectual property: the Talmud. They contributed to its further development in the Byzantine era.

The "Jerusalem Talmud" from the Byzantine era is considered to be less significant than the "Babylonian Talmud". But that should be of no concern to us. The Christian rulers must be given some credit for the fact that these works were allowed to develop with few obstructions under Byzantine rule. The Talmudic scholars completed their grandiose work just in time as an increasing number of anti-Jewish measures began to take place in the late phase of Byzantine rule in the Holy Land, namely since the reign of Emperor Justinian (527–565).

It is no wonder that the Jews in the Holy Land hoped for a change in occupiers at the very least. This occurred in 614 when the Persians came and in 634 when Islamic Arabs arrived.

Re-orientalisation: Arabisation, Turkification

(From the Seventh to the Eleventh Century)

In the seventh century, the Christian Occident took leave of the Holy Land when it was conquered and occupied by other peoples and religions. Again we can witness a new wave, which would not be the last. But a dramatic and revolutionary change in occupiers was taking place: the Arabisation and thus the Islamisation of the Holy Land.

It would be absurd to consider this change in possession to be a change in ownership, especially if you follow the previous arguments.

Before that, there was a Persian interlude, although only a short one. This interlude, too, was purely oriental and not Christian. In 614, the Persians wrenched the Holy Land from the Byzantine Empire and lost it again after only 15 years (in 629). The Byzantine Emperor Heraclius triumphantly returned to Jerusalem. He fell quickly and steeply because as early as 634 Islamic Arabs arrived outside the gates of the Holy Land. They opened them by force.

The Jews of the Holy Land welcomed the Persian conquerors with open arms. No wonder. They were fed up with being bullied by the Christians. They were much happier being bullies themselves, a role they quickly adopted when they unexpectedly became the masters of Jerusalem. Persia handed it over to them to look after on Persia's behalf. Now Christians were expelled and their churches were destroyed. Is this poetic justice? By no means. It is pure meanness and malice. Unfortunately, inhumanity is interconfessional, intercultural and international. This went too far even for the Persians. They again assumed command themselves. As mentioned above, however, they had to give way to the Christians in 629.

© The Author(s), under exclusive license to Springer Nature Switzerland AG 2021
M. Wolffsohn, *Whose Holy Land?*, https://doi.org/10.1007/978-3-030-74286-7_20

The Jewish elites now courted the Byzantine emperor, who (falling prey to various temptations) promised to spare them. But even the emperor was not almighty. And besides, he had already enjoyed the cordialities of the Jews. Why should he protect them now? Anti-Jewish lobbying by the state and church began. The Emperor did what many before and after him did: he gave in. He gave in to pressure, and that meant murders and massacres of the Jews and their expulsion from Jerusalem. Yet again, the Holy City was to become "free of Jews".

But the Jews soon welcomed the liberators and new occupiers of the Holy Land: Islamic Arabs. This is almost unbelievable from today's perspective. But Spain, too, had a "golden" Arab-Islamic-Jewish era between the eighth and fifteenth centuries.

It is a comfort that not even allegedly "eternal" enmities last forever. Almost all relationships follow a cyclical pattern. This means that there are ups and downs. Unfortunately, we normally do not know in advance how long the "downs" will last. Nothing is more constant than change.

From 634 to 1099, Arab Muslims ruled over the Holy Land. They joined the ranks of occupiers. The Umayyads ruled Jerusalem until 750. Then their rivals, the Abbasids, assumed control.

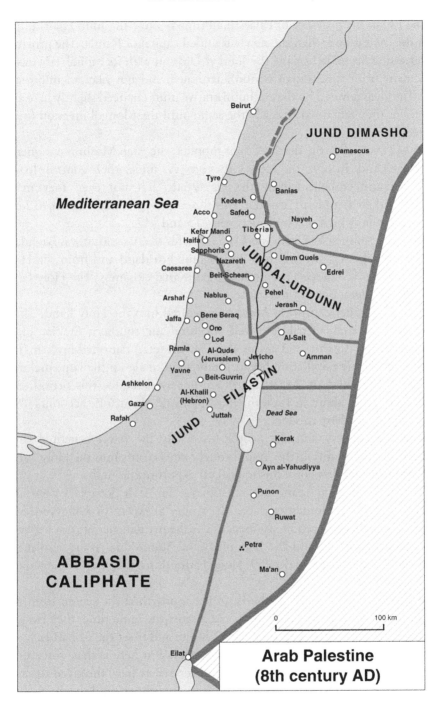

Arab Palestine
(8th century AD)

The Byzantine province of Palaestina Prima became the Jund Filastin, first with the capital Lod, then the newly founded capital of Ramla. The province of Palaestina Secunda became the Jund al-Urdunn with its capital Tiberias (a settlement from the Roman period). Jerusalem did not play an important role. The areas covered by these administrative units changed slightly here and there, but they remained basically the same until the Mongol invasion (mid-thirteenth century).

Only 2 years after the death of their prophet, the Arab Muslims conquered the Holy Land. In 638, the Holy City, too, was under their control. It was protected and embellished by the Umayyads, but not even they made Jerusalem their temporary capital. This function was initially given to Lod, then to Ramla, which was built between 715 and 717.

The centre of the Umayyads was Damascus; for the Abassids it was Baghdad. The distance both from the Arab and Islamic heartland and from the Holy Land had grown—despite the undeniable internal closeness. The Holy Land was close to them, but not that close.

Unlike in earlier centuries, Arabs now poured into the Holy Land. There were northern Arabian tribes as well as central and southern Arabian ones. The Byzantine, Roman, and before that, Jewish (etc.) dam had broken. The Arabisation of the population began. Arabs soon made up the large majority of the local population. Exact figures are not available for this period. But there is no doubt about it. Even the most patriotic of patriotic accounts from Israel would not deny this fact.

Both the country and the people (especially the Jews) benefited from Arabisation. For example, the Arabs brought citrus fruits into the Holy Land. That means Israeli Jews owe this important export to the Arabs.

Like the Jews (and many other peoples), the Arab occupiers were also unable to maintain domestic peace. The rivalry between the Umayyads and Abbasids has already been mentioned, as has the permanent contrast between the urban population and the Bedouins. The Sunni-Shia rivalry also made itself felt in the Holy Land. In 969, Shiite Fatimids from Egypt conquered the Holy Land.

At the same time, rivals of the Fatimids approached the region from the north. These rivals were Seljuk Turks. At almost the same time, they banged on the gates of the shrunken Byzantine Empire and beset the Abbasids.

The obvious and seemingly confusing conclusion here is that, since time immemorial, various peoples from almost everywhere have thronged towards the Holy Land. They came from the south, the southeast, and the north. The same story is told in the Old Testament.

This time it was Arabs, Turks, and Egyptians. Since the seventh century, Egypt's population had been Arabised and Islamised to a large extent, but not completely.

Even Byzantium saw its chance. The Abbasids had become so weak that Byzantium felt strong enough to attempt to conquer the Holy Land. In addition, the Muslims (unlike in the seventh century) were fragmented. The Christians from Byzantium had legitimate hopes from a military point of view, but this says nothing about who owned or occupied what. All the same, Byzantium advanced into the area south of the Sea of Galilee.

Chaos reigned around the year 1000. Almost everyone was fighting everyone else. Raids by the Bedouins ruined the economy and destabilised local regimes. The actual masters of the region were now the Bedouins. Nomads as possessors? A contradiction in terms. There is no need to ask who owned the land.

Possession changed at a swift pace. In 1071, the Seljuks were successful. Even Jerusalem was Turkish now—until 1098 when the Fatimids came roaring back. The former occupants (the robber of a good stolen time and again) were back. This had much to do with rule and war, but nothing with justice and ownership. Population movements depended on who ruled and possessed the land. All in all, the mixture of peoples in the Holy Land was given a good shake.

Who had possession and ownership *rights*? We can look for them. But the search will be futile—unless you legitimise possession by the length of occupation.

Initially, the Arab conquerors liberated the Jews, too. The Jews were certainly better off than in the late Byzantine period. The Christians also had little to complain about. Like the Jews, they occasionally reached top-level administrative positions.

But as always in the Holy Land—there also occurred some extremely unholy things. Ups alternated with downs. Like the Umayyads did (for a while) in Spain, the Abbasids in the Holy Land passed laws requiring non-Muslims to wear special clothing and markings. Jews sometimes, but not always, had to wear a yellow turban, Christians a blue one, and Samaritans a red one. Human history has a long and sad tradition of distinguishing one group of people from another. In the Middle Ages, especially since the thirteenth century, the Christian Occident adopted the idea of excluding certain groups by requiring them to wear distinctive clothing, mainly the yellow Jewish hat or patch. We all know such signs of intolerance. Not to mention the yellow badge under National Socialism.

Re-europeanization
(The Crusades, Eleventh to Thirteenth Century)

In 1099, the crusaders arrived in Jerusalem after the Seljuks and the Fatimids. Their manners were not very knightly. The reader may remember the section on Jerusalem and the holy places. Islamic-Jewish cooperation in the face of Christian conquerors is again worth mentioning. The Christian conquerors were never in a position to seriously claim ownership. They were occupiers at best. Nobody today would seriously think along these lines. Or would they?

In 1187, Islam was poised to return to the Holy Land. At Hattin, Saladin won a decisive victory. This was not far away from the Sea of Galilee, which is closely related to the history of Christianity. At Hattin, the Christians experienced more damnation than salvation.

By the way, Saladin, the liberator of the Islamic world, was of Kurdish descent. From our perspective, this is a remarkable detail, because Kurds and Arabs do not live in what we would call brotherly Islamic harmony. When the Arab world today invokes Saladin's legacy against Christian Europe (and its alleged appendage, Jewish Israel), this is as unconvincing as the ancestral link between the Philistines and the Palestinians. The Kurdish Saladin as the liberator of the Arab world?

The Arab world today often compares the Jewish State of Israel with the former Christian state of the crusaders.

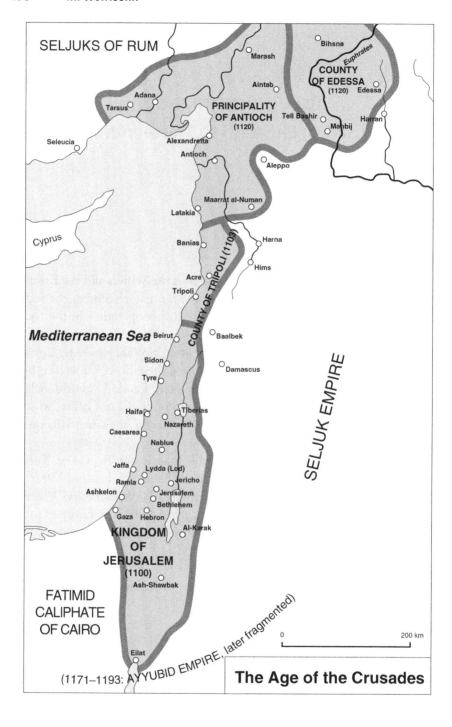

SELJUKS OF RUM

Bihsna

Marash

Euphrates

COUNTY
OF EDESSA
(1120)   Edessa

Aintab

Adana

Tarsus

PRINCIPALITY
OF ANTIOCH
(1120)

Tell Bashir

Manbij

Harran

Seleucia

Alexandretta

Antioch

Aleppo

Maarrat al-Numan

Latakia

Cyprus

Banias

Harna

COUNTY OF TRIPOLI (1109)

Hims

Acre

Tripoli

Mediterranean Sea Beirut

Baalbek

Sidon

Damascus

Tyre

Haifa

Tiberias

Nazareth

Caesarea

Nablus

Jaffa

Lydda (Lod)

Ramla

Jericho

Ashkelon

Jerusalem

Bethlehem

Gaza Hebron

Al-Karak

KINGDOM
OF
JERUSALEM
(1100)

SELJUK EMPIRE

Ash-Shawbak

FATIMID
CALIPHATE
OF CAIRO

Eilat

(1171–1193: AYYUBID EMPIRE, later fragmented)

0   200 km

The Age of the Crusades

As in the past, the artificial, foreign structure will disappear, if not today, then tomorrow or the day after tomorrow. As in the past, the Islamic world will not give up, so people say. This comparison is rather convincing at first sight. But if we look at it more closely, it is not, because at that time the Crusaders claimed *new* possession and ownership rights to the Holy Land. But Jews and Arabs insist on actual or alleged *old* rights.

Hattin (1187) marks the beginning of the end of the Christian interlude, which ended in 1291.

The Return of Islam

(Mamluks and Ottomans, Thirteenth to the Twentieth Century)

The next temporary occupier (not owner) of the Holy Land was Saladin, the founder of the Ayyubid dynasty. At that time, some parts of the Holy Land were still in the hands of Christian crusaders.

The Ayyubids ruled the Holy Land from faraway Egypt as did the Pharaohs in ancient history and later the Fatimides.

This well-known model causes enormous problems even in the present day. For Arabs from North Africa to Iraq, the Jewish state is a wedge driven between them. This is by no means solely a religious or national matter. Israel comes across (without intending to) as a wall between the eastern (Mashriq) and the western part (Maghreb) of the Arab world. The Holy Land was and still is a land bridge between these parts. Some ancient structures are not affected by the passage of time. They existed in ancient times and continue to exist today. They apply to Muslims, Jews and Christians alike.

Let us return to the Middle Ages. After the crusades, the Islamic world was well aware of the importance of the Holy Land. Its political significance has increased considerably. And this is how things have remained. Even under Ayyubid rule, however, the Holy Land did not become a central region for Muslims. The same can be said of the Islamic heartland—the Arabian Peninsula—at this time. The diversity of the Islamic world had reversed the process of "Arabisation" as it were. In other words, the Arabian element was no longer as dominant as it once was. The same applies to the Holy Land, which Khwarezmians overran in the year 1244 at the invitation of the Egyptian Ayyubids.

In 1250, the Mongols from East Asia invaded the Fertile Crescent. They brought violence and destruction with them. The Mongols were expelled in 1260 by the Mamluks, who had assumed power over Egypt 10 years before.

© The Author(s), under exclusive license to Springer Nature Switzerland AG 2021   **161**
M. Wolffsohn, *Whose Holy Land?*, https://doi.org/10.1007/978-3-030-74286-7_22

Step by step, the Mamluks conquered the remaining crusader strongholds in the Holy Land. The Fall of Acre in 1291 also meant the fall of the last crusader outpost. The Christian interlude had come to an end.

"Mamluk" referred only to warriors and not to the entire Ayyubid people in Egypt, which is comparable to the early historical terms "Canaanites" and "Hebrews". The Mamluks changed little although they undertook many construction projects, especially in Jerusalem. The city gained in significance, and the administrative region of its governor was extended to include Hebron. This was intended to serve as both an external and a religious signal.

But the cities of Ramlah and Gaza, in particular, were economically and socially much more important than Jerusalem. Jerusalem was the Holy City, but it was located far from the great trade routes. And holiness alone does not pay. In addition, few pilgrims travelled to the city because Bedouin raiders had made the routes unsafe.

What is important about the era of Mamluk rule is without a doubt the renewed Islamisation of the Holy Land. This can be seen in the many new mosques and Koran schools and in the population. Jews continued to live in this area, but their numbers had shrunk even more since the crusades. Even according to the Encyclopaedia Judaica, which celebrates almost every single Jew living in the Holy Land before the First Aliyah (1882), only a few Jewish families were scattered throughout this region. For example, the encyclopaedia says that in 1481 three hundred Jewish families were living in Safed, which was "four times the number of Jews living in Jerusalem". Seventy Jewish families in Gaza are documented while only thirty-eight families were living in Kfar Kanna near Nazareth at this time. And this despite the "great numbers" of Jews who were expelled from Spain in 1492 and from Portugal in 1497.

Especially those Christian European readers who are outraged (and rightly so) about the intolerance of contemporary Islamic fundamentalists should acknowledge that it was Muslims, more specifically Mamluks, who granted Jews (expelled by Spanish and Portuguese Christians) asylum and even a new home. Tolerance, like intolerance, is not a trait of a certain religion, ethnic group or nation.

The Mamluks did not gain any proprietary or ownership rights over the Holy Land. And anyway, who would be able to claim them today? What people or nation can be considered the descendants of an occupational group? No one, of course.

We should make no secret of the fact that the (few) Jews living under Mamluk rule were in a favourable political situation. But how can we measure tolerance when it is extended to a small and thus politically, economically and socially completely harmless minority?

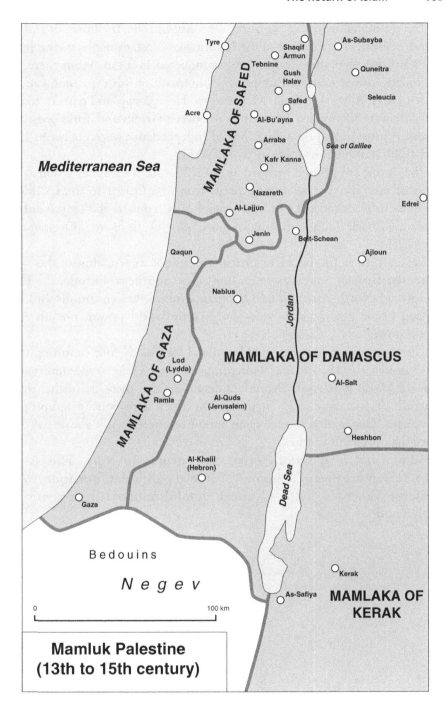

Tyre

Shaqif
Armun

As-Subayba

Tebnine

Quneitra

Gush
Halav

MAMLAKA OF SAFED

Seleucia

Safed

Acre

Al-Bu'ayna

Mediterranean Sea

Arraba

Sea of Galilee

Kafr Kanna

Nazareth

Edrei

Al-Lajjun

Jenin

Beit-Schean

Ajloun

Qaqun

Nablus

Jordan

MAMLAKA OF DAMASCUS

MAMLAKA OF GAZA

Lod
(Lydda)

Al-Salt

Ramla

Al-Quds
(Jerusalem)

Heshbon

Al-Khalil
(Hebron)

Dead Sea

Gaza

Bedouins

N e g e v

Kerak

0   100 km

As-Safiya

**MAMLAKA OF
KERAK**

**Mamluk Palestine
(13th to 15th century)**

The triumphal march of the Turks was unstoppable. The fifteenth and sixteenth centuries were the age of the Ottomans. Constantinople, the capital of the Christian Byzantine Empire, was conquered in 1453. From there, the Ottomans moved towards Europe. The aftermath of this expansion can still be felt today. Albania, Bosnia, Montenegro, Herzegovina and parts of today's Bulgaria were Islamicised. The conflict between Greeks and Turks goes back to this expansion and the Greek War of Independence waged between 1821 and 1829. It also has its roots in World War I.

The Ottomans pressed forward as far as Vienna. Twice they stood at the gates of the city. The wave now swept from the Orient to the Occident. Only in 1683, when the Ottoman assault was repulsed at Vienna, did the wave roll back (although much more slowly) from the Occident to the Orient.

Let us return to the early Ottoman conquests. At almost the same time, the Turkish wave was extending across southeast Europe, the Holy Land, and North Africa. The Ottoman Empire was enormous and had indeed become a world power—an Islamic world power, not an Arab world power.

The Ottomans ruled over the Holy Land for exactly four centuries, from 1517 until 1917/18. This was a long time, almost as long as the sum total of years of Jewish statehood. The only difference is that these are further in the past, which does not change anything with regard to ownership and proprietary rights. Occupation is once again a topic of interest. As it always has been since the thirteenth century.

Administrative questions often bore people to tears. This is sad because they are potential sources of crucial political information. What does the structure of the Ottoman administration tell us about the Holy Land?

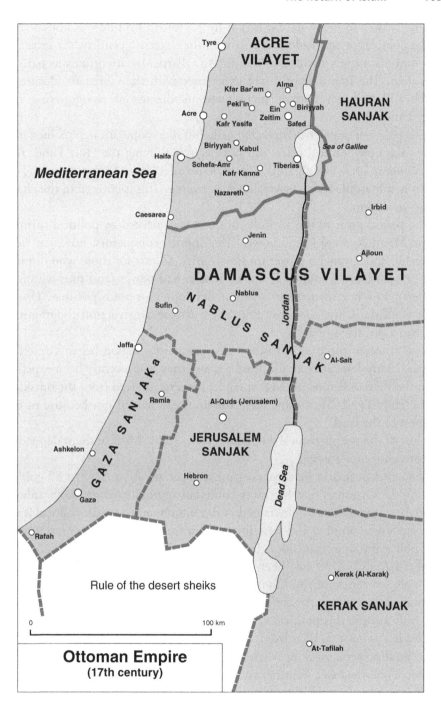

Tyre

ACRE VILAYET

Kfar Bar'am   Alma

Peki'in   Ein   Biriyyah   **HAURAN SANJAK**
Acre   Zeitim
Kafr Yasifa   Safed

Biriyyah   Kabul
Haifa   Schefa-Amr   Sea of Galilee
Kafr Kanna   Tiberias

Mediterranean Sea

Nazareth

Caesarea   Irbid

Jenin

Ajloun

DAMASCUS VILAYET

Nablus

Sufin   *NABLUS SANJAK*   *Jordan*

Jaffa   Al-Salt

Ramla   Al-Quds (Jerusalem)

GAZA SANJAK a

Ashkelon   **JERUSALEM SANJAK**

Hebron

Gaza   *Dead Sea*

Rafah

Kerak (Al-Karak)

Rule of the desert sheiks

KERAK SANJAK

0   100 km

At-Tafilah

Ottoman Empire
(17th century)

One answer to this question is that the Ottoman Empire was not considered a political or an ideological entity. In the sixteenth century, the territory was administratively divided into four parts. Particular attention was paid to Jerusalem. The Islamic world had experience with the Christian Occident, which still had not entirely abandoned its dreams of reconquering the Holy Land.

The political superstructure changed, but the population remained the same. The new political rulers did not begin turkifying the Holy Land. But the economy grew rapidly in the first five decades under Ottoman rule. This boom is still visible today especially in Jerusalem. This is covered in the chapter on Jerusalem.

The period prior to the Turkish conquest was marked by political turmoil as the Mamluks were losing power. The Turkish conquerors, however, were powerful, and sovereign power meant security, at least for those who did not face persecution. As soon as it was clear who had power (and thus who had property, but not ownership), certain developments were possible. Under these conditions, the economy flourished. Major construction programmes also had a positive impact.

As is so often the case in history, this prosperous region began attracting people. Many Jews arrived, not least because they had recently been expelled from the Iberian Peninsula. Most people, however, arrived from the outskirts of the Holy Land. They came for economic reasons and not because of the holiness of the land.

Most of the people from the outskirts were Arabs. Most of them depended on agriculture for a living.

The new Ottoman rulers even organised a census. After the first 50 golden years under Ottoman rule, the Holy Land had approximately 300,000 inhabitants. The population had increased in size but remained small. Political leaders were few in number and were imported from the Ottoman central power. The politically important local families originally came from northern and southern Arabia. They had been extremely powerful since the Mamluk era. The political centre of the Mamluks was in Cairo, that of the Ottomans in Istanbul. The rivalrous Arabic/Palestinian families of the Holy Land increased in significance in this political vacuum.

This is a pattern familiar from the history of Jews in the Holy Land. When the central power is weak or when a political vacuum emerges, the possibility of independence arises. Autonomy could only occur if the foreign power was weak. The basic facts of history apply to both Jews and Palestinians alike.

The majority of the population were Arab peasants. "Arab" is the operative word in this sentence. There are no two ways about it. The same can be said about the argument that a majority can do many things, but it cannot create rights or even justice and ownership rights.

At the beginning of Ottoman rule, there were almost no Jews in the Holy Land. According to the Encyclopaedia Judaica, there were approximately 5000. Although the encyclopaedia is a scholarly and reliable work, it often gives higher rather than lower estimates (for things that are difficult to quantify anyway)—it does this seemingly for political reasons. At the end of this first period under Ottoman rule, which had been a golden era even for Jews, there were approximately 10,000 Jews living in Safed alone. This Galilean city became a new centre of Jewish mysticism (Kabbalah), spirituality and piety. At this time, most of the (nevertheless small number of) Jews inhabiting the Holy Land lived in Safed. In the middle of the sixteenth century, this figure was hardly more than 15,000.

Their numbers were small, but they had grown since the end of Mamluk rule as many Jews of Spanish and Portuguese origin had found refuge here. This is another example of Islamic tolerance, first shown by the Mamluks and now by the Ottomans. Islamic tolerance in Spain lasted until 1492. The Jews only started to flee the country after intolerant Christians got the upper hand in the power struggle with Muslims.

The Holy Land remained under Ottoman rule for a long time. The decline of the empire began early but its dissolution was slow. Ottoman hegemony grew increasingly porous starting in approximately 1600. Local strongmen gradually filled the vacuum. The Bedouins in particular grew in strength. They were Arabs, but they were nomadic and did not permanently establish and extend bases of power. For them, filling the political vacuum in and around the Holy Land was a question of opportunity. These opportunities were also sought by the Druze in the Beirut area and on Mount Carmel (in the Haifa region).

The Ottoman Empire was also weakened by military defeats in Europe, especially after 1683. Failure simply breeds more failure. Unhappy about their defeats, the Ottoman warriors, the Janissaries, mutinied again and again. Conquered peoples were forced to pay heavy taxes. They therefore tried to escape Ottoman control wherever possible. The Ottomans in turn desperately needed the tax income. To stem the loss of power, they had to prepare for war. And wars cost money. Pressure and counter-pressure set in motion a slow but inevitable development.

The inhabitants of the Holy Land also attempted to rid themselves of occupiers and taxes. This was the case with the largest ethnic group, the Arabs. Mutiny and rebellion call for leadership.

In this way, certain influential Arab/Palestinian families living in the Holy Land expanded their power. Open rebellion would have been suicidal, but by acting as intermediaries between the local Arab/Palestinian population and the Ottoman state, the leaders of the large families increased their status. At the same time, this role became a major pillar of their power over the long term, at least among their own people.

The constant attacks and assaults by Bedouins and Druze scared away the Jews living in the Holy Land and those who were willing to immigrate. By the end of the seventeenth century, there was not a single Jew living in Tiberias, and the Jewish stronghold of Safed was becoming weaker and weaker. The Jews living in the Holy Land were now moving to Jerusalem, Hebron and Gaza. Jerusalem once again became one of the most important places in the entire region.

Gaza also attracted many Jews, as it had become an important and prosperous city on account of the trade routes along the Eastern Mediterranean. Times have changed, especially since 1948. As mentioned above, the establishment of Israel as a Jewish state drove a wedge between the eastern (Mashriq) and the western part (Maghreb) of the Arab world. Israel disrupted important trade routes. This, of course, was unnecessary. What is wrong with peacefully trading with your neighbours? Unfortunately, politics have taken a different course and today Gaza is a city of strife.

Things were different then and Jews were well liked by local Arabs, i.e. Palestinians. It becomes apparent once again that Islamic intolerance is nothing but a popular misconception. It is people and not religions who are relentless, unreasonable and intolerant.

The historical events can be easily memorised. The decline of the Ottoman Empire began around the year 1600. It started to collapse around the year 1700. Shortly before 1800 (in 1798), Napoleon advanced through Egypt to Acre to the Holy Land. Around 1900, the Zionists arrived. They began immigrating to the Holy Land in 1882. But let us take a step back.

In 1683, the Ottomans were forced to stop their siege of the city. The retaliation of European Christianity began. One foot after another, the Europeans entered the Holy Land. With the Treaty of Karlowitz, the Ottomans ceded large territories to the Tsar in 1699. He also obtained control (called "protection") over the holy places in Jerusalem as well as overall Orthodox Christians in the Ottoman Empire. The terms of this treaty meant that Russia was now the protector of the Greeks, Serbs and Hungarians living in the Ottoman Empire. This was a great tool for unhinging the Ottoman Empire.

External and internal enemies of the Ottomans began forging coalitions at the end of the eighteenth century. An Ottoman rebel even formed an alliance with Russia, but in 1775 his revolt failed. In many cases, Ottoman rebels raised armies by recruiting peoples oppressed (or at least conquered) by the Ottomans, such as North Africans, Arabs, Albanians, Greeks, Bosniaks and Hungarians.

The Ottoman Empire was crumbling on the inside, but it was broken from the outside. First by Russia, which penetrated deeper and deeper into the Ottoman Empire during the eighteenth and nineteenth centuries (e.g. in Crimea), and then from Britain and France in the nineteenth and twentieth centuries.

The only reason why the Ottoman Empire survived for so long in the nineteenth century was that the European superpowers had to make up their minds about who was to receive what part of its territory. At first, they quarrelled.

In 1798, Napoleon Bonaparte advanced with his troops through Egypt into the Holy Land. He did not come peacefully. Neither did he have any religious plans for the Holy Land. For this reason, he had no particular interest in taking the Holy City. The Arabs in the Holy Land welcomed Napoleon. Not because they were longing for European Christian rulers like in the time of the crusades. In fact it was just the opposite. "The enemy of my enemy is my friend"—this was the thinking and approach of the Arabs. Independence from the Ottoman rulers appeared to be at hand.

So what were Napoleon's objectives in the Holy Land? He wanted to weaken England. By conquering the Holy Land, he hoped to possess an important key that the British needed for the route to India. Napoleon had a keen understanding of geography and strategy. The British fleet under Nelson's command, however, played an unpleasant trick on the Corsican. Napoleon's operations on land were not successful either. He failed to advance farther than Acre, at the northern end of Haifa Bay. What mattered even more to him than a victory over England was the struggle for power in France. He returned to France to seize power. This gave the Ottomans a brief respite.

The peoples controlled by the Ottomans had learned, however, that their rulers were mere paper tigers. This gave them the courage to intensify their struggle for independence and self-determination. At the same time, they had to acknowledge that they were militarily and technically inferior to the Europeans.

This led Muslims to ask themselves whether this inferiority was based on their religion. Some answered yes, others answered no. But it is here that we can find the roots of Islamic fundamentalism. Those who answered no reasoned that the defeat of the Islamic world was punishment for the fact that Muslims had gone astray from the right path. They believed that Muslims should not turn their backs on their religion but should instead focus even more on Islam in order to become stronger against Christian Europe. Industrial achievements of European civilisation could be used, they reckoned, but it was important to foster the content and substance of their own culture. In short, they said yes to technological and industrial modernisation but no to westernisation.

Others within the Muslim community welcomed both modernisation and westernisation. They therefore pursued a pro-Western policy. One of them was Muhammad Ali, an Albanian who was first appointed governor of Egypt by the Ottomans and who then governed independently. He took advantage of the situation. The Ottomans had lost the war against the Greeks and their European allies in 1829. They had lost military and political power. What was even worse, the Ottomans had to endure moral scorn for trying to deny the Greeks their right to self-determination. This is something most European rulers did both within and beyond their borders. They believed they were entitled to do so.

From 1832 to 1840, Muhammad Ali and his stepson Ibrahim Pasha ruled over the Holy Land and Syria. This period was marked once again by temporary changes in power and possession without changes in ownership.

Under the reign of Ali and Pasha, the major Palestinian families did not do well, unlike the Jews. Christians were arriving from France, in particular, and even from the United States. They were modernisers, missionaries, schoolteachers and university lecturers and were active especially in the region of Lebanon and Syria. In the long term, these Christians were digging the grave of Western civilisation in the Middle East, since the educational institutions where they worked became centres of Arab nationalism. This movement turned against the West in the twentieth century, first against the European colonial rulers (who had only arrived in the nineteenth and twentieth centuries) and then today against the West in general and the United States in particular.

Why did Christians, of all people, become the standard bearers of Arab nationalism in the Middle East? The answer is relatively simple. Christians were outsiders in the Islamic Middle East. By positioning themselves at the forefront of the Arab movement, they hoped to be integrated into the Arab community and to overcome their isolation. It is hardly surprising that today radical Palestinians like George Habash or Nayef Hawatmeh or the founder of the pan-Arab Ba'ath movement are or were Christians.

When the reign of Ali and Pasha ended, the Ottomans returned to the Holy Land with strong European support. They were even weaker now that they depended on European power. As a result, they had to allow Europeans into the region. As early as under Ibrahim Pasha's rule, Britain opened a consulate in the Holy City in 1838. The dam had finally broken. One European state after another followed. After 1840, it was clear that the weakened Ottomans were unable to close the floodgates.

Not only did the Europeans open consulates, Christian missions and schools, France became the protective power of Roman Catholic Christians and the holy sites in the Ottoman Empire, just like Russia had become the protector of the Orthodox Christians. In 1847, the French helped to restore the Latin Patriarchate of Jerusalem. Other Christians did not want to be left behind. Internal rivalries flared up among Christians. It would be unfair to blame only Jews or Muslims for the irrational struggles fought inside or because of the Holy Land.

Britain decided to become the protector of the Protestants, but there were few of them in the Ottoman Empire. As a consolation and in order to secure proportional political power, London assumed protection of the Druze and the Jews living in Palestine. The British needed an instrument to destabilise Istanbul from inside, if necessary, or at least to threaten the Ottomans. The only ones left to support were the Jews. The Druze were analogous to the Maronites, who lived in Lebanon and were protected by the French.

The Prussians just looked to heaven since there was no one left in the Holy Land for them to protect. Instead, the German Templers began arriving in 1868. They established small German settlements in Jerusalem, Jaffa, Haifa and Sarona. Alex Carmel has written several books on the Templers in the Holy Land which are worth reading.

Istanbul did not stand idly by. The Ottoman Empire in no way abandoned itself to what was seen as Islamic fatalism. On the contrary. After their defeat against the Greeks, they launched an enormous and comprehensive modernisation programme to save what could be saved. When it came to the military, they sought Prussian support and advice. Even Moltke the Elder was an active and successful military advisor to the Ottoman Empire. Let us not forget that, against all expectations, the Ottomans fought long and successfully during World War I. The foundation stone for this had been laid in the middle of the nineteenth century although (or actually because) the Ottoman Empire increasingly resembled Swiss cheese. The Ottomans were able to plug some of the holes but the overall structure nonetheless remained porous.

The power of the possessors of the Holy Land became even more porous during the nineteenth century as a result of what were known as capitulations. As a result of these contracts, citizens and protected peoples of the European powers who were living on Ottoman territory were no longer subject to Ottoman law. Their countries of origin and their protecting powers were now responsible for them. The Ottoman occupiers watched their power erode.

One often hears in Germany that this is when the "traditional German-Arab friendship" began. The people who say this, however, are confusing Turks with Arabs and they are also overlooking the fact that the strengthening of Turkish power was ultimately directed against the Arabs. As a result, World War I saw Arabs seek help against the Ottomans not from Germany but from its enemies, above all the British.

Construction schemes in Jerusalem were also part of Istanbul's modernisation programme. With an increase in construction projects and careful treatment of the Holy City, the Turks hoped to send a political signal, namely: We may be weaker than ever before and we may even have to accept your consulates in Jerusalem, but you should know that Jerusalem is a city that is holy to Muslims and is therefore important.

The leaders in Istanbul also had a political and inner-Islamic objective. They attempted to create a united Islamic front against Christian Europe and played the pan-Islamic card. They also wanted to integrate and control the Arabs. They did not, however, succeed.

With the new administrative division of the Holy Land, they hoped to send a pan-Islamic signal to the Christian European world.

The significance of Jerusalem is especially interesting in this context. With the promulgation of the Vilayet Law in 1864, the Holy City was split from Damascus Province (Vilayet) and declared an independent district that was directly subject to the Ottoman central government in Istanbul. Administrative structures are generally an important topic if we hope to learn more about political power and its distribution.

The European powers were followed by people, Christians and Jews. Around the year 1800, some 300,000 people were living in the Holy Land. Some authors provide even smaller figures. This means that the population had not grown since the middle of the sixteenth century. Living conditions in the Holy Land were apparently so poor that the indigenous population was unable to grow and people from abroad had no interest in moving there. In other words, the occupiers had not taken due care of their possession and the land was desolate.

As mentioned above, around the year 1800 there were some 5000 Jews among the 300,000 inhabitants, according to the Encyclopedia Judaica.

According to the Israeli Bible Atlas, there were 6700 Jews among a total population of 275,000 people. These figures result in a higher (although still small) percentage, namely 2.4%. Be that as it may, ownership rights cannot be justified or refuted by higher or lower population figures.

The number of Christians living in the Holy Land around 1800 is, by the way, estimated at 25,000.

At the end of the reign of Ali and Pasha around 1840, the total population was unchanged but the number of Jews had doubled according to the Encyclopedia Judaica. This sounds impressive, which is presumably the intention. However, what do ten to twelve thousand people matter, even in relation to such a low total population? At best, they are a sign of uncertainty about one's own legal standpoint. This uncertainty is justified, but this does not entitle Arabs and Palestinians to claim ownership of their possession.

But then there arrived the first Zionist immigrants in the Holy Land.

The Return to Zion
(Nineteenth and Twentieth Century)

Why did so many more Jews flock to the Holy Land starting in the first third of the nineteenth century than in previous centuries? There are two main answers to this question.

First, the Jews received a warm welcome from their hosts in the Holy Land (if they did in fact present themselves as guests and not as actual possessors or even owners). These hosts were the Western-oriented and enlightened moderniser Muhammed Ali, his stepson Ibrahim Pasha, and the Turks. Despite being weak, the latter had opened up and taken major steps towards modernisation since the 1830s.

Second, the European Jews were able to feel more protected than ever before. The Ottomans could not afford to be inhospitable. As citizens of various European countries, the Jews enjoyed the protection of the "capitulations". They lived in the Ottoman Empire, but under the law of their respective country of origin. What is more, the British lion could make himself heard if need be, as London had become the patron of the Jews.

Preposterous situations arose. For example, the government of His Majesty the Emperor of Russia was everything but favourably disposed towards the Jews. Domestically, one pogrom came after the other, particularly during the late nineteenth century. Externally, the Russian bear sank his teeth firmly into the Ottoman prey. In this situation, it seemed perfectly opportune for Moscow to "protect" Russian Jews in the Holy Land against the central power in Istanbul. The Tsar and his advisors had not, of course, discovered their love for the Jews. Instead, they were trying to expand their sphere of influence and deprive the Ottomans of their power.

But there were other reasons for the growth in Jewish immigration. Europe was engulfed by the fires of nationalism, and flared tempers saw Jews as the problem. Jews had long been victims of persecution, particularly in Russian territory (which included Poland). In 1881, Tsar Alexander II was murdered by anarchists. Who was "allegedly" to blame? The Jews of course. A wave of pogroms followed.

Russian Jews realised that they needed a way out of their ill-fated situation. They availed themselves of current thought. At the time, many peoples believed that the solution to their problems was to establish their own state, a national state. Similar voices began to be heard among European Jews.

There was no mention of a state among these Russian Jews. "To Zion, back to Zion" was the slogan of the "Lovers of Zion" (Hovevei Zion). "O House of Jacob, come ye and let us go (to Zion)", they would say, quoting the Hebrew Bible. They used the first letters of this Bible quotation to form the name of their group: "Bilu". The Jews in the Bilu movement really went to Zion—as Zionists!—and arrived in Palestine in 1882 (this was the first Aliyah, i.e. the first wave of immigrants).

They made their way to Zion to survive and establish a new community there, and not to pray, die and be buried in holy ground. It was about life, not about religion. As mentioned above (more than once, because it is an important point that is often overlooked), there was no talk of a state.

They never or hardly ever thought about the people already living in the Holy Land. They did not want to meddle in the affairs of those residing there. They were mainly concerned with their own affairs. Their story is tragic because (as in Greek tragedy) they meant well. Like most Zionist immigrants who came after them, all they wanted was to survive and save themselves. The conflict they sparked is something they would have wanted to avoid.

The fact that they wanted to avoid this conflict is demonstrated in the way they purchased Arab land. They always sought out places where few Arabs lived. They wanted their territory to be separate from that of the Arabs, not because they had something against the Arabs but because they finally wanted to be among themselves, among only Jews. This was a upright wish that had very unfortunate and unintended consequences. By the end of the 1920s, there was hardly any such land left. Now the Zionist buyers were reliant on land that was close to the Arabs. The conflict drew nearer, with Jews and Arabs unable to avoid each other—even in geographical terms—but at the same time each wanting their own (preferably politically independent) territory.

This practise of purchasing land was a ludicrous idea, and to this day it still angers supporters and opponents of Zionists and Palestinians alike. In the United States, Kenneth Stein has published what is likely the most insightful book on this subject, namely "The Land Question in Palestine, 1917–1939" (Chapel Hill 1984). In Germany, the German-Israeli political scientist Dan Diner has published a book that is stimulating but often distorts the facts and is quite difficult to read: "Keine Zukunft auf den Gräbern der Palästinenser" (Hamburg 1982).

Purchasing land was a strange undertaking from the outset because, by doing so, the Zionist buyers wanted not only to possess the land but also to own it. They wanted everything to be legal and moral. But if the Jews were the true owners of the land (as they had always claimed), then surely there was no need for them to purchase land in the first place. Whoever owns a territory also owns its land. Or is that not so? Whatever the case, the fact that land was being bought indicates a sense of doubt.

It was not, of course, an act of anticipatory atonement either. Land was acquired on the property market, where only individuals and not nations do business. A nation does not buy another nation's land. History has shown that land is usually seized rather than bought. The Holy Land is no exception.

The land purchases were thus either a sedative for the bad conscience of Zionists or a narcotic for Palestinian landowners and families (who, despite their political protests against the Zionists, were nevertheless happy to do business with them). Or perhaps they were a way of distracting third parties. Perhaps all these explanations are correct. At least the appearance of legality was guaranteed—although the justification of the Zionist's position was unintentionally called into question (although this went largely unnoticed). After all, the message behind the land purchases was clear: nobody knew for sure who owned the Holy Land.

The Palestinian Arabs were not intent on a conflict with the Zionists either. But these newcomers troubled them. They felt uneasy with the first Zionist immigrants. This feeling grew when more Zionists arrived between 1904/1905 and 1914 (the second Aliyah) because these Zionist Jews were different from their fellow believers who had come to the Holy Land earlier. The first wave of Jewish immigrants simply wanted to live in the Land of the Fathers as more or less middle-class Jews. For the worldly-minded Zionists who came with the second wave, the goal was to establish a new, highly modern community that was financed by Western Europe. Even worse, the men and women who came with the second wave of Zionist immigrants, particularly the women, wore modern and revealing clothes. The promiscuity of the immigrants provoked religious Muslims. Incidentally, the religious Jews who had come to Zion only to pray and to die felt the same. Here we can find the roots of the coalition between Arabs and strictly orthodox Jews.

The men and women of this second Aliyah also caused a stir with their Marxist leanings, which they mixed with Zionism (which was also regarded by devout Jews as blasphemous) to create "socialist Zionism".

Although the political movement of Zionism in the nineteenth century had ideological forerunners (e.g. the "Lovers of Zion" in Russia), Zionism was not established as an organisation until 1897 by Theodor Herzl.

In short, these developments unsettled the pre-modern, traditional and, as a rule, deeply religious Arab Palestinians. They sensed almost instinctively that danger was imminent. It was not long before they took up arms. One of the numerous legends surrounding the Arab-Israeli conflict is that everything was sunshine and roses between Jews and Arabs until 1917–18 (when the British arrived).

A clash of civilisations and cultures was looming. Neither side—neither the Zionist Jews nor the Arabs—wanted it to happen. Objectively, however, it was unavoidable. And fate took its course.

Immediately before the Zionist immigration began in 1882, the overall population of the Holy Land, including the Jewish population, had increased dramatically for the reasons mentioned above. Scholars (although they disagree, of course) generally provide the following population figures for 1882:

• Overall population: 450,000
• Palestinian Arabs: 426,000
• Jews: 24,000

From 1882 to the outbreak of World War I, a huge development occurred in the Holy Land. This is reflected in the population figures (again only estimated by experts) for 1914:

• Overall population: 685,000
• Palestinian Arabs: 600,000
• Jews: 85,000

Compared with the figures for the Palestinian Arabs, the Jewish population increased rapidly. This was the result of immigration and was not a natural increase.

This was not the case with the Palestinians. The increase in their numbers was mainly the result of natural population growth. This is an important historical point because we often hear that the improved economy in the Holy Land from 1882 had attracted many Arabs from other regions. This assertion is not true and does not apply to later periods up to 1948 either, when the Jewish state was established. Population growth maintained the same pattern until 1948. This means that approximately 75% of the growth in the Jewish population can be attributed to immigration. The growth of the Palestinian population was the result of a natural increase. Up to 1948, the annual growth in the number of Jewish inhabitants was approximately 9%, while the same figure for the Palestinians was just under 3%.

Hospitality: yes; foreign domination: no. This was the opinion of the powerless rulers in Istanbul. The Palestinian Arabs felt the same, of course. They were not owners or possessors of the Holy Land either, but they were its inhabitants. They lived in an area that was largely populated only by them. This created peace and security. As is almost always and everywhere the case, insecurity arises when areas are populated by different peoples. And this is precisely what was happening again in the Holy Land. Disaster was inevitable. Even the British, who ruled in the Holy Land from 1917 to 1948, tried to prevent the population groups from mixing, starting in 1922. But it was too late to stop it. Not even Britain, a world power, could do anything about it.

The British in the Holy Land
(Twentieth Century)

Step by step, Britain—the world power—had drawn closer to the Holy Land. In 1704, Gibraltar was conquered during the War of the Spanish Succession. In 1757, the British took control of India. There was a need to establish a permanent and reliable link between the mother country and India. At least that was what politicians in London wanted. And this is precisely what happened over the course of the next two centuries. And between London and New Delhi lay the Holy Land. This made it strategically important for the British.

The British lion crept towards the Holy Land from different directions, closing the circle ever tighter. Malta was conquered in 1800, Aden was occupied in 1839, and in 1875 Britain acquired shares in the Suez Canal, which was inaugurated in 1869. The British had also ruled Egypt since their occupation of the country in 1882. By the end of the nineteenth century, "defence agreements" had been concluded with almost every small principality on the Persian Gulf (with Kuwait in 1899, for example). In 1907, the British shared power and influence with the Russians in Iran.

Britain tried to prevent other countries such as Germany from entering and advancing into the region. Construction of the Berlin-Baghdad railway, for example, met with fierce resistance from the British.

Finally, so the British hoped, the Ottoman Empire appeared to be losing control over the Holy Land and Arabia. World War I broke out. Britain wanted to achieve even more "security" in the Middle East along its route to India. But the foray into the Holy Land was in no way quick. On the contrary. Thanks to help from the Germans, the supposedly weak Ottoman

© The Author(s), under exclusive license to Springer Nature Switzerland AG 2021
M. Wolffsohn, *Whose Holy Land?*, https://doi.org/10.1007/978-3-030-74286-7_24

Empire was initially successful on the battlefield. London had not expected this. It thus went looking for allies in the Middle East. It found them in the Arabs.

Like the Turks, the Arabs were Muslims, but they saw the Ottoman rulers with good reason as foreign occupiers. They too wanted self-determination. The beginnings of Arab nationalism date back to the nineteenth century. Their cause appeared to attract support because Britain hoped to win their favour.

Above all, the British promised an independent Arab kingdom to Sharif Hussein from the Hashemite family, the keeper of the holy Islamic sites in the cities of Mecca and Medina. In view of the world war, London wanted to establish "a firm and lasting alliance" with the Arabs. Their intended result was formulated by Sir Henry McMahon, the British High Commissioner, on behalf of his government on 24 October 1915: "... the expulsion of the Turks from the Arab countries and the freeing of the Arab peoples from the Turkish yoke, which for so many years has pressed heavily upon them."

The promised region was also specified in this infamous McMahon letter. To this day, Arabs, British and Jews as well as historians and politicians still argue over whether Palestine was part of this agreement. This debate is pointless for two reasons. Firstly, the borders are plain to see for anyone who reads the letter and who consults a map. He will see that the Holy Land belonged to the promised Arab territory. But the debate is also pointless for a much more important reason. The British government had no intention whatsoever of keeping the promise they were making. (Incidentally, this issue is accurately depicted in the film "Lawrence of Arabia".)

The military contribution of the Arab Revolt against the Turks, which began on 5 June 1916 on the Arabian Peninsula (not in the Holy Land), was of little significance to the British. But this does not justify their misleading promise.

It is easy to prove the deceitful and shameless nature of the promise the British government made to the Arabs. At almost the same time (1915–16), the British were planning an entirely different partition of the expected Ottoman prize, together with the Russians, the French, the Italians and the Greeks. But, as many English politicians asked themselves, why share this with so many rivals? The answer was the Anglo-French Sykes-Picot Agreement of 16 May 1916. This agreement largely awarded to Britain control of the Holy Land and Mesopotamia. France was to receive Lebanon and Syria. At the time, of course, these areas still belonged to the Ottoman Empire.

But that was not all. 'Better safe than sorry' was the thinking of the British government. This is why, on 2 November 1917, it also promised the Holy Land to the Zionists, having previously offered it to the Arabs as well. In reality, however, it had always intended to keep this region for itself. This promise went down in history as the Balfour Declaration. The then British foreign secretary Balfour set it out in writing in a letter to Lord Rothschild: "Dear Lord Rothschild, I have much pleasure in conveying to you, on behalf of His Majesty's Government, the following declaration of sympathy with Jewish Zionist aspirations which has been submitted to, and approved by, the Cabinet. 'His Majesty's Government view with favour the establishment in Palestine of a national home for the Jewish people, and will use their best endeavours to facilitate the achievement of this object, it being clearly understood that nothing shall be done which may prejudice the civil and religious rights of the existing non-Jewish communities in Palestine, or the rights and political status enjoyed by the Jews in any other country'. I should be grateful if you would bring this declaration to the knowledge of the Zionist Federation."

The text is extremely interesting in the context of the history of Zionism and the Israeli-Palestinian conflict (these themes are covered, for example, in the book "Nahost", which I wrote together with Friedrich Schreiber). But our sole concern here is the question of who owns the Holy Land, and only in the context of changes in possession.

Before London had even taken possession of the Ottoman Empire or parts of it, Britain behaved as if it were the owner. It audaciously promised everybody everything but ultimately kept it all for itself. A thing that was acquired unlawfully was then deliberately, i.e. for reasons of power, given to others. The British government acted as if the Holy Land were something it owned. In Yiddish, this is called "chutzpah", or audacity. Or should we call it fraud?

Its French ally was fobbed off with a small region that, as of 1920, it had to defend against the Arabs using military means and against the British using political and diplomatic means with no holds barred.

Following his government's political scam and the victorious battle for Jerusalem, the British conqueror acted out a scene. On 9 December 1917, General Allenby entered the city with his troops. Upon reaching the Jaffa Gate, he descended from his horse because he wanted to enter the Holy City as a pilgrim and not as a conqueror. Of all things! In front of him was the Holy City, behind him were his armed forces. However, neither the Jews nor the Palestinians challenged the general about his claim to be a pilgrim. The Jewish inhabitants received General Allenby with enthusiasm, while the Palestinians gave him a friendly welcome. But the new occupier only gained military control over the Holy Land, Syria and Lebanon by autumn 1918. The death of the "sick man of Europe" was slow and long.

There was eager excitement amongst Zionists and Palestinian nationalists. Everyone hoped that Britain would "liberate" them, grant them independence, and hand the land over to them—their land, the Holy Land, the territory they considered their own. There is no need to discuss the pan-Arabian perspective here. It is more of an internal Arabian issue. The objective was a single Arab state and not several smaller Arab states. This idea has been seen in the Palestinian national movement. It was unable to truly gain acceptance among the Palestinians and other Arabs.

Once again, the Holy Land had new occupiers. Britain now was in control of the region and acted as if it were the owner. On 24 July 1922, the British had their coup with regard to Mesopotamia and the Holy Land (called "Palestine" since the Roman era) legitimised on an international level by the League of Nations. The French did the same with regard to Syria and Lebanon.

And so this sham became international law. It was a scandal for its treatment of the Arabs and the Zionists alike. It was victor's justice. But it was passed off as international law. The term used in "international law" was "mandate". This word is related to the Latin word "manus" (or hand). The mandate was thus a trusteeship. Trusteeships are assumed, for example, for under-age persons. And this is precisely how the League of Nations regarded the inhabitants of the Middle East and of the Holy Land. Independence would not be granted to them until they were "mature" enough to receive this status. In other words, neither Britain nor France was willing to one day *voluntarily* give up their trusteeship. On the contrary, they intended to convert their mandated territories into colonies—with the aid of international law.

Neither the Zionists nor the Palestinians harboured any illusions about this situation. They disagreed intensely about how to rid themselves of the mandate. It would be a mistake to lump together all Zionists or all Palestinian groups and to lose sight of their fundamental differences of opinion. But apart from collaborators, everyone was waiting for their opportunity—to take action against the British. Essentially, the Zionists wanted to realise their own state at the expense of the Palestinians, while the Palestinians wanted to realise their own state at the expense of the Zionists. Again, these objectives were of course not expressed as such, and each of the two camps of course consisted of two groups: the militant "hawks" and the gentle "doves". The "hawks" and "doves" agreed on their objective but disagreed vehemently on how to achieve it.

There is no doubt that the Zionists acted and thought more politically than the Palestinians. In other words, they never lost sight of their strategic goal but made tactical compromises. They were willing and able to take a step back in order to take two leaps forward. Zionist politicians had realised that (for the time being) nothing could be achieved against the will of the major powers or the various occupiers of the Holy Land.

Even Theodor Herzl, the founder of the World Zionist Organization, was guided by this realisation. Indeed, he seemed at times to have no other principle. He negotiated with the Ottomans to persuade them (incidentally with the assistance of the German emperor Wilhelm II and others) to grant the Jews the sought-after "national home in Palestine". It is clear that the Turks had no interest in seeing their already weak position undermined by even more Jewish immigrants or by a national home.

It must be emphasised that there was no official mention at the time of a Jewish *state*, despite the fact that it was Herzl's actual objective. The title of his programmatic book (which was published in 1896, one year before the World Zionist Organization was founded) was "The Jewish State". The strategic goal was a state, while the tactical goal was a "national home" protected under international law.

After World War I, most Zionist politicians believed that they would initially be able to achieve more by acting *alongside* rather than *against* Britain. Gradually, however, this policy become increasingly controversial among Zionists.

Many historians disagree about whether British politicians were "pro-Zionist" or "pro-Arab". This dispute among historians (like many others) is pointless because the answer is simple: the British were pursuing British policies.

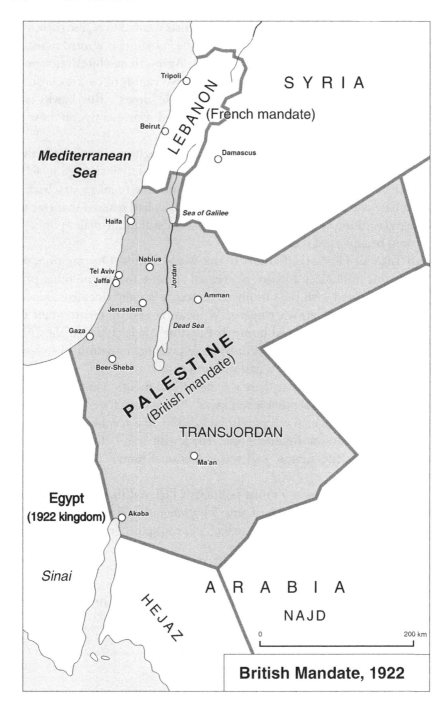

British Mandate, 1922

They played Zionists off against Palestinians and vice versa. They wanted neither the Palestinians nor the Jews to have Palestine. They wanted to keep it. Divide et impera—"divide and rule"—has been the name of this cruel game since Roman times.

The British Mandate for Palestine passed by the League of Nations in July 1922 consisted roughly of the following areas:

* Israel proper of today within its borders prior to the conquests of the Six-Day War
* The territory east of the Jordan River
* The territory west of the Jordan River and
* The Gaza Strip

But by 1921 the British government had already set aside four fifths of the mandated territory: not for the Zionists or the Palestinians, but for the Hashemite family. It was an act of compensation—at the expense of the Jews and the Palestinians.

The head of the Hashemites in 1915 was Sharif Hussein. The British had promised him independence and control over the Holy Land, which they had taken and kept for themselves in 1917–18. Their intention was to compensate the Hashemite family with Syria and Lebanon. This upset France, which used military power in July 1920 to drive Emir Faisal, one of Sharif Hussein's sons, out of Damascus. The ball was now in London's court. It had far too blatantly deceived the Hashemites. Emir Abdallah, another of the sharif's sons, stormed northwards with his troops to "liberate" Syria from the French for his family, but London had to prevent this to avoid problems with Paris and a role in a military conflict. What should they do? The first answer the British came up with—primarily advanced by the colonial secretary Winston Churchill in March 1921—was to keep Mesopotamia, convert it into a kingdom, and name Faisal king of Iraq in 1921.

The second answer was to give Emir Abdallah the territory east of the Jordan River (Transjordan) as a consolation. This did not satisfy the Hashemites, who were understandably upset, but it did pacify them, especially because they were stumbling into a conflict with the House of Ibn Saud in their homeland (the Hejaz, a region in the west of the Arabian Peninsula). They lost the conflict and, in turn, their control over the Hejaz in 1925. The new ruler was now Ibn Saud, who named his kingdom "Saudi Arabia".

But back to the Hashemites in Transjordan, which became an emirate in 1921 although it was still part of the British mandated territory of Palestine. The British imported the ruling family of this emirate, which became a kingdom in 1946 (Kingdom of Jordan).

The Zionists described this step as the "first partition of Palestine". And the Palestinians were rightly also outraged. Winston Churchill had simply forced a foreign ruling family upon them. It was an Islamic family and an Arab family, but it was nonetheless foreign—and it remains so today.

King Hussein of Jordan (an honest, friendly, brave and tactically skilled man) was the grandson of the first emir (and later king) of Transjordan. No matter how wisely he governed, the Palestinians remained hostile because they no longer wanted foreign rule, not even Arab rule. At the time, the Palestinians represented the overwhelming majority of the population of (Trans)Jordan. This is even more true today, when they make up as much as sixty to seventy-five percent of Jordan's population. It is therefore only a matter of time before they rid themselves of this foreign rule. Although they deny that they are planning this, they have made several attempts (for example in 1958 and from 1968 to 1970). Will the volcano erupt? It is certainly not extinguished.

And so, since 1921 the Hashemites (and King Hussein) have only actually represented themselves and some of their minions, but not "their people". They do not even have a people as such, apart from the traditional support they receive from Transjordanian Bedouins and their descendants. The latter have been happy about any partners who can help counterbalance the power of their urban Palestinian rivals.

Even in 1921, the decision made by the British was "reactionary" because it was intended to turn back the hands of time. Someone who wishes to turn something back or "reverse" (Latin: reagere) something is "reactionary". Churchill wanted to continue, in the twentieth century, to make decisions behind closed doors without taking into consideration the will of the majority.

British politics were not only immoral. On closer examination, they were a violation of international law, a fragile construction that had not always distorted the political truth about the Holy Land but had considerably whitewashed it. The text of the 1922 mandate dealing with the territory of Transjordan (Article 24) states: "In the territories lying between the Jordan and the eastern boundary of Palestine as ultimately determined, the Mandatory shall be entitled, with the consent of the Council of the League of Nations, to postpone or withhold application of such provisions of this mandate as he may consider inapplicable to the existing local conditions".

And so the British were able to do or not do whatever they wanted in the territory. And they wanted to give the Hashemites some form of compensation, albeit at the expense of the Palestinians and Zionists. At the same time, they had pledged in the preamble of the mandate to keep the promise they had made to the Jews: "The Mandatory should be responsible for putting into effect the declaration originally made on 2 November 1917." What this refers to is the Balfour Declaration, i.e. the "establishment in Palestine of a national home for the Jewish people".

Was this promise now more important than the others, even more important than the "land-grab" politics of the British and the French? Far from it, because Article 25 wrenched from the Jewish people four fifths of the gift that the giver only had at its disposal by virtue of its power and not by virtue of ownership rights.

The British showed their lack of interest in the "establishment in Palestine of a national home for the Jewish people" just three months after the adoption of the Mandate for Palestine. In June 1922, Winston Churchill published a white paper. In it, it said: "Palestine as a whole should not be converted into a Jewish National Home." Moreover, "[Jewish] immigration cannot be so great in volume as to exceed whatever may be the economic capacity of the country at the time to absorb new arrivals." And finally, "... a Legislative Council [should be established] containing a large proportion of members elected on a wide franchise." This meant that now, instead of a Jewish national home (not a state!), a Jewish-Arab home should be formed pro forma—not a national but a binational home, i.e. a home for both peoples. Naturally, Britain intended to continue being the "master of the house". London acted and ruled in the name of international law because the natives were apparently not "mature" enough yet for independence. This was a cynical farce.

Despite being annoyed and angry, the immigrant Zionists remained on the defensive because at the time they were still far too weak to attack anyone (whomever that may have been). They needed to gain time to allow more people to come to strengthen their position.

Passions were inflamed in the Arab world too, particularly among the Palestinians. They wanted self-determination, considered (and still consider) the Holy Land to be theirs, and clearly realised that they were facing an imminent threat, either in the form of British or Jewish rule or from both sides.

The Palestinians thus went on the offensive, and they were brutal even then. On the very first anniversary of the Balfour Declaration on 2 November

1918, violent anti-British (and of course anti-Zionistic) demonstrations broke out in Jerusalem. In April 1920, a fanatical Arab mob stormed Jerusalem's Jewish quarter during the Nabi Musa festival in Jerusalem. In May 1921, there was violent unrest above all in the port city of Jaffa. The Arab-Palestinian population felt that the Zionists were acting not only on behalf of British capitalism but also on the basis of blasphemous Communist ideas. A strange political mixture was being assumed here, but fear does not necessarily lend itself to clear thinking. And we must understand that the Palestinians felt threatened and cheated by everyone around them. But we must also understand the anger of the Zionists, particularly the socialist Zionists, who meant so well in everything they did and yet made so many mistakes—at least as far as the Palestinians were concerned. The latter did not want to be ruled by the English or to be "liberated" by the socialist Zionists.

The Zionists also wanted to liberate the Jewish people (and thus themselves too), namely from the agony of several hundred years of diaspora. They believed that the place of liberation could only be the "Land of the Fathers". They only wanted to return and not to conquer or seize land as was the case approximately 3300 years before, i.e. in Biblical times. The opponents of the socialist Zionists, the right-of-centre nationalist "revisionists" under Vladimir Jabotinsky (one of the spiritual fathers of Menachem Begin, Yitzshak Shamir and Ariel Sharon), did not harbour many illusions. They did not believe that the Arabs were willing to be liberated by the Jews. Instead, they believed that the Arabs would forcefully defend the land that they too regarded as their own. And understandably so. This is why Jabotinsky argued that the Zionists should build an "iron wall" around their community. The Arabs would repeatedly bang their heads against it but would ultimately realise that the wall came away better than their heads. As is so often the case with the socialist Zionists, good intentions do not equal good policies because

- The British intended to continue their occupation and
- The Palestinians—like the Jews—regarded (and still regard) themselves

as the true owners of the Holy Land.

The conflict was predestined and unavoidable but at the beginning deferrable. The deferral came after the year 1922 for two reasons. Firstly, the British had stabilised their position in the Middle East, and secondly, the number of Jewish immigrants began to drop again. Only in the confusion after World War I and the Russian Revolution did Jews set off for Palestine. In any case, the majority favoured the United States over the Holy Land. A typical pattern in Zionist and Israeli history is clearly seen here. Only a minority choose to go to Zion. The majority (insofar as they want to or have to move) prefer "the good life".

The Palestinians were hopeful, the British were pleased, and the Zionists were worried. But not for long. By 1928–29, the crisis of the Zionists was over. Once again, Jewish immigrants arrived. The autumn of 1929 marked the beginning of the Great Depression. The "good life" was becoming less and less common outside the Holy Land.

Germany under Adolf Hitler went from persecuting Jews in 1933, to murdering them in 1938, to destroying them in 1941. Poland too witnessed a dramatic surge in anti-Semitism at the beginning of the 1930s (before the country was invaded by the Germans). The majority of Jews who immigrated to the Holy Land starting in 1932–33 came from Poland. Only 18% came from Germany. But this was still a new German-Jewish record. Prior to this time, the German Jews had shown little interest in Zionism. The majority of them even rejected it. They repeatedly proclaimed they were doing fine in Germany.

"Why should we suffer the consequences of Polish and German anti-Semitism?", asked the Palestinians, but the question was mostly rhetorical. They went from defence to attack and, in August 1929, massacred Jews above all in Jerusalem and Hebron. Ironically, most of the victims were Orthodox Jews, who (as we know from the first part of this book) also to this day oppose Zionism.

Even this cruel slaughter failed to help the Palestinians, although a report issued by the British government took sides with the Palestinian perpetrators. Nevertheless, even more Jews came to Palestine. As a result, the Palestinians attempted to revolt from 1936 to 1939, initially against the Jews and later against the British and the Jews. In the end, they lost in military terms (despite receiving military assistance from Germany, i.e. the National Socialists) but won in political terms.

They won politically because World War II was approaching, and Britain needed peace in the Middle East. The Arabs, however, were anxious because the Palestinians had been brutally overpowered by the British until early 1939. In other Arab regions too, especially Egypt and Iraq, the supporters of independence were becoming louder and louder. For these Arabs, independence meant: "Out with the British." This would have been a catastrophe for London because the Middle East was of major strategic importance. This assessment was proven right during the war.

The British now had to use every means available to win the Arabs over as a partner in their fight against Hitler. If nothing else, the Arabs were to remain outside the conflict. A highly symbolic and effective step for the British mandatory power was to put a stop to Jewish immigration to Palestine. This option became official government policy on 17 May 1939, when it was published in a white paper. It also became illegal to sell Palestinian land to Zionists. The end of Zionism appeared to be near.

World War II—and hence the Holocaust—began. British policies appeared to have failed in Palestine in light of the blatant hardship of the Jews of Europe. But wasn't the objective of defeating Hitler so morally right that it was necessary to tolerate this immorality? This at least was the argument in London (and Washington!)—even during World War II, when millions of Jews were being murdered.

The assertion that Hitler inadvertently promoted the establishment of Israel is heard again and again. Repetition of an untrue statement does not, however, make it true. I have discussed this issue in detail in my book "Ewige Schuld? Vierzig Jahre deutsch-jüdisch-israelische Beziehung". Here are just a few points that are relevant in this context:

- The Holocaust may have accelerated but did not make possible the foundation of Israel.
- The Holocaust was a major boost for Zionism within Judaism. It proved to the majority of Jews, who until then had been opposed to Zionism, that Zionism was right because it had always warned about the threat of homicidal anti-Semitism.

Some people (including historians, particularly Israeli historians) have even claimed that Zionist leaders, above all David Ben-Gurion, deliberately did nothing about the Holocaust precisely because they hoped it would make Zionism more legitimate. But what could they have done? Utter passiveness, on the other hand, would have been foolish—even suicidal. The Jews who did come voluntarily to Palestine were Eastern European Jews. And they were the main victims of the Holocaust.

It is said that, after 1945, supporters of the establishment of Israel repeatedly cited the Holocaust as a justification for their cause. But we must see the withdrawal of the British and the founding of Israel in a global historical context, namely in connection with decolonisation. What Africa's less modern peoples have achieved as a result of decolonisation could surely also have been achieved by the well-organised Zionists, who had been single-mindedly developing their community since 1882.

"We have to foot the bill for the Holocaust", claim many Palestinians. Their anger at the establishment of Israel is understandable. But their reasoning is wrong. A British plan for dividing Palestine already existed in 1937 but was withdrawn with the White Paper of May 1939. Nevertheless, the Zionist train had already left the station and was hurtling through the political landscape.

In one respect, however, the Palestinians did indeed have to foot the bill, namely for a state of affairs they themselves had created. Like some Arab nationalists (e.g. in Egypt and Iraq), the Palestinians had sided with Germany in World War II. The Palestinian leader Amin al-Husseini (the Grand Mufti of Jerusalem) sought help and guidance from the German Führer, Adolf Hitler, in the struggle against the British. This pious man from the East even offered active support for the annihilation of the Jews. We must not forget that German troops fought in Northern Africa from February 1941 to November 1942. Many Jews lived there, and North African Jews began to be transported to Eastern European extermination camps.

This type of active cooperation was largely unknown to Western politicians after the war. The decisive point for them was that the Palestinians had sided with the adversary and were thus unreliable. Nonetheless, Western politicians (particularly in London) were happy to forget certain things in the early phase of the Cold War. As its goal was to curb the advance of the Communists, Britain could not afford the luxury of putting morals above realistic politics and did not want to either.

British politicians did not sense a moral connection between themselves and the Zionists anyway. Even before World War II, some right-wing Zionists demanded that action be taken not only against the Palestinians but also against the British. They were unable to assert their demand at that time, but in 1944 there was no stopping them. In this year, Menachem Begin, the leader of the military arm of the revisionists (Etzel), announced a "rebellion" against the mandatory power. This small militant group was a great embarrassment for Britain in the Holy Land. The means used by Begin and his followers were anything but holy. Their approach and mind-set were reminiscent of the Zealots. They themselves found (and still find) this comparison rather flattering. We are told that you cannot argue about questions of taste. But sometimes we should in order to show where we stand. Because the way we interpret the past is always a political signal in the present.

Even after the murder of millions of European Jews, the British government refused to allow survivors to immigrate to Palestine. The obstinacy of the British annoyed not only Zionists but also the general public in the Western world. The Zionist leaders expected and took advantage of this. They leased one refugee ship after the other, knowing full well that the British navy would intercept them off the coast of the Holy Land and place the refugees in inhumane internment camps. This was fuel for anti-British and thus pro-Zionist propaganda. The story of the refugee ship "Exodus" is well known, either from the bestseller by Leon Uris or from the film based on this book.

The militant right-wing Zionists under Begin bombed the British out, while the left-wing Zionists opted for the equally effective weapon of propaganda (see "Exodus"). The Palestinians too wanted to see the immediate withdrawal of the British from the region. In the United States, the people (and President Truman, beginning in October 1946) were appalled at the stupidity, obstinacy and immorality of the British. In February 1947, the British government gave up. It left the problem of Palestine to the UN. The two remaining parties to the conflict, the Zionists and the Palestinians, now increased their military and diplomatic efforts.

The Founding of Israel: Palestine Becomes Jordan

On 29 November 1947, after a long diplomatic struggle, the United Nations General Assembly believed that it had found the solution to the Zionist-Palestinian conflict: the division of the Holy Land.

The rationale behind it was simple. Since the two peoples in that region appeared to be unable to live together, they had to be separated. Jerusalem was to be placed under international administration.

Dividing the region did not solve the problem, however. The two-thirds majority in the UN General Assembly, which was required and achieved, should have known that. This is because, in August 1947, British India had been partitioned into two independent states. Millions were murdered and killed in the resulting population transfer.

Strictly speaking, the plan of the UN minority was a provocation for the Jewish side. It provided for the following. There was to be a federal state consisting of a Jewish and an Arab state. Jerusalem was to be the capital of this federal state, the government of which would be responsible for defence and foreign affairs. This concept would have led to a Lebanon-like scenario. Disruption and paralysis would have been inevitable.

In addition, the plan allowed for the immigration of Jews into the Jewish state for 3 years—in accordance with the "absorptive capacity" of the country. That was a clear drawback. Moreover, the "absorptive capacity" was to be determined by three Jewish, three Arab and three UN representatives. It is understandable that the Zionists rejected such measures in and for their own state, all the more so after the Holocaust.

© The Author(s), under exclusive license to Springer Nature Switzerland AG 2021
M. Wolffsohn, *Whose Holy Land?*, https://doi.org/10.1007/978-3-030-74286-7_25

Because of the partition and the resulting possibility of founding a state of their own, albeit on a small territory, the Zionist politicians reluctantly accepted the partition plan.

The Palestinians rejected the plan outright. They immediately took up arms (as early as 30 November 1947)—and lost everything in the end. They even forfeited a state of their own, which the UN had intended for them.

Even before the foundation of the State of Israel on 14 May 1948, the Palestinians had been militarily defeated by the Zionists. Some had already been expelled or had fled. Both things happened and each side propagated their own views. The most objective and self-critical views can be found in Israel (which comes as no real surprise), where much has recently been uncovered about the issue of expulsion. Probably the best analyses have been made by Benny Morris. Interested readers should consult his book "The Birth of the Palestinian Refugee Problem, 1948–1949" (Cambridge 1987). Meir Pa'il, the Israeli military historian (and retired major), also gave an accurate and self-critical account of the controversy over "flight or expulsion": "About one third of Palestinian refugees decided to flee of their own free will, especially at the beginning of the war [i.e. since November 1947]. Another third fled because of psychological measures of the Jews. They were told it would be better for them to leave of their own free will than to be conquered. The final third were expelled by force."

Israel since 1948

What were these "psychological measures"? Here one example from 15 May 1948. Israeli soldiers gave Palestinian inhabitants of a Jerusalem district the following advice through loudspeakers: "Leave this bloodshed. Surrender with your weapons. You will suffer no harm … If you stay, you will cause a disaster."

Two thirds of the Palestinians were expelled; one third fled hoping soon to return to "their own country" as winners. "Hundreds of thousands decided to leave their home country. Their decision was reinforced by several "national committees" founded mainly in Jaffa by militant nationalists who assured them that their exile would only be temporary, only weeks or months. This time would be needed by allied Arab armies to beat the Zionist armed forces." This was reported not by an Israeli "court historian" but by Salah Khalaf, since assassinated, also known as Abu Iyad. He was the head of intelligence of Fatah, the largest PLO group.

How many people were living in the Holy Land in 1948? How many Jews, how many Palestinians? Let us look at the figures. On the eve of the foundation of the State of Israel,

- Around 600,000 Jews
- And almost 1.3 million Palestinians were living there

That means roughly one Jew for every two Palestinians. In other words, about as many Jews were living in the Holy Land in 1948 as Palestinians were in 1918. At the end of World War I, only a small number of Jews were living in the Holy Land, i.e. about 54,000. That was almost 30,000 less than before World War I. Most of them had emigrated.

Let us now look at the figures on the date of Israeli independence, which take into account flight and expulsion.

On 15 May 1948 (one day after independence), the State of Israel was home to

- Around 650,000 Jews
- And only 156,000 Palestinians

A dramatic change had occurred as a result of dramatic developments. In other words, the Jewish state had become almost "free of Arabs".

But it was not only the Israelis who took away from the Palestinians "their land" during the war (which, by the way, was more than the UN had earmarked for the Jewish state). On 14 May 1948, the State of Israel was proclaimed by David Ben-Gurion, the first prime minister of Israel. The Palestinians, who had already been defeated in the civil war, asked their Arab brothers for help and they came: for example Egyptians, Iraqis, Lebanese, and Syrians. One of them took from the Palestinians the rest of the territory assigned to them by the UN. It was Emir Abdullah of Transjordan (king since 1946). He conquered the Old City of Jerusalem and the entire West Bank. In December 1948, he was celebrated by his supporters as a "liberator" and incorporated the West Bank and East Jerusalem into his kingdom. He called it Jordan, because he now "owned" both banks of the Jordan River, not only the east bank (Transjordan). Abdullah announced that the next step would be the "liberation" of the entire territory of Palestine.

That was the public message. Behind the scenes, he had long ago signalled to his old Israeli friends that he had not the slightest interest in doing this. He wanted to pacify the Palestinians (who had a grudge against him since his rule in Transjordan). His motto was control by annexation. It was an ill-conceived approach because now the population of Jordan was more Palestinian than before.

Jordan's gulp from the Palestinian bottle was too large, and between 1948 and 1967 Abdullah and his successors were faced with discontent. The Palestinians of the West Bank and East Jerusalem were rightly rebellious and dissatisfied since nearly all the money for further development in Jordan flowed into the East Bank, including the money earned from tourism in Jerusalem.

Jerusalem was not a priority for the Jordanian kings because Amman remained the capital. This pattern has been repeated since the times of Islamic conquest. Political analysts should pay more attention to deeds than to words. This is illustrated by the example of Arabic policy and propaganda when it comes to Jerusalem. Jerusalem was not irrelevant to the Arabs (not since the times of the crusades) but it was never of central importance despite assertions to the contrary.

The Palestinians also lost the Gaza Strip. While Egypt did not annex the Gaza Strip, it "administered" it. Here again, the Palestinians had to obey, this time Egyptian leaders.

By annexing the West Bank, Jordan violated international law because the UN had allocated it to the Palestinian state. East Jerusalem was to be placed under international administration and was to belong neither to Israel nor to Jordan. As a result, only two states recognised this annexation: Britain, which was Jordan's traditional protecting power, and Pakistan.

"Returning" these territories to Jordan today would therefore not restore international law. This land never belonged to Jordan. It was part of the British mandate and this area was subdivided. But the moral basis of that mandate, which was fully supported by international law, is shaky. I have emphasised this on several occasions to show that international law in this case does injustice to nations.

Egypt controlled the Gaza Strip like Jordan controlled the West Bank and East Jerusalem. But Egypt adhered to international law by merely "administering" the Gaza Strip. But administration and control are by no means mutually exclusive.

The United Nations, which is an entity of international law (like the League of Nations with respect to the British mandate), has been indignant at Israel's Jerusalem policy since 1949. Contrary to international law, Israel declared West Jerusalem its capital. But the same United Nations was much less bothered by Jordan's annexation of East Jerusalem. There are numerous examples of the dubious moral authority of this institution. These doubts also apply, by the way, to the consent to the partition of Palestine, which was a major contribution to the foundation of Israel. (Israel would have been founded without the UN, but it would have been at a later date and more difficult.)

Non-involved third states (with highly dubious justifications and not always clean records) decided for and about two others. That was rather presumptuous. But can and should we simply accept a conflict between two contentious parties without trying to contain or even settle it? That, too, would be immoral. We thus face a dilemma. The closing section will briefly discuss this issue and possible solutions. But before that, an account of the remaining changes in possession should be completed.

The following fact must be borne in mind: today, about three quarters of the inhabitants of Jordan are Palestinians. So how Jordanian is Jordan?

"Greater Israel": Jewish or Democratic? Of Federations and Confederations

From a historical perspective, the state of Israel that was founded in 1948 was outside the ancient Jewish heartland. This area included the territories west and east of the Jordan River, rather than the coastal plains where the Philistines used to live, or Galilee, which was Judaised during the time preceding the birth of Jesus and which is home to a majority Arab population, or the Negev Desert. Although this desert played an important role along the trade route between the Red Sea and the Mediterranean Sea, we must not forget that many Arab tribes moved through this territory or lived there. Tourists, for example, can still today admire the desert city of Arad.

From a state, political and geographical perspective, in other words in terms of borders, the Jews did not actually "return". Only reluctantly did Israel accept this "mini-Luxembourg", as some Israeli "hawks" call it. The Six-Day War in June 1967 created a new situation. The causes and the history of this war are not our focus here; our attention will remain on changes in possession. During the Six-Day War, Israel captured

- East Jerusalem
- The West Bank
- The (Syrian) Golan Heights
- The (Egyptian) Sinai Peninsula, and last but not least
- The Gaza Strip

The "return" was completed, the "land of the fathers" was once again in Jewish possession. Although this territory did not include the East Bank, even the most greedy Israeli "hawks" were satisfied with this (partial) return.

© The Author(s), under exclusive license to Springer Nature Switzerland AG 2021
M. Wolffsohn, *Whose Holy Land?*, https://doi.org/10.1007/978-3-030-74286-7_26

As a result of this "return" of the Jews to "their land", many Palestinians from the West Bank had to flee "their land" once again. Let us be clear about one thing. For many Palestinians, this "return" meant expulsion.

This is a statement that is bound to cause great indignation among many people, but I have a witness above all suspicion: former Israeli president Chaim Herzog. In 1967, he was a military commander and was responsible for this operation. Approximately two hundred thousand Palestinians (an enormous but unfortunately realistic number) were "persuaded" that they had to leave the territory. Israeli vehicles were "generously" made available to them. In November 1991, Herzog reported about this "human expulsion".

One can easily imagine what fate the Jews would have suffered if they had lost the Six-Day War. The reader is reminded of the various massacres that took place in the Arab world: in Lebanon (since 1975 during the civil war), in Syria (1982), in Iraq (1991), in Kuwait (1990/91) and in Jordan (1970). The hate propaganda was unambiguous. No, the Arab side in general and the Palestinians in particular have no right to throw stones. They too are sitting in a glass house. This has repeatedly been demonstrated by terrorist acts of the PLO, especially since 1968. Murder is murder, no matter how pure the motives may be.

Israel did not fully *incorporate* all the territories. It incorporated *East Jerusalem* and did so immediately after the conquest in June 1967. This is an important fact that explains why the Israelis stubbornly insisted before and since the beginning of Middle East Peace Conferences that no Palestinian from East Jerusalem represented the Palestinian people. The Israelis regarded these Palestinians as inhabitants (but not citizens) of their state. The (Oslo II) accord on Palestinian autonomy that was signed by the Rabin-Peres government and PLO Chairman Arafat in September 1995 brought about a fundamental change: Palestinians in East Jerusalem were granted the right to vote and to stand as candidates in Palestinian elections.

The Golan Heights were annexed in December 1981, exactly one day after the imposition of martial law in Poland. The world's attention was focused on Eastern Europe. In the Middle East, Prime Minister Menachem Begin and his Israeli "hawk" government took advantage of this (for them) favourable situation. In this respect too, the Rabin and Peres governments signalled a fundamental change. They informed the Israeli public in rather unambiguous terms that they would have to relinquish the Golan Heights in exchange for peace with Syria.

A large piece of land was returned during the period from 1974 to 1982: Egyptian territory on the west side of the Suez Canal, which had been captured (in October 1973) during the Yom Kippur War. By 1982, the entire

Sinai Peninsula had been returned to Egypt. As a result of the peace treaty that was concluded between Israel and Egypt (with considerable assistance from the United States), Israel withdrew from this land area, which is of huge strategic importance (a buffer zone and access to the Red Sea) and huge economic importance (oil and tourism).

In 2005, Israel withdrew from the Gaza Strip hoping to gain "peace for land". It turned out to be a misjudgement. Israel got rockets for land.

The Jewish State has pursued an intensive settlement policy since 1977. This has been a time when the nationalist Likud party shaped the policies of the Jewish state. Mostly, that is. Menachem Begin, Ariel Sharon and Benjamin Netanjahu were the strategists behind this settlement policy.

The Palestinians could have avoided this development if they had joined the Israeli-Egyptian peace process in 1978–79. Palestinian participation in both the pertinent Camp David framework agreement (September 1978) and in the Peace Treaty (March 1979) had been envisaged. The Oslo Accords of 1993/94 presented yet another chance. In 2000, at Camp David, Maryland, Yassir Arafat rejected Prime Minister Ehud Barak's offer: 97% of the West Bank plus East Jerusalem. In September 2008, Israel's Premier Ehud Olmert offered President Mahmud Abbas more or less the same, received no answer and was soon ousted from office (for internal reasons).

Palestinian autonomy or, in other words, Palestinian self-government in the Palestinian territories, even demilitarized Palestinian statehood was among the objectives of these agreements. It is true that full national sovereignty was not envisioned but the establishment of a democratically elected and internationally approved Palestinian authority would have made it far more difficult for Israel to implement its settlement policy.

Even if it intended to do so, no Israeli government today would be able to force Jewish settlers to withdraw without risking a civil war within the Jewish community. Anyone who remembers how difficult it was for the Israeli government in April 1982 to evacuate a single settlement (Yamit) in accordance with the Egypt-Israel Peace Treaty or the 2005 Gaza Strip withdrawal can easily imagine that the evacuation of approximately 140 settlements, not to mention the number of settlers (2021 about 600,000) involved, would hardly be possible. This was the enormous problem that Rabin and Peres had to solve when they (officially) initiated the peace process with the Palestinians in September 1993. This process began in public with the signing of the Declaration of Principles (Oslo I) in Washington, DC, on 13 December 1993 (but had actually started almost one year earlier). On both sides, "hawks" opposed a peace compromise and mobilised their supporters against the peace process. Since the autumn of 1993, they have killed "enemies" on the other side and "enemies" on their own side. The most prominent victim of Israeli hawks, who even claimed religious motivations for their behaviour, was Prime Minister Yitzhak Rabin, who was assassinated by a nationalist religious fanatic in Tel Aviv on 4 November 1995. From a subjective perspective, hawks from the two sides are mortal enemies. From an objective perspective, they have been working hand in hand. They have sabotaged and derailed the peace process together, though for fundamentally different reasons.

In early 1992, I wrote in the first and second German editions of this book:

> Does time work in favour of Israel? This is what the Israeli 'hawks' believe; they continue to build settlements. They are, however, wrong because Israel should be a Jewish and democratic state. If, however, approximately 2.5 million Palestinians live alongside (or in hostility towards) approximately 4.5 million Jews in the same state, this is no longer a Jewish state but a Jewish-Arab one.
>
> The Palestinians in the occupied territories do not participate in elections in Israel because the territories have not (yet?) been incorporated into the Israeli state. The rules of democracy do not apply to these Palestinians. Israel will not grant the Palestinians an independent state, something Jordan apparently wants as little as almost all other Arab states, which always claim the opposite.
>
> If the Palestinians living in the Gaza Strip and the West Bank were granted the right to vote in Israel as Israeli citizens, Israel would no longer be a Jewish state. With these territories, Israel can thus be neither Jewish nor democratic. The Israeli 'hawks' have given themselves the gift of a Trojan horse.
>
> The (highly unlikely) return of the territories, however, would not be a solution to this fundamental dilemma either. Even if the territories were evacuated, approximately 800,000 Palestinians would still live in Israel proper (based on current data) and would form a large minority that is likely to grow larger. As a result of natural population growth, the Palestinians in Israel proper (i.e. without the occupied territories) would probably constitute the majority of the population by 2040 even if approximately two million Jews from the former Soviet Union—which is an unlikely high number—immigrated to Israel.
>
> A Greater Israel is thus not a solution; and this applies to both Jews and Arabs.

What should they do?

Accept compromises and make peace. This is exactly what Rabin, Peres and Arafat started to do behind the scenes in 1992 and continued to do in front of the scenes in the late summer of 1993.

Between 1993 and 2000, Rabin, Peres, Barak and initially also Arafat took the "risk of peace". They failed. Intentionally or not? This is not the question. The fact alone matters. The hard-line stance has been a historic failure and will inevitably contribute to a political impasse. Military means are not an option for Israel to resolve the conflict. And what about the Palestinians and Arabs? Unfortunately, the answer is not encouraging (at least in my opinion). Violence has been the only way for Arabs and Palestinians to obtain political and territorial concessions from Israel: this applies to Egypt and Syria in 1973–74 after the Yom Kippur War and to the Palestinians after the First Intifada from 1987 to 1993 and the Oslo Accords. Last but not least, the Hezbollah forced Israel to withdraw from South Lebanon in May 2000 and Hamas forced Israel to withdraw from the Gaza Strip in 2005. Apparently, the purpose of the Second (Al-Aqsa) Intifada, which started in the autumn of 2000 and lasted to 2005, was to create a "small Palestine" or even "Palestine" (in what boundaries?) from the "mini-Palestine" that was on the verge of becoming a reality at that time. And then? A happy ending? Or more likely a new basis for further conflicts? Does the wheel of history never stop turning?

These forced concessions are far from being successful politically. Palestinian Statehood is as far as ever. Moreover, more and more Arab states seem to be tired of almost permanent Palestinian nays . In 2020 the United Arab Emirates, Bahrein, Sudan and Marocco have begun normalizing relations with Israel. Much to the dismay of the Palestinian leadership.

Injustice for Injustice—Conclusion—Solution?

Right versus Right. This is the usual answer to the question: "Whose Holy Land?" This is considered to be the truth among moderate and thus reasonable people, who can be found on both sides. I support their stance too, but unfortunately they are wrong when they defend the "right versus right" argument.

My view is: wrong versus wrong. I regret to say that this is the only way to describe the situation in the Holy Land.

Both the Jews and the Arabs were temporary *possessors* but not *owners* of the Holy Land. Today it is impossible for us to identify the legal successors or direct descendants of the original owners, even if we conducted genealogical and racial research, which is controversial (not only for Germans).

The Holy Land is a cemetery of nations. This is where the Canaanites rest. Neither the Palestinians nor the Jews are their descendants. There were, however, many successors. All of them regarded themselves as the real owners during the four-thousand-year history of the Holy Land. They thought that taking possession of the land was the same as obtaining ownership.

Since the time of the Romans, the acquisition of ownership through adverse possession has been a familiar concept in the European legal tradition. This also applies to the laws of the ancient Near East, for example the Code of Lipit-Ishtar (around 1934–1924 BCE) and the Code of Hammurabi (Babylonian period, 1792–1750 BCE). Ownership, however, could be acquired through adverse possession only if the original owner was unable to pay his debts or fulfil his feudal obligations. This has never been the case with the different possessors of the Holy Land.

But what is the point of this legal dispute? Such a dispute is in fact pointless because law has seldom delivered justice. One example is the British Mandate, which is firmly based on international law but morally highly questionable.

In many cases, however, justice is a double-edged sword. Too many attempts to achieve or restore justice have turned into brutality and terrorism or, in other words, into the destruction of human lives on behalf of humanity.

All possessors of the Holy Land, including Jews and Arabs, came as conquerors or took possession of the land through violence. As a result, their reputation was stained from the beginning.

Historically, there was no moral justification for taking possession of this land. Possession was always based on power. This is probably why the Jewish conquerors looked for and found a religious justification. They referred to the divine promise in the Bible (which they themselves wrote). The Conquered Land thus became the Promised Land. In other words, the Jewish possessors issued themselves a certificate of ownership: the Bible.

This touches on matters of faith; it is, however, not my intention here to refute divine inspiration. The Hebrew Bible gave the Canaanite owners (as well as the Moabites, the Ammonites and the Edomites) a good kick (Genesis 9:21): Noah "drank of the wine, and was drunken; and he was uncovered within his tent." Ham, the youngest of Noah's three sons, saw his drunken father lying naked in the tent. Ham's brothers, Shem and Japheth, lowered their eyes and covered Noah with a garment. After Noah woke up, this otherwise kind and honest man cursed Canaan, Ham's completely innocent son. Noah cursed Canaan to eternal servitude. For some, this story provides a religious and at the same time pseudo-historical justification for the subjection of the Canaanite people. For devout Jews this story is true.

But what if there are people who do not share this belief and doubt its ability to justify ownership? The result is a religious war, which is something that any reasonable person would want to avoid.

What remains is a "Holy War". A highly dubious concept that has been abused too often. Anyone who qualifies a war as holy should take care not to lose sight of heaven. This applies equally to Jews, Muslims, Christians, and others.

The Palestinians have not stepped on the thin ice of religion. With the exception of those (including some Islamic fanatics) whose intention it is to render the Holy Land "clean of Jews". It is no surprise that the Palestinians refer to the holiness of the land and the city of Jerusalem only in very general terms. I have shown that it is not altogether heretical to suggest that the Quran can be interpreted as a Zionist source. Some readers may indignantly claim that this is a "misinterpretation" on my part. Before doing so, however, they should first read the texts presented and explained here, compare them with the Quran and consider the Jewish roots of the Quran.

The Palestinians thus do not focus on religious sources but instead on their ancestors: the Canaanites and the Philistines. This ancestral line, however, is wrong, in spite of all the speeches, essays and books that may be well intentioned but are less well researched.

So, who owns the Holy Land? The Holy Land belongs to no one—and everyone. To all survivors. To all people who want to live there or have to live there.

Anyone who claims a right to the land must be aware that such a right has absolutely no solid foundation. The Holy Land belongs to the survivors of different peoples, including, of course, the Jews and the Arabs. As a transit region, the Holy Land has always been multinational, multiconfessional and multicultural. The idea of turning it into the state of a *single* nation, i.e. a nation state, is understandable. It is, however, unrealistic.

A "Solomonic" Solution: A Mixture of Federalism and Confederalsim

1. In the long run, a compromise may be possible since there will come a time when the Kingdom of Jordan is "Palestine". In demographic terms, Jordan is today already a Palestinian country since about three quarters of its population are Palestinians. This development began in 1921 when Emir (later King) Abdallah imposed himself (with British help) on the mostly Palestinian population of Jordan's East Bank and was strengthened in 1948, when he carelessly incorporated an additional peace of Palestine into his territory by illegally annexing the West Bank and East Jerusalem. Although all of these Palestinian entities became a part of Jordan in 1948, today's Jordanian Kingdom of the East Bank will become "Palestine" in the long term. Due to its demographic structure there is every reason to believe that this will be the case. The King could help shape this process and play a role similar to that of the federal president in Germany. He could be a "moral" and representative rather than a political authority.
2. While all eyes are on the occupied territories, the Palestinians living in Israel are a domestic challenge that remains unnoticed.

What we must keep this in mind:

- Like it or not: The West Bank, East Jerusalem and Israel proper have a mixed Jewish and Arab population. A "separation of the population groups" would be possible only with blood and violence, by unacceptable "ethnic cleansing". For his reason, such an approach must be rejected.

- Palestinian Arabs constitute the overwhelming majority of the population in today's Jordanian Kingdom.
- Self-determination as such is what matters to people, not the geographical location of self-determination. Personal rather than territorial *self-determination. In other words: Self-determination for the people rather than the territory.*

This suggests that a compromise may be possible and could involve both a Jewish as well as an Arab federal state (like "states" in the US or in Germany) in Israel proper Add to this an Arab-Palestinian "state" plus a Jewish "state" in the West Bank and an exclusively Palestinian-Arab "state" in the Gaza Strip. In other words, this would be a mixture of a federal state (federation) and a union of states (confederation). The *federal state* would consist of component US-like states, i.e. Israel (= Israel proper), the West Bank and the Gaza Strip. The *union of states* (confederation) would be formed by Jordan, Israel, the West Bank and the Gaza Strip (= Palestine).

Here is a summarizing scheme:

A—Federal States

(I) Federal State of **Israel** (Personal Self-Determination) - Israel proper (4 June 1967 borders)

  (a) Jewish Israelis
  (b) Palestinian-Arab Israelis

1 State Legislature for the Jewish and Palestinian-Arab population respectively (elections by each people)
1 Federal Legislature (nationwide elections) forming and controlling the Executive

(II) Federal Palestinian-Jewish **West Bank** State (Separate Police Forces only, no Military)

  (a) Palestinian-Arabs vote for

  - the West Bank Palestinian-Arab State Legislature
  - the joint Legislature of the West Bank, Gaza, Palestinian-(Jordanian) Legislature forming and controlling the All-Palestinian Executive

(b) Jewish Israelis vote for

- the Jewish-Israeli State Legislature
- the Legislature of the Federal State of Israel

Disputes between (a) and (b) are to be solved a mixed Arbitration / Mediation Council

(III) Federal Palestinian **Gaza** State (Police only, demilitarized)

Gaza Palestinians vote for

- the Gaza Palestinian-Arab State Legislature
- the joint Legislature of the West Bank, Gaza, Palestinian-(Jordanian) Legislature forming and controlling the All-Palestinian Executive

B) **Single, Central State**: Constitutional Kingdom of **Palestine-Jordan** (Military + Police Forces)

- National elections for its Legislature forming and controlling the Executive
  C) Israeli-Palestinian **Confederation**
  A + B

Self-determination should be for people, not territories. As a result, every ethnic group would elect its representation regardless of where they live. In other words, Palestinians living in Galilee, Haifa and Jaffa as well as Palestinians living in East Jerusalem, Hebron, Nablus, Amman and Aqaba would elect the Palestinian parliament. Jews living in Tel Aviv and West Jerusalem as well as Jews living in East Jerusalem, near Hebron and Nablus would elect the Israeli parliament. The powers of the different parliaments and governments would have to be defined in detail.

During a period of transition, foreign and security policy decisions affecting Israel proper, the West Bank and the Gaza Strip would have to be taken by the Israeli-Jewish government.

The Palestinian component state in the West Bank and Gaza Strip would have foreign and police but no military powers.

In the long term, the West Bank and the Gaza Strip could be and would have to be demilitarised. International control of this demilitarisation is a pipe dream. Since this approach would be in the interest of both sides, it should work nevertheless since only mutual interests create ties that bind and bond.

The Palestinian-Arab government (elected by Palestinians in Israel, the West Bank, the Gaza Strip and, of course, Palestine-Jordan) would have a traditional foreign and security policy that would cover the territory of present-day Jordan, which would be the Palestine of tomorrow. When will this vision become a reality?

This solution would imply the continuation of conventional statehood in the territory of present-day Israel and present-day Jordan and a division of power in the West Bank and Gaza Strip. The Jewish state would not lose its Jewish character. And the Palestinians could finally exercise their right to self-determination, though not without restrictions: self-determination or rather sovereignty in all matters would be limited to Palestine (present-day Jordan). The Palestinians would not have achieved everything but definitely more than they possess today. There is nothing to suggest that they will be successful if they demand even more.

A complete withdrawal from the West Bank would make it impossible for Israel to survive. Not for military but for pragmatic reasons: Israel would not have enough water. Without the underground water resources of the West Bank, the Israeli population would die of thirst. At the same time, however, the Palestinians will not allow themselves to be deprived of their water. This issue too must be solved through cooperation and not a power struggle. Otherwise, blood will be shed for water.

The ideas of that time were on the cusp of becoming reality. But the election of the Netanyahu government in 1996 marked a turning point. Barak then tried to revive these ideas, but this attempt failed during the Al-Aqsa Intifada and paved the way for Sharon. The situation was similar to that in 1992.

Now as then, Jews and Arabs must draw a line and must reach a compromise. Otherwise, they will end up as losers. The arms race in the Middle East has reached a dangerous stage. Middle Eastern countries have stocked up on biological and especially chemical weapons. And then there are nuclear weapons and their destructive power.

Israel has long possessed a nuclear bomb. Iraq has tried to develop one again and again (even after the Gulf War of 1991). Iran and Algeria (at least until the 1992 coup) as well as Libya's Gadhafi until 2003 have tried everything to acquire a nuclear bomb. The build-up of nuclear capabilities in the Middle East is well underway.

This could lead to a "Samson effect". Samson was a Jewish judge from the Old Testament. He was seduced by Delilah. The Philistines imprisoned him, gouged out his eyes, and enslaved him. God gave Sampson his immense strength back one last time. Samson brought down the columns of the building where the Philistines were holding a festival in honour of Dagon, their god. The building collapsed, and the Philistines as well as Samson were killed.

Should such a disaster be the future of the Holy Land?

Chronology

Around 2350 BCE: Egyptians control rebelling city-states in (what is today) the Holy Land.

Around 2000 BCE: West-Semitic invasion (Amorites). Progenitors as part of that invasion?

Around 1900 BCE: The Amorites are defeated by Egypt.

Around 1500 BCE: Canaanites. First sources mention the "Hebrews".

14th century BCE: The ruling Egyptians call the area of (today's) Holy Land "Canaan".

Mid-13th century BCE: Egypt's rule over Canaan is weakened. Invasion of the "children of Israel". "Jewish" conquest. Time of the "Judges".

Around 1025–1006 BCE: Kingdom of Saul. Union of the twelve tribes.

990–968 BCE: King David.

968–928 BCE: King Solomon. After his death, the kingdom is divided into "Judah" (consisting of the tribes of Judah and Benjamin) and "Israel" (the remaining ten tribes).

722 BCE: "Israel" is destroyed by the Assyrians.

586 BCE: Destruction of Judah and the First Temple in Jerusalem by the Babylonians. First Jewish diaspora (in Mesopotamia).

Around 550 BCE, the Persians defeat the Babylonians.

538 BCE: The Persian king Cyrus allows the Jews to return to Judah, which becomes an autonomous province of the Persian Empire; until 332 BCE.

515 BCE: The Second Temple is built in Jerusalem.

332 BCE: Conquest by Alexander the Great. After his death, rule by the Ptolemies; after 200, rule by the Seleucids.

167–164 BCE: Successful revolution of the Hasmoneans or Maccabees.

142 BCE: Establishment of a Jewish kingdom by the Hasmoneans.

63 BCE: Pompey conquers the Jewish State.

66–70 CE: The "Jewish War" against Rome. The Second Temple burns to the ground in 70 CE. Beginning of the European diaspora of the Jews. The last Jewish resistance is broken at Masada in 73 CE. Rome calls the country "Palestine".

132–135: Another revolt of the Jews under Bar Kokhba.

After 395: After the division of the Roman Empire, "Palestine" belongs to the Eastern Roman or Byzantine Empire.

614: The Persians conquer Palestine.

634: The Arabs conquer Palestine.

969: Shiite Fatimids from Egypt conquer Palestine.

1098: Seljuk Turks conquer Jerusalem.

1099: The crusaders conquer Jerusalem.

1187: Saladin defeats the crusaders at Hattin.

1250: Mongol invasion

1260: The Mamluks, who ruled Egypt since 1250, expel the Mongols.

1291: The Mamluks conquer Acre, the last stronghold of the crusaders.

1453: The Turks conquer Byzantium and in

1517 the Holy Land. Turkish rule lasts until 1917.

1917–18: Britain defeats Turkey in World War I.

1918–22: "Palestine" becomes British mandate territory.

29 November 1947: The UN General Assembly decides on the partition of "Palestine" into a Jewish and a Palestinian state. Beginning of the civil war between Jews and Palestinians, who are supported by neighbouring Arab states.

14 May 1948: David Ben-Gurion declares the independence of the "Jewish State of Israel".

15 May 1948: Invasion by Arab states. The first Arab-Israeli war lasts until January 1949.

1948-1951: Jewish mass immigration and economic problems

29 October–5 November 1956: Suez War

5–10 June 1967: Six-Day War. Israel captures the Sinai Peninsula from Egypt, the Gaza Strip under Egyptian administration, the West Bank, which was illegally annexed by Jordan in 1948, and the Golan Heights from Syria.

1 March 1969–7 August 1970: War of attrition along the Suez Canal

6–26 October 1973: Yom Kippur War against Egypt and Syria

1 September 1975: First disengagement agreement with Egypt

19–21 November 1977: Egyptian President Sadat visits Jerusalem.

17 September 1978: Camp David Accords with Egypt

26 March 1979: Peace treaty with Egypt

26 April 1982: Return of the Sinai Peninsula to Egypt. Israeli war against the PLO in Lebanon starting in June.

9 December 1987–September 1993: Intifada (uprising of Palestinians in the West Bank and Gaza Strip against Israeli rule)

16 September 1993: Oslo I Accord between Israel and the PLO signed in Washington, D.C.

1 July 1994: Yasser Arafat takes over as head of the Palestinian Authority in Gaza.

26 October1994: Peace treaty between Israel and Jordan

4 November 1995: Prime Minister Rabin is assassinated because of his peace policy by a nationalist and religious fanatic.

20 January 1996: Arafat is elected Palestinian President and receives 88% of the votes cast.

29 May 1996: Netanyahu defeats Rabin's successor Peres.

17 January 1997: Agreement between Israel and the Palestinians on Israeli withdrawal from Hebron

23 October 1998: Wye River Agreement, Washington mediates between Israel and the Palestinians and brokers a further withdrawal of Israeli troops. The slogan is now "land for security" (instead of "land for peace").

17 May 1999: Ehud Barak (Labour Party) is elected Prime Minister. The voters expect him to conclude a peace deal with the Palestinians.

24 May 2000: Israeli withdrawal from Lebanon

5–25 July 2000 Camp David Summit. US-President Clinton, Israel's Barak and Arafat or the Palestinians. Barak offered 97% of the West Bank + East Jerusalem, confirmed at Taba in January 2001 by Barak's caretaker administration

30 September 2000: Beginning of the Al-Aqsa Intifada

9 December 2000: Barak resigns.

6 February 2001: Ariel Sharon (Likud Party) is elected Prime Minister by 62% of the votes cast. The voters expect him to use a heavy hand against the Palestinians.

22 March 2004: Execution of Hamas founder Sheikh Yassin by Israeli armed forces

11 November 2004: Death of Yasser Arafat. The moderate Mahmoud Abbas (Abu Masen) becomes the new President.

July 2005: In July 2005, Sharon ensures Israel's withdrawal from the Gaza Strip despite strong domestic opposition.

January 2006: Hamas, an Islamist organisation, wins parliamentary elections. Ismail Haniyeh becomes Prime Minister.

12 July–14 August 2006: Second Lebanon War. The problems of Israel, Palestine, Lebanon, Syria, and Iran are increasingly linked.

June 2007: Hamas expels PLO Fatah from the Gaza Strip. Division of "Palestine" into two or division into three (?) with Jordan or division into four (?) with Israel from a greater Palestinian perspective.

September 2008 Israel's Prime Minister Ehud Olmert offered 97% of the West Bank and East Jerusalem as the Palestinian Capital

Summer + Fall 2020 Normalization of relations between Israel and these Arab states: Bahrein, United Arab Emirates, Sudan, Morocco. Half-open relations between Israel and Saudi Arabia, Oman. Palestinan protests

Recommended Reading

Indispensible Religious Texts

The Bible
The Quran

Helpful Encyclopediae

Encyclopedia Judaica
Encyclopedia of Islam

Atlases

Aharoni, Yohanan /Michael Avi-Yonah, The Macmillan Bible Atlas, New York–London 1977, latest edition 2014
https://bibleatlas.org/

Gilbert, Martin, Atlas of Jewish History, 8th edition, London–New York 2010
Gilbert, Martin, Atlas of the Arab-Israeli Conflict 10th edition, London–New York 2012

© The Author(s), under exclusive license to Springer Nature Switzerland AG 2021
M. Wolffsohn, *Whose Holy Land?*, https://doi.org/10.1007/978-3-030-74286-7

Basic Reading

Asbridge, Thomas, The Crusades, New York 2010

Cleveland, William L. and Martin Bunton, A History of the Modern Middle East, New York–London 2018

Fawcett, Louise, ed., International Relations of the Middle East, Oxford 2019

Finkelstein, Israel and Neil A. Silberman, The Bible Unearthed, Archeology's New Vision of Ancient Israel and the Origins of its Sacred Texts, New York 2002

Finkelstein, Israel and Neil A. Silberman, David and Solomon: In Search of the Bible's Sacred Kings and the Roots of the Western Tradition, New York 2007

Finkelstein, Israel, The Forgotten Kingdom: The Archaeology and History of Northern Israel, Atlanta, Ga., 2013

Fisk, Robert, The Great War for Civilization, The Conquest of the Middle East, London etc. 2006

Khalidi, Rashid, The Hundred Years' War on Palestine, London 2020

Lewis, Bernard, The Middle East, 2000 Years of History, 4th edition London 2004

Mansfield, Peter, A History of the Middle East, 5th edition, London etc. 2019

Shapira, Anita, Israel. A History, London 2015

Recommended Documentaries

- See the documentary series "History of the World" (Youtube)
- Entire History of the Neo-Assyrian Empire (911-609 BC)//Ancient History Documentary
  https://www.youtube.com/watch?v=tizdco2i85w
- Ancient Israel +Ancient Babylon - The Bible's Buried Secrets Documentary (the title is misleading)
  https://www.youtube.com/watch?v=I7lmS68KO20

Ancient Mesopotamia

- The Kings: From Babylon to Baghdad 1
  https://www.youtube.com/watch?v=xnQGjmdUGCI

Persian Empire

- Entire History of the Persian Achaemenid Empire (550-330 BC)/Ancient History Documentary
  https://www.youtube.com/watch?v=34oQfaJiy7w
- The Epic Journey To The Holy Land (Religious History Documentary)
  https://www.youtube.com/watch?v=XitSlNH4KL4
- Alexander the Great/Hellenism
  #EpicHistoryTV #Alexander theGreat
- Alexander the Great (All Parts)
  https://www.youtube.com/watch?v=K7lb6KWBanI
  or
  https://www.youtube.com/watch?v=anJNKLII3NA
- Hellenism and Alexander the Great in Ancient Israel (300s BCE)
  https://www.youtube.com/watch?v=nFZcKcTbim4

Roman Empire

- Ancient Rome: The Rise and Fall of an Empire | BBC Documentary
  https://www.youtube.com/watch?v=wjJNJsVL8Rc
- The Siege of Jerusalem (70 AD) - The Great Jewish Revolt
  https://www.youtube.com/watch?v=y741QbT1YEo

Byzantium

- Byzantium and Islam: Age of Transition
  https://www.youtube.com/watch?v=%2D%2D8oApudpEE
- History of the Jews in the Byzantine Empire
  https://www.youtube.com/watch?v=DI0keRKIqhs

Islam and Jews

- Verses and Interpretations: Quranic Attitudes towards Jews and Their Relevance to Our Times
  https://www.youtube.com/watch?v=gbp_MYHo1DQ

Prof Bernard Lewis Lecture

- Islam, the West and the Jews
  https://www.youtube.com/watch?v=XGQVnK9Ztjk
- Crusades
  https://www.youtube.com/watch?v=vOyswuA8wEs&t=1s

Mongolian Empire

- Genghis Khan - Rise Of Mongol Empire - BBC Documentary
  https://www.youtube.com/watch?v=XAFnxV2GYRU

Mamluks

- Mamluk Sultanate's army: an introduction
  https://www.youtube.com/watch?v=BB5f_GMrm1Q
- Ottoman History
  https://www.youtube.com/watch?v=1oean5l__Cc

Arab-Israeli Conflict

- Pillar of Fire Series
  See
  https://www.youtube.com/watch?v=qjBSmqgkbxE

- The 50 Years War Israel and the Arabs Part 1 and others Documentary
  https://www.youtube.com/watch?v=ZxSoa6AF4e4
  https://www.youtube.com/watch?v=Pj0zQC2W1Go

- Six Days War 1967
  https://www.youtube.com/watch?v=rIx0UXfu68s, Part 1
  https://www.youtube.com/watch?v=ZoC5mQd1qt0, Part 2

- Jerusalem, History
  https://www.youtube.com/watch?v=r7HYh1Ihi2k

Made in the USA
Columbia, SC
06 November 2023

25569711R10135